Linux System Administration Recipes

A Problem-Solution Approach

Juliet Kemp

Apress®

Linux System Administration Recipes: A Problem-Solution Approach

Copyright © 2009 by Juliet Kemp

ISBN 978-1-4302-2449-5

ISBN 978-1-4302-2450-1 (eBook)

9 8 7 6 5 4 3 2 1

Trademarked names may appear in this book. Rather than use a trademark symbol with every occurrence of a trademarked name, we use the names only in an editorial fashion and to the benefit of the trademark owner, with no intention of infringement of the trademark.

Lead Editor: Frank Pohlmann
Technical Reviewer: Sean Purdy
Editorial Board: Clay Andres, Steve Anglin, Mark Beckner, Ewan Buckingham, Tony Campbell, Gary Cornell, Jonathan Gennick, Jonathan Hassell, Michelle Lowman, Matthew Moodie, Jeffrey Pepper, Frank Pohlmann, Douglas Pundick, Ben Renow-Clarke, Dominic Shakeshaft, Matt Wade, Tom Welsh
Project Manager: Kylie Johnston, Sofia Marchant
Copy Editor: Kim Wimpsett
Production Support: Patrick Cunningham
Indexer: Ron Strauss and Ann Rogers
Artist: April Milne

Distributed to the book trade worldwide by Springer-Verlag New York, Inc., 233 Spring Street, 6th Floor, New York, NY 10013. Phone 1-800-SPRINGER, fax 201-348-4505, e-mail orders-ny@springer-sbm.com, or visit http://www.springeronline.com.

For information on translations, please contact Apress directly at 233 Spring Street, New York, NY 10013. E-mail info@apress.com, or visit http://www.apress.com.

Apress and friends of ED books may be purchased in bulk for academic, corporate, or promotional use. eBook versions and licenses are also available for most titles. For more information, reference our Special Bulk Sales–eBook Licensing web page at http://www.apress.com/info/bulksales.

The information in this book is distributed on an "as is" basis, without warranty. Although every precaution has been taken in the preparation of this work, neither the author(s) nor Apress shall have any liability to any person or entity with respect to any loss or damage caused or alleged to be caused directly or indirectly by the information contained in this work.

The source code for this book is available to readers at http://www.apress.com.

Contents at a Glance

Contents

About the Author

Juliet Kemp first started messing around with Linux when she discovered it was more interesting than Finals revision, then began taking it more seriously when she discovered that part-time systems administration was better than bar work for subsidizing post-graduate education. After a couple of years in political research, she found that the systems administration was more interesting than the M.Phil it had funded.

Despite not being an astrophysicist herself, she spent the next several years at Imperial College, London, sorting out the IT crises of astrophysicists and improving the group's server back-end software. She began writing when she realized how much time she spent digging up information online and concluded that making her own experiences available to others might be helpful.

She wrote most of this book while temporarily living in Sydney, Australia, but is now back in London. Sadly, there is rather less sunshine and ocean available in London than in Sydney, but she likes it anyway. She spends a lot of time on a bike and encouraging other people to ride bikes, has recently started going climbing in place of surfing (you can't surf on the Thames), and is currently rather taken with the freelance lifestyle.

About the Technical Reviewer

Sean Purdy first encountered a computer when he was seven, his uncle's Apple][. He learned to program on the BBC Microcomputer, like so many protogeeks did in the 1980s. During his electronics degree, he was exposed to SunOS, which kick-started a lifelong interest in Unix-like operating systems.

Linux came along in the mid-1990s in the form of Slackware, about the same time he finally got his hands on a 386sx machine capable of running it. Since then, he has been trying to run Linux on everything and anything—games consoles, PDAs, and tiny laptops. The toaster is starting to worry

Sean has worked for several ISPs and technology companies, with almost 15 years of experience of Linux, FreeBSD, and Solaris. He now works as a systems guy for Consolidated Independent, delivering music and video content to iTunes, Amazon, and other digital music services.

Sean lives in London with two cats and a person.

Acknowledgments

Many thanks to the various people from Apress who worked on this book with me: Frank Pohlmann, who handled the technical editing and who helped me work out the original plan for the book; Kim Wimpsett, who patiently copyedited out my assorted verbal tics and U.K. English; and Kylie Johnston, who took over project management from Sofia Marchant and who navigated everything through the publication process with impressive speed and good humor. I was particularly happy to have Sean Purdy as technical reviewer, because he's been a good friend of mine for a long time now—thank you for all the painstaking checking and electronic red pen, Sean! The input from them all has made this a much better book.

I've been fortunate in my career as a sysadmin to have managers who've been happy to let me operate freely and who have been very encouraging. In particular, Anne Wilson, the IT manager when I was working at St Hilda's College, Oxford, was incredibly supportive and helpful at a time when I was very much just starting out and doing a lot of learning on the job (read: making numerous mistakes). I've also learned a great deal through the various IT-related problems that my colleagues in the Astrophysics Group at Imperial College brought to me when I was working there, and I enjoyed my time there.

On a more personal level, I want to thank my parents. They've always been incredibly supportive of me, and they've already assured me that they will be reading this book despite not knowing anything at all about Linux!.

Finally, gratitude and love as ever to my partners, Pete and doop, and to my best friend, Marna, who have patiently put up with my complaints; made encouraging noises at appropriate points; provided tea, rocket-fuel coffee, and/or chocolate when necessary (my burgeoning caffeine habit is entirely their fault!); and in general continued to be the awesome individuals that they are, even when 10,000 miles and quite a few time zones away. Special thanks to Pete for allowing me to mess about with his machines in the name of ~~science~~ testing.

Introduction

This book is a collection of recipes for the working Linux sysadmin—a set of stand-alone quick guides and tips that you can keep on your desk for easy reference. Hardcore in-depth manuals are great when you have the time to sit down and read through them thoroughly, but that's not always the case when you have a bug that you needed fixed yesterday. This book is aimed at giving you tools to fix problems faster but also to help you set up software and systems to avoid problems showing up in the first place. Or at least to help you catch them sooner and solve them faster when they do show up. I wrote this because when working as a sysadmin, I spent a lot of time hunting for just this sort of information. This is a collection of things that I've personally found useful and wanted to share with other people in my position.

Who This Book Is For

I've aimed this book primarily at the Linux sysadmin who's been doing the job for a year or so and is starting to get to grips with how things work. New sysadmins should find some things useful, but you'll need at least some knowledge of how Linux works and how to fix it before you'll really be able to use the book. There'll also be some tips that are useful to people who have a bit more experience—I know I keep learning new things myself!

The book will be particularly useful for someone working as a solo sysadmin in a smallish group or company, such as when you're the person who has to fix both the user-level problems and the back-end issues, rather than having the luxury of concentrating on one particular area.

How This Book Is Structured

All recipes should be more or less stand-alone; although there are some sections with several recipes for one piece of software, in which case the basics will be covered only in the initial recipe(s), and later ones will assume some knowledge of the software. In particular, there's a lot of interdependence in the Kerberos and LDAP recipes in Chapter 2.

Here's the chapter breakdown:

Chapter 1, "Saving Yourself Effort," includes tips to help you document your work better, to improve your shell and Perl scripting (because you will have to read it again someday...), and to help you keep a history of your configuration files by using version control.

Chapter 2, "Centralizing Your Network: Kerberos, LDAP, and NFS," includes recipes to get an LDAP and Kerberos setup running smoothly and also contains a few hints on adding NFS to the mix.

Chapter 3, "Monitoring and Updating," covers how to set up Nagios to monitor your servers and how to set up Puppet to make configuration easier.

Chapter 4, "Taking Backups and Managing Data," covers how to get your backups properly set up *before* the first time you need them and how to have rapid-restore in place in case of a server emergency. Finally, you will learn how to rescue data from bad disks when for whatever reason your backups aren't useful.

Chapter 5, "Working with Filesystems," covers editing and resizing your filesystems on the fly and using RAID to your best advantage.

Chapter 6, "Securing Your Systems," covers SSH, password policy, sudo, Kerberos, Apache—there are many parts of your systems where security matters. Test password strength yourself before an intruder does!

Chapter 7, "Working with Apache," includes a handful of recipes to help you out when you're using the preeminent web server on the Internet.

Chapter 8, "Using the Command Line Better," covers bash, which is incredibly versatile. It pays to learn more about it. This chapter also includes a find and xargs quick reference. Both find and xargs are great tools, but the man pages can be a bit alarming if you're not already familiar with them.

Chapter 9, "Working with Text in Files," covers less, sed, awk, and Perl, which all do useful things with text files. The final recipe looks at getting text out of other files, too.

Chapter 10, "Things Going In, Things Going Out," covers keyboard maps, printers, and remote desktops.

Chapter 11, "Tracking Down Bugs," contains recipes about best practices and the best tools when you're bug hunting, which sysadmins spend a lot of time doing, so it's a good idea to make the process as pain-free as possible.

Chapter 12, "Managing Time and People," covers managing time and people. (Un?)fortunately, we don't spend all of our time with computers. Especially if you do any first-line user support, thinking about how you deal with your colleagues can make an enormous amount of difference to how your working life goes on a day-to-day basis. Similarly, managing your time between the multitude of demands on it is challenging but incredibly important to your well being at work.

Conventions

Lines starting with # indicate a root prompt. The code continuation character ↵ indicates that what would be a single line at the shell prompt or in a text file has been split onto multiple lines for ease of typesetting in this book.

Prerequisites

The recipes have been tested on Debian 5.0 (lenny) and Ubuntu 9.04 (Jaunty Jackalope), which were the stable versions of both distributions at the time of this writing. Other Linux distros may vary slightly in file names and the way that various system issues are handled. I've tried to note some differences, but you might need to make your own additional changes. The basic theory or idea behind each recipe should be valid for any modern Linux distribution. Software versions are given in the text (in general, these will be the versions as packaged for Debian 5.0 and Ubuntu 9.04 at the time of this writing).

Downloading the Code

The code—config files and scripts—for this book is available to readers at http://www.apress.com in the Downloads section of this book's home page. Please feel free to visit the Apress web site and download all the code there. You can also check for errata and find related titles from Apress.

Contacting the Author

I can be contacted at juliet@earth.li or via my website at http://the.earth.li/~juliet/. I write regularly for http://www.serverwatch.com and http://www.linuxplanet.com/, as well as for the magazines *Linux Format* and *Linux Pro Magazine*.

CHAPTER 1

■ ■ ■

Saving Yourself Effort

This chapter covers the essential attribute of a sysadmin: laziness. The more time and effort you save overall, the more time you have to do other things: whether that's fixing other problems, setting up more systems, or surfing the Internet while you wait for the next thing to break. Documentation, good scripting practice, and version control are all ways of saving yourself time (sometimes quite a lot of time) in the long run, so they are worth investing time in up front.

1-1. Documentation: Knowing It's a Good Thing

The problem with documentation (specifically, with motivating yourself to actually do it) is that it's easy to think that *of course* you'll remember exactly what you did to fix a particular problem. Immediately after you've just spent several hours, or even several days on it, it's all very clear in your mind and seems incredibly memorable, even obvious. So, you don't stop to document it but instead hurry on to the next problem in your queue.

Unfortunately, whatever you may optimistically think, you really don't have that good a memory (sorry!). In six months, when something else similar, or even the same thing on a different machine, crops up, you'll be left with a vague feeling of recognition and maybe a detail or two.

Even while you're actually in the process of investigating a problem, it can be easy to lose track of what you're doing. You make lots of changes in a hurry, changing various factors in the hope of getting more information or finding a fix, and then you forget what you just changed, what you changed before that, why you changed it, and whether you tested properly between times.

That's why proper documentation, even if only for yourself, really is worth the effort both while you're working and as a record afterward.

1-2. Documentation: Keeping Track of What You're Doing

The first part of the documentation problem is to keep track of what you're doing while you're doing it. This recipe assumes that you're using **bash** and a fairly standard Linux setup.

While you're actively troubleshooting, do your best to make at least a brief note of everything you try. A dead-tree notebook can be really helpful here. As well as helping you keep track of what you've already tried, the act of writing things down can sometimes generate new realizations. If you lose track of where you are or what you've done, scrolling back through your **bash** history (or looking at **~/.bash_history**) will remind you. There are a couple of history settings that you can change to make this easier and more informative. Try adding these lines to your **~/.bashrc**:

```
01   shopt -s histappend
02   PROMPT_COMMAND='history -n;history -a'
03   HISTSIZE=100000
04   HISTFILESIZE=100000
```

Line 01 fixes the problem whereby if you have multiple terminals open, information may be lost. This happens because the default bash behavior is to overwrite the history across sessions, rather than to append.

Line 02 extends this to give you real-time appending to history across multiple terminals. The PROMPT_COMMAND setting executes the given command at every prompt; here it means that the shell writes to the history and then reads the history file every time you hit Enter. (The default behavior is that you'll get the history from a given terminal written to file only when you close that terminal.) Bear in mind that this means that when you go back through your history (with the up arrow or with a shortcut such as ! !), you'll be accessing whatever your last command on that machine was, not just your last command in that terminal window.

Lines 03 and 04 extend the history past the 500-command default. These 500 commands come around pretty quickly, and with that as a limit, you're highly likely to lose information you want to keep. You can increase these numbers if you want.

Finally, line 05 prefaces each line of the history file with a timestamp in the format 2009-03-08 10:54:31.

If things get really chaotic and you don't want to go hunting through your ~/.bash_history, try the following find command to find any file that has been modified in the last ten minutes:

```
find / -fstype local -mtime -10m
```

Note that you'll need to run this as root (or use sudo) to avoid getting lots of error messages, because it searches from /. It will also take a long time on any machine with large filesystems: looking through ~/.bash_history will be faster, especially if you've used the previous recipe to make sure that your ~/.bash_history file is up-to-date in real time! -fstype local searches only directories mounted on the current system so will exclude NFS-mounted filesystems. For more information on find, see Chapter 8. All the previous comments about keeping careful track of commands become twice as important when you're installing something. In that case, not only do you want to be able to repeat them if need be, but you might also want to be able to automate the commands, which requires even more accuracy. See Chapter 2 for hacks for, and more information on, centralizing and automating installs.

1-3. Documentation: Using a Wiki

So, you've improved your ability to keep track of what you're doing while you're doing it; what about documenting it properly afterward? This is the second part of the documentation problem.

A wiki is arguably the best solution—something like MediaWiki (there are plenty other options if you prefer those) is free (in both the speech and beer senses), works well, and is easy to install. See recipe 1-4 for how to run multiple wikis on the same base installation.

A wiki is also handy if two (or more) sysadmins are working together. If this is the case, it's probably worth taking turns to cast an eye over it every week to do any necessary tidying or rearranging. (This is an example of preemptive laziness: it's worth a small investment of time and effort up front to keep the tool working well so that you don't waste time and energy when you really need it.) If it's just you, this may seem less necessary (since it'll probably reflect your brain and its organization fairly well), but it's worth bearing in mind that there may come a time when you have to pass it onto a successor or to someone who's holding the fort while you're away. Also, it's good practice to remind yourself of what's in there at intervals.

There are of course other potential solutions:

- *Notebook*: The classic solution is the notebook. Notebooks are great for keeping track of what you're doing while you're actively troubleshooting, as discussed previously, but they suffer the major drawback of being searchable only by eye. They're also inherently linear: you can't readily rearrange them to keep similar problems or notes together. They're good to have around for scribbled notes or brainstorming, but they're not a good permanent documentation solution.

- *Text file*: A plain-text file will do the trick, but it will also get increasingly difficult to navigate (even with search) as it gets longer, and you can't make links between notes. It's better than nothing, but again it's not an ideal permanent solution (think about how many problems you encounter in the average day). HTML and the GNU info format both enable you to make links, but in this case you might as well use a wiki to handle your link formatting for you.

- *Database*: You could use a database, but at this point, you start needing to think about an interface. So, again, you may as well use a wiki, especially since MediaWiki at least uses a database back end anyway.

- *Third-party solution*: Various commercial or open source note-making products are available, all of which have their advantages and disadvantages; examples include OmniOutliner (which is Mac-only but may be useful if you have a Mac laptop), Tomboy, BasKet (KDE), and Springnote.

1-4. Documentation: Running Multiple Independent Wikis on the Same Install

If you're setting up a wiki for your own notes, as discussed in the previous recipe, you may already have an existing wiki install. Or after you set up yours, someone else may demand one. You probably don't want to share the information between wikis, so you need an independent setup; however, it's a waste of time and space to reinstall all the files when you don't need to, since most of the information is in the databases that MediaWiki uses as a back end. It's entirely possible to run multiple wikis off basically the same installation of MediaWiki, and you have two options: use the same database but different tables or use a different database.

For a basic MediaWiki install using MySQL on Debian or Ubuntu, just use the following:

```
sudo apt-get install php5-mysql mediawiki
```

If you don't already have MySQL set up, make sure you install `mysql-server` first. If you prefer, you can also use Postgres; the configuration will be very similar.

See the description of the second install for the configuration details. Make a note of what database name you use for your first install. You'll need to either add or uncomment this line in `/etc/mediawiki/apache.conf`:

```
Alias /mediawiki /usr/share/mediawiki
```

In Ubuntu, the directory is **/var/lib/mediawiki**.

Now you can set up the second install (you can repeat this as often as you like, for as many wikis as you like). Here, **/main/wiki** is the directory where you've put your first install (what **http://server.example.com/wiki** points to, which in the previous example would be **/var/lib/mediawiki**), and **/new/wiki** is where you want your second (or third or...) install, which is where **http://server.example.com/wiki2** points to.

```
cd /new/wiki
ln -s /main/wiki/* .
rm images config LocalSettings.php
cp -r /main/wiki/images .
cp -r /main/wiki/config .
```

This sets up most of the files to simply use the already installed ones but copies across the **images** and **config** directories, which must be independent in order to be able to set different configuration options for the different wikis and to keep the images separate. (If your wikis are closely linked, you might prefer to have a shared image directory, but bear in mind that this will mean you can't use generic names, such as **logo.jpg**, for any files that are not the same for all the wikis sharing the image directory.) **LocalSettings.php** is generated when you install, so you don't need to copy that.

Set the ownership on the files and directories (including **/new/wiki** itself) to be correct for your web server:

```
chown -R wwwdata /new/wiki
```

▉ **Note** The **www-data** username is correct for a default Debian install but may not be correct for your setup. If you have permissions problems, check the ownership on **/main/wiki** (or any other working web directory) with **ls -ld /main/wiki** and substitute for **www-data** as appropriate.

Next you need to reconfigure Apache to deliver this new directory. Copy the existing MediaWiki config file:

```
sudo cp /etc/mediawiki/apache.conf /etc/mediawiki/apache-wiki2.conf
ln -s /etc/mediawiki/apache-wiki2.conf /etc/apache2/conf.d/mediawiki2.conf
```

Edit the **/etc/mediawiki/apache-wiki2.conf** file to change all occurrences of **/main/wiki** to **/new/wiki**, and then restart Apache (**/etc/init.d/apache2 force-reload**).

Now you can do the final wiki setup. Go to **http://server.example.com/wiki2/**, and click "setup wiki."

The first page (as shown in Figure 1-1) asks for a wiki name (for example, MySAWiki), e-mail contact, and license settings and then requires you to set an admin password. There's a memcached option; for a small wiki, there's no need to use caching.

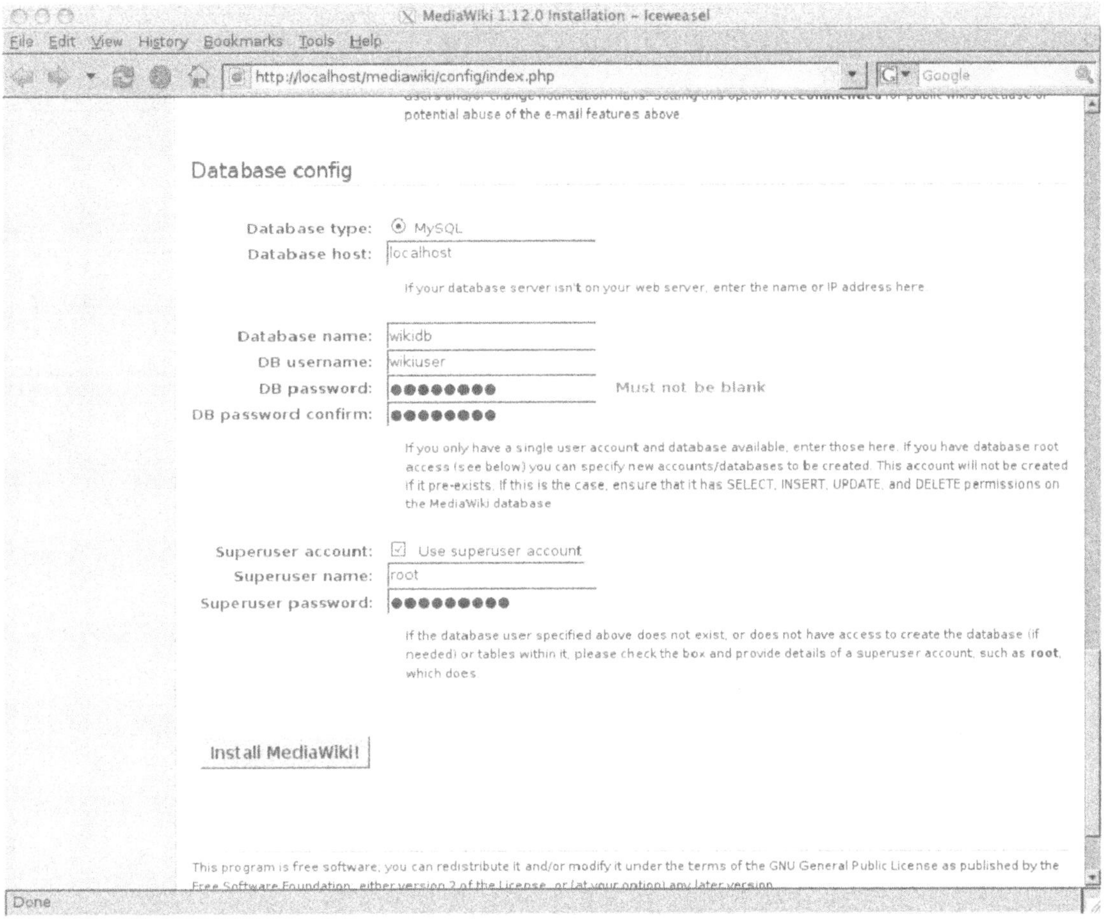

Figure 1-1. The database setup page for your first wiki

The second page sets up various e-mail features, which you can enable or disable as you prefer.

The third page (see Figure 1-2) is the important one for our purposes, because it handles database setup.

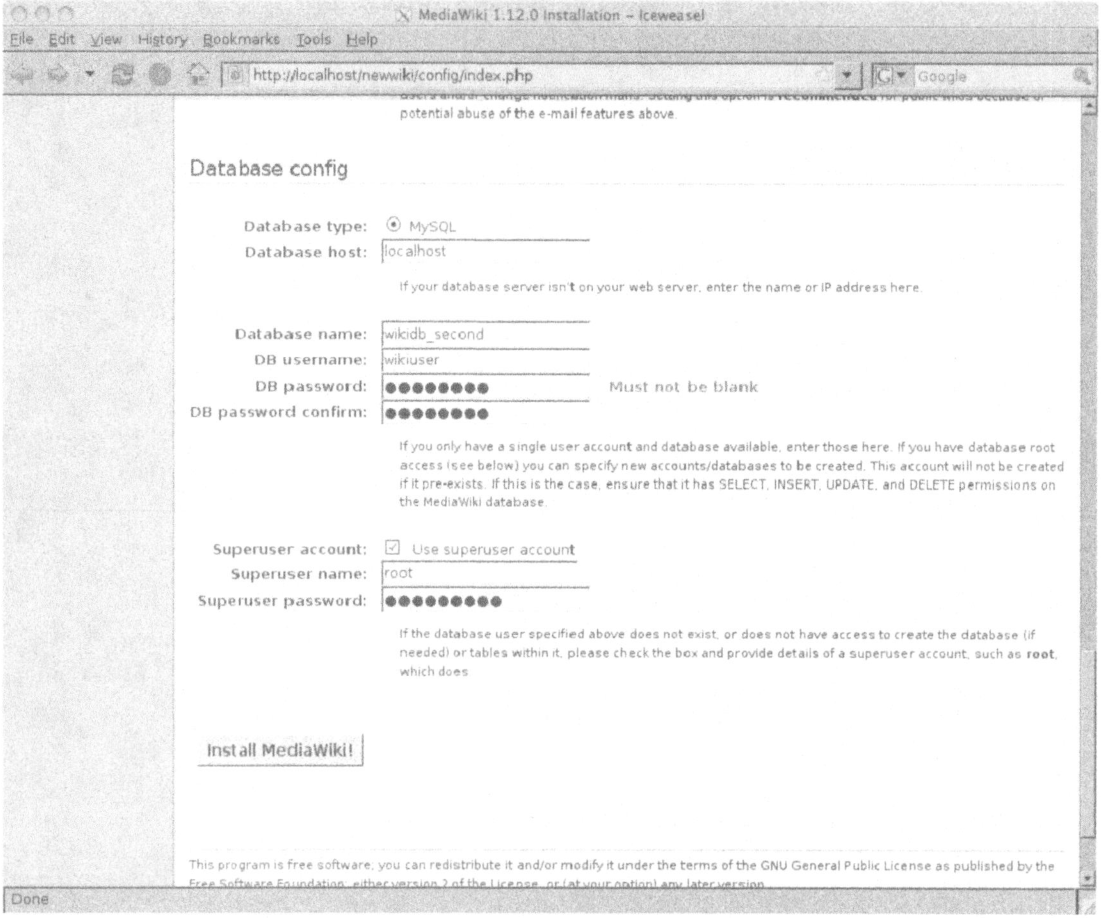

Figure 1-2. The database setup page for your second wiki. Note the changed database name.

You need to use a separate database to keep your two wikis separate, so change the field with the database name. You'll also need to set the database username and password. If the user doesn't yet exist or doesn't have database-creation permissions within your MySQL setup, you'll need to provide the name and password for a MySQL user (possibly root) who does.

Once the setup is finished, if it has all gone well, you should see an "Installation success" message. After this, you should move **/new/wiki/config/LocalSettings.php** to **/new/wiki/**, delete the **/new/wiki/config/** directory, and make sure that other users cannot read the settings file:

```
chmod og-rw /new/wiki/LocalSettings.php
```

> ■ **Note** MediaWiki's "Installation success" message may tell you to move `LocalSettings.php` to
> `/etc/mediawiki`. Ignore this!

1-5. Scripting: Setting the Display Style

Contrary to many an argument on the Internet, style choices (tabs or spaces, line lengths, cuddled `else`s, or whatever) don't really matter. The important thing is to make a decision and stick with it.

It is, however, a good idea to set all your text editors on all your machines (see Chapter 3 for centralization tips) to have sub-80-character lines. For vim, add the following line to your `~/.vimrc`:

```
set tw=78
```

For emacs, add this in `~/.emacs`:

```
(setq-default fill-column 78)
```

For nano, add this in `~/.nanorc`:

```
set fill 78
```

This is because someone else will have to read that script after you, or you might wind up reading it on a text console that doesn't have your proper setup. In those cases, the lines won't wrap properly, and you will cry. Keep it short. Use \ in `bash` to break up a line; with Perl, newlines are ignored since `;` ends a statement, so break the line wherever you want.

1-6. Dealing with Variables in Perl

When you need a quick-fix script, Perl and `bash` are fantastic tools. They're comprehensive, they're flexible, and they can be tied together with other system tools. Having said that, while you *can* do a lot with `bash`, you probably shouldn't unless there's a very good reason, such as a need for major portability, in which case you need to consider a number of other factors—check out *Beginning Portable Shell Scripting* by Peter Seebach (Apress, 2008). If the task is going to take more than about ten lines or require much more than stringing a series of shell commands together, it's best to use Perl (or your preferred scripting alternative).

The other issue to bear in mind is whether you need a script at all. Really large projects might be better in another language; see recipe 1-16 later in this chapter for making sure that you're not reinventing the wheel.

Anyway, scripting languages may be great tools for getting something working in a hurry, but their very greatness can lead to cutting corners in the name of speed. Then six months down the line your "quick hack" is still there, has developed add-ons and a bug or two, and you can't remember what on Earth you were thinking when you wrote it. As with the documentation mentioned earlier in this chapter (recipes 1-1 through 1-4), spending a little extra time now can save you a lot of time and mental energy later.

Ideally, most of your code should be crystal clear without comments (this is where coding practices such as sensible variable names come in). But, as with this script, having at least a comment up top saying what the script does, what input it expects, and what output it provides will be incredibly helpful at that later date I keep mentioning. (I like to add my initials and the date as well, but that's optional—it depends on if you want to know who to blame when something breaks.) Checking for the correct number of arguments (as in line 09 of the script later in this recipe) and printing a usage message are both good ways of making a script self-documenting.

If you're doing anything remotely complex, a line or two of comment never goes amiss. While you're at it, consider whether you want to turn what you're doing into a subroutine, as in lines 22 to 26 of the script—this is another good way of increasing readability and extendibility. In this case, instead of just printing out the regular users, you could use this subroutine to import them into your LDAP database. See recipes 2-9 to 2-11 for more on LDAP scripting.

If you're wedded to a scripting language other than Perl or **bash**, there's no need to skip reading this—most of it should be of general applicability. So, feel free to substitute $language-name at will.

As an example, let's look at a script that parses **/etc/passwd** and prints out the regular users (as opposed to the system users), as indicated by whether they have a UID greater than 1,000. Depending on your setup, this may not be 100 percent accurate; check the output before doing anything permanent with it!

```perl
01  #!/usr/bin/perl -w
02  # Script to print non-system user lines from /etc/passwd
03  # JK 25.03.2009
04
05  use strict;
06
07  # Declare subroutines before they're used; this one is defined after
08  # the main script logic, lines 25-29.  You could if you preferred define
09  # it here.
10  sub printuser;
11
12  die "Usage: $0" unless @ARGV == 0;
13
14  my $file = "/etc/passwd";
15
16  open FILE, $file;
17  while ( <FILE> ) {
18      my @userarray = split /:/;
19      if ( $userarray[2] && ( $userarray[2] >= 1000 ) ) {
20          printuser(@userarray);
21      }
22  }
23  close FILE;
24
25  sub printuser {
26      my @userarray = @_;
27      my $userline = join "\t", @userarray;
28      print "$userline\n";
29  }
```

Lines 01 and 05 demonstrate the single best way to make life easier in Perl. You should put these two lines at the top of every single script you write.

The -w flag turns on warnings. This means that if Perl thinks you might be doing something wrong, then it'll tell you so before running the program. It's not always right—in particular, if you're reading from files, you may get some warnings if your data isn't always complete—but most of the time it's worth at least taking another look at the warning.

use strict means that you have to declare all your variables before using them (or at least at the same time). This is demonstrated in line 11. You could also use this:

```
my $file;
// some stuff
$file = "/etc/passwd";
```

But if you just have $file = "/etc/passwd", the script will complain and die. This is an absolute godsend if you are remotely prone to typos or to variable name forgetfulness (because if you declared $file and then try to set $dile, you will be told what you've done). If you're not remotely prone to either of these events, then you are unusually fortunate; you should use strict anyway because it'll be even harder to find the mistake the one and only time your fingers or memory betray you.

It's best to declare all your variables up top, before you start, as in line 11. (Obviously, there's no need to do this for temporary variables such as loop variables.) Again, it makes it much easier to keep track of what you're doing.

Don't hard-code *anything*. Put it in a variable, and put it at the top of the file. Put this sort of possibly-might-change variable (for example, the e-mail address that you want to send output to or the location of a particular file) before any other variables, as well, so they're easy to spot. Resign yourself to the fact that things will change, and the just-one-time script will still be here in six months' time when you rearrange your filesystems and all your directories change. At this point, first some of your scripts will break, and second you will have to fix them. Make that fix a two-second job rather than a search-and-replace-through-every-file job.

When you pass variables into a script or a subroutine, don't just use the default names (for example, $_[0] or @_ for a Perl subroutine).

Instead, give them real names immediately, and use those thereafter—as in line 23. It's a single extra line of code, and it makes it far, far easier to remember what exactly it is that you're doing with what you're passing in. It will also help you remember what it is that you're passing in, rather than having to repeatedly check what variables are expected.

And, while you're naming variables, name them something sensible that is going to be meaningful when you return to the file, say, tomorrow morning. So, use $file, not $f.

1-7. Testing Scripts Fully

Books can and have been written on proper testing, but that's overkill on a quick script. However, you should do basic testing on even a junk script. (If there's any possibility of it being used more than once, put in basic error handling as well.) If you don't test it and you accidentally delete something important or wipe the log data you've spent the last month collecting, you'll be very irritated with yourself.

Test edge cases, and check what happens if the input is bad (too many or too few arguments, a word instead of a number, or vice versa). Testing in chunks is also useful—check that the first half of the script is generating what you want it to before you start writing (or at least before you start testing) the processing in the second part.

Printing to screen (print in Perl or echo in bash, as in line 25 of the script in recipe 1-7) is a quick and easy way to debug. Remember to comment it out afterward if you don't need it; even better would be to set a debug variable and use that to control whether the debug output is printed:

```
my $debug = 1;  # set to 0 to turn off debug output
print "At step 1\n" if $debug;
```

This may seem like too much hassle for a quick-fix script—I admit I don't always bother myself. But you will be very grateful to yourself in three months' time if you do it. To make it easier, set up an alias in your editor to insert if $debug;. For vim, add this line to your .vimrc:

```
iab db if $debug;
```

For emacs, type $debug in an open document, and then type C-u 2 C-x a g db (this adds the word before the cursor as a global abbreviation). You'll also need to type M-x abbrev-mode to turn on abbrev-mode. Then, in whichever of vim or emacs you've set up, when you're editing your Perl script and want to type a print line, type db (then hit Enter) at the end of it. Thus, the following:

```
print "Reached point 3",db;
```

will be expanded to this:

```
print "Reached point 3" if $debug;
```

A mere two keystrokes generates a massive timesaving later when you don't have to either reinsert all your debug output or go looking for comments.

1-8. Version Control: Using Subversion Aliases

It's a good idea to keep more or less every file you touch in version control. For config files, you may want to tie this in with your centralization setup (see Chapter 2). On a smaller level, you can use a version control system for your own scripts, notes, and documents. Using version control, if you make an edit to a file and then realize that you deleted stuff you wanted to keep, you can still get it back! (This happened to me recently—I accidentally erased 50 percent of a nearly complete 4,000-word article and didn't realize until I went to finish it. I retrieved the previous version from Subversion, and that one incident has more than made up for any minor time impact that using version control has day to day.)

But, being lazy means trying to reduce that minor time impact still further. If nothing else, the easier you make this for yourself, the more likely you are to use it regularly, which is what you need in order to make it useful. The following applies to Subversion, which works in much the same way as CVS but with some of the more irritating aspects of CVS removed. The excellent online documentation should get you started if you aren't already familiar with it; I'm not going to go into the basics of using Subversion here.

Here are a couple of aliases to reduce your typing. Add this to your .bashrc file:

```
alias sva='svn add'
alias svc='svn commit -m'
alias svs='svn status'
```

The first two aliases both need an argument after them.
sva file.txt will schedule file.txt to be added to the repository.
svc "Commit message" will commit with the given message.

`alias svs='svn status'` just outputs the status of the current directory, showing which files are modified and which haven't been added. It's a good idea to get into the habit of doing this before you run a commit; plus, it reminds you of what you're about to commit so you can write a useful commit message.

1-9. Version Control: Adding Labels to Subversion Log Messages

Something that can be an issue when using Subversion is that the default `svn log` command won't show you what files were changed in each commit; it shows only some revision information and the log message. `svn log -v` gives path information, or you can add more information to the log message itself. For example, say you have three big projects that you're working on, A, B, and C; the following script will add labels for them:

```perl
01  #!/usr/bin/perl -w
02  # svnl.pl: script to add labels to SVN commit message
03  # usage: svnl.pl A|B|C "commit message"
04  # Juliet Kemp 23.03.2009
05
06  use strict;
07
08  die 'usage: svnl.pl A|B|C "commit message"' if $#ARGV > 1;
09
10  my $label    = $ARGV[0];
11  my $msg      = $ARGV[1] || "";
12  my $project;
13
14  if        ( $label eq "A" )    { $project = "Project Able:"; }
15  elsif ( $label eq "B" )    { $project = "Project Beta: "; }
16  elsif ( $label eq "C" )    { $project = "Project Code:"; }
17  else      { $project = "Other: $label"; }
18
19  `svn commit -m "$project $msg"`;
```

Note that this script allows for the usage `svnl.pl "message text"`. In this case, `$label = "message text"` (line 10, since `message text` is the first and only argument) and `$project = "Other: message text"` (line 17), so that is what's committed as the log message. Your labels can be as simple or as complicated as you like.

1-10. Version Control: Adding Multiple Files to Subversion

Occasionally, you'll find that you have a large stack of files to add all at once. `sva *` will add everything in the directory and just give you a warning message about anything that's already there. But first, that's a bit untidy, and second, you might not want to add everything.

The following script, which must have a commit message as an argument, will look for all the files that haven't been added to the repository, ask you whether you want to add each one (you can shortcut with all to add all the remaining ones or end to skip all the rest at any point), and then add and commit them with your message:

```perl
01  #!/usr/bin/perl -w
02  #
03  # Script to add multiple files to Subversion by running SVN status and asking
04  # for confirmation.
05  # Usage: svnmultiadd "message"
06  # Juliet Kemp  04.03.2009
07
08  use strict;
09
10  die "Usage: svnmultiadd 'message'\n" if $#ARGV != 0;
11
12  my $msg = " -m '$ARGV[0]'";
13
14  my $filelist;
15  my $all;
16  open ( SVN, "svn status 2>&1 |" ) or die ("Couldn't get svn status: $!");
17  while (<SVN>) {
18      die "Not a SVN working copy directory" if (/not a working copy/);;
19      my ($status, $file) = split;
20      next unless $status eq "?";
21      unless ($all) {
22          print "Add $file? (Y/n/all/end) :";
23          my $add = <STDIN>;
24          chomp $add;
25          last if $add eq "end";
26          next if ($add eq "n") || ($add eq "N");
27          ($all = 1) if $add eq "all";
28      }
29      $filelist .= "$file ";
30  }
31
32  print "Adding files $filelist \nGo ahead? (Y/n)\n";
33  my $confirm = <STDIN>;
34  chomp $confirm;
35  if ( $confirm =~ /[^Yy$]/ ) {
36      `svn add $filelist; svn commit $msg`;
37  } else {
38      print "Add cancelled.\n";
39  }
```

As it stands, this will commit everything in the directory, not just your adds; in other words, it will also commit any edited files. To commit only the added files, change line 36 to this:

```perl
`svn add $filelist; svn commit $msg $filelist`
```

1-11. Version Control: Telling Subversion to Ignore Files

Finally, you may find that there are particular files or types of file that you never want to add, such as automatically generated backups. To remove these on a global basis, edit either your own `~/.subversion/config` file (to affect just your own repositories) or `/etc/subversion/config` (to affect all users on the system). Add this line (or uncomment it if it's already there):

```
# global-ignores = *.o *.lo *.la #*# .*.rej *.rej .*~ *~ .#*
```

and edit it to include whatever specific wildcard or full file names you want. For example, if you often have scratch-pad files called **notes.txt** that you don't want to keep in SVN and you also don't want to store any file with a **.bk** extension, your line will look like this:

```
global-ignores = *.bk notes.txt
```

You can also exclude a specific folder locally. If you want to ignore ~/**scripts/test**, then **cd** to ~/**scripts** and type this:

```
svn propset svn:ignore test .
```

The dot at the end is important because it tells Subversion to use this directory as its base for the ignore. Similarly, you could replace **test** in that with ***.bk** to ignore all files ending in **.bk**.

The next time you run **svn status**, you won't see any output for that file.

Unfortunately, when using **propset**, it replaces the value rather than adding it; so, if you use this line again to ignore another file, the first file will be unignored. There are three ways to get around this: one is to create a directory **ignores** where you put anything that you don't want in version control and then ignore that directory with **svn propset svn:ignore**:

```
mkdir ignores
mv unwantedfile.txt ignores
svn propset svn:ignore ignores/
```

The second is to add the file name(s) in the **global-ignores** line mentioned previously:

```
global-ignores = *.bk notes.txt unwantedfile.txt
```

And the third is to list the files, one per line, in a text file:

```
unwantedfile.txt
unwantedfile2.txt
```

and then to use the following, which will give you the list of files that you've ignored:

```
svn propset svn:ignore -file list_of_files
svn propget svn:ignore
```

13

1-12. Subversion: Dividing Repositories

You can keep going for a long time with the basic stuff with version control—as long as you're remembering to commit all your changes, you're fine. However, eventually you may need to mess around a bit with your repositories. Dividing, branching, and merging repositories are all things that may be necessary at some point and are straightforward with Subversion.

So, you've decided that your single repository would be better off as two repositories. Maybe you want to divide the config files from your scripts or from your notes. Before you start, make sure all working changes are committed (or you'll lose them when tidying up afterward) and that no one else is going to commit to the repository while you're moving things around.

To get a list of the directories in the repository and decide what to move, type the following:

```
svn list file:///path/to/repository
```

Then use this to get a dump of the repository (which may take a little while if you have a large repository):

```
svnadmin dump /path/to/repos > repos.dump
```

■ **Note** Although svn will use http:// or file:// repositories, svnadmin takes only a plain path. So, you can't use it on a repository that you have only remote access to. You have to be logged in on the machine where the repository actually lives.

Next, create the directory for your new repository:

```
svnadmin create /path/to/newrepos
```

The tool **svndumpfilter** allows you to choose a particular directory or directories. The command you want is as follows:

```
cat repos.dump | svndumpfilter include testdir | svnadmin load newrepos
```

This pipes the old repository through **svndumpfilter**, tells the filter to include only the **testdir** directory, and then loads it into the new repository. (You can specify multiple directories if required.)

All that's left to do after this is to tidy up. If **/local/checkout/testdir** is where your existing working copy of **testdir** is living, use this:

```
rm repos.dump
cd /local/checkout/
svn delete testdir
svn commit -m "Deleting testdir from repository"
svn checkout /path/to/newrepos/testdir testdir
```

This deletes the dumpfile, deletes the migrated directory from the old repository, and checks a working copy out from the new repository.

Note Unfortunately, there's no way in Subversion to remove a directory from the database altogether, in other words, including all of its change history; this recipe just deletes it from this point in time, with all the past information still kept. If you want to erase it altogether, you'll have to use `svndumpfilter exclude` to create a new repository without the unwanted directory. This code will do that:

```
svnadmin create /path/to/new_main_repos
cat repos.dump | svndumpfilter exclude testdir | svnadmin load new_main_repos
```

After you've checked your new main repository, you can delete the old one altogether and then check everything out again from the new one.

1-13. Subversion: Branching Repositories

The canonical situation for coders where you'd want to branch is when you want to create a dev branch of a project so that the main fork can be the stable code. (Or vice versa.) For sysadmin purposes, it might be useful to branch your config file tree when you upgrade some machines to a different version of your distro—so you can also merge across changes from the main version when they apply and then merge the whole branch back in when you upgrade the other machines.

To create a new branch, you need to make a copy of the main project:

```
svn copy /path/to/repos/proj/trunk /path/to/repos/proj/branch
```

Now check out that new directory to start working on the branch, and that's it:

```
cd my_branch_dir
svn checkout proj/branch
```

In due course, you'll probably want to merge the changes back into the main tree (for example, when all your machines have been upgraded). This is going to be a little more complicated, because chances are, you've made a few changes to the stable branch as well, and it may not be possible to automatically merge them all.

To merge changes from the trunk back to your branch, use this:

```
cd my_branch_dir
svn merge /path/to/repos/proj/trunk
```

Check for conflicts with **svn status**, resolve them if necessary, run any appropriate tests (for example, config file syntax checkers) to check for conflicts, and then commit the changes as usual.

To merge your branch back into the trunk, first check out a clean copy of the trunk. Then (from that checked-out directory), run this:

```
svn merge --reintegrate /path/to/repos/proj/branch
```

Again, check for conflicts and problems; then commit the changes, and you're done! Now, create a new branch, and get going on your next stages of development!

1-14. Subversion: Merging Repositories

To merge two separate repositories while keeping both of their histories intact, you again need to use `svnadmin dump`.

■ **Note** If you don't care about the history, you can just check one of them out into a working directory and then import that working directory as a new project into the second repository. The second repository won't have a record of the revision history of this newly imported project, but it will have all the current information and file contents, and any further changes will of course be recorded as normal.

The code to do this is as follows:

```
svnadmin dump /path/to/repos1 > repos1.dump
svnadmin dump /path/to/repos2 > repos2.dump
svnadmin create /path/to/big_repos
svn mkdir file:///path/to/big-repos repos1
cat repos1.dump | svnadmin load --parent-dir repos1
svn mkdir file:///path/to/big-repos repos2
cat repos2.dump | svnadmin load --parent-dir repos2
```

This works as follows: two existing repositories are dumped out, and a new repository is created that will hold both of them. Then the `svn mkdir` command is used to create a new directory within the new repository for the first of the old repositories. This is to keep the two old repositories separate. The `svnadmin load` command is used to put the first old repository into the new one, within the specified parent directory. Then a directory is created for the second repository, and this is loaded into the new repository.

Again, once you've checked that everything is in place as expected, you can delete `/path/to/repos1` and `/path/to/repos2` and check everything out again from the new repository.

1-15. Testing: Knowing It's a Good Thing

Whether you're implementing something new or fixing a bug, proper testing is absolutely vital. And you really need to think of it *before* you start work. If you're fixing bugs, you need to set up a test that currently fails and that demonstrates the bug. If you don't do this in advance, you can't be certain that you've fixed the problem, because you have no baseline. This is particularly true with multiple users and multiple machines. A reported bug may turn up only for a particular user, and if you don't establish that up front, you'll think you've fixed it when you haven't. Establishing a baseline test can also give you useful information and help you narrow down the problem before you even start, as in the case of a user-specific problem. (See Chapter 11 for more on bug fixing and bug hunting.) Try to reduce the test to be as small and as straightforward/limited as possible while still exhibiting the problem. This too is a way of narrowing down the problem before you start.

For example, let's say that a user, Angela, complains that she can't print from Firefox. Before you start looking at potential causes, you should run some or all of these tests:

- Try printing from Firefox from your own machine.

- Try printing from Firefox from Angela's machine, logged in as yourself.

- Try printing from Firefox from Angela's machine, logged in as her.

- If both of these fail, try printing from Firefox from Angela's machine, logged in as root. (If you can print from her machine as you or as root, then you may be looking at a user-specific problem rather than a Firefox or printer problem.)

- Try printing from the command line on Angela's machine. (Again, you can try this as yourself, as Angela, and as root, depending on what results you're getting.)

- While you're doing the previous tests, make sure that you're always printing to the same printer. Then, try some or all of the previous tests but print to a different printer.

Change only one thing at a time when you're implementing new features or bug fixing, and test after every stage. It's much easier in the long run to do it this way than it is to have to go back and untangle exactly what you did when and which bit is failing, even if it seems irritatingly slow at the time. (Also, it gives you a nice motivational warm glow of satisfaction when a particular test passes, which is arguably worth it in itself and cheaper than the warm glow of satisfaction you get from eating a motivational bar of chocolate, if less tasty.)

So, in our printing problem example, if you log onto the CUPS console (at `http://localhost:631`) and make a change to one of the printer settings (for example, to the default paper size), run the appropriate tests from your initial setup again *before* you change anything else. In particular, rerun the tests before you try restarting the printer; it's very useful to know whether you *just* need to change the setting or whether you need to restart the printer for the change to be applied.

Not only that, but make sure the change really has been applied (refresh the CUPS console page, in our example) and that you're testing the right machine (are you sure you're in the right terminal window?) and test again. *Then* you can change something else. This is along the same lines as being careful to make comprehensive initial tests. Change one thing at a time whenever you're testing so that you can be clear on what changes have an effect on the problem.

And of course, you should make sure you keep notes while you're doing it, as per the earlier discussions about documentation in recipes 1-1 through 1-4.

Another example of good testing practice is to test against either a known-good machine (when bug fixing) or a known-unchanged machine (when implementing something new). Make sure that whatever you're testing on the machine you're working on checks out correctly on the comparison machine. If you're chasing down a bug and test A fails on both your buggy machine and your comparison machine, then either you've discovered a bug of wider scope than you thought or you're not testing the right thing. Either way, it indicates that you need to rethink. So, in the printing case, if you find that you can print from Firefox on your own machine, whoever you're logged in as, but can't print from the command line (but not vice versa), then the comparison between this and Angela's machine will tell you something useful.

Similarly, if you're implementing something on box 1 and one of your interim tests also passes on box 2, which you haven't changed, then you may be doing more work than you need to do. This is particularly true when working on client-server software, when a change to the server can affect all the clients without you having to do any more work. Checking against your comparison client can find these sorts of problems.

Testing regularly can also be a useful part of a system monitoring setup; see Chapter 3 for more on system monitoring.

1-16. Reinventing the Wheel

When you come across something that needs to be fixed or implemented, it can be very tempting to crack straight on with rolling your own solution. Writing stuff yourself is fun, and it can seem a lot more appealing than the process of looking for a solution that already exists, checking that it really does do what you want it to, getting it installed, and so on.

Here's some reasons why you should ignore the impulse to reinvent the wheel and instead should take yourself to Google, reread this book, check out the many others available for specific or broader admin topics to see whether they have anything useful to say, or solicit recommendations from other sysadmins:

- It's quicker. It may feel like less interesting work, but it really will be quicker than going through the design-implement-test process.

- More support is available—even just a couple of users (and most existing projects will have more than that) is a couple more than your self-constructed tool, and that's a couple more people than just you to get input from when something does go wrong.

- When eventually you move on to bigger and better things, the person who replaces you will have more chance of picking the tool up smoothly and may even have previous experience with it.

- Documentation should already exist, so you won't have to write it yourself! (OK, this isn't always an absolute guarantee with open source software, unfortunately, but there should be at least *some*. And if you do have to write more, you can get a nice warm altruistic glow by making it available to the rest of the user community.)

- If it really doesn't have everything you want, you can patch it—without having to write *everything* from scratch. And again, you can hand that over to the community as well.

- Someone else has done all the testing for you.

This list applies to things like Perl modules (CPAN, which is great in many ways but is sadly unrated; try http://cpanratings.perl.org/ to get more information on modules). Use other people's hard work so that you can direct your own hard work more usefully.

CPAN is an enormous collection of free Perl modules—reusable Perl toolboxes in effect. There's a pain-free installation method, as described in the main tutorial on the site. If you're writing Perl at all regularly, it is well worth checking out. Because anyone can upload to CPAN, quality does vary, but there's good stuff there, and the documentation can be very helpful. At its best, it can save an awful lot of wheel reinventing.

To identify the most valuable CPAN modules, helpful options are checking the "kwalitee" scores on the CPAN Testing Service page (`http://cpants.perl.org/kwalitee.html`), looking at the recommended CPAN modules on the Perl Foundation web site (`http://www.perlfoundation.org/perl5/index.cgi?recommended_cpan_modules`), and checking out the CPAN ratings (`http://cpanratings.perl.org/`). Google can also be useful.

SourceForge (`http://sourceforge.net`) also has stacks of Linux software projects available for free and is well worth checking out. Freshmeat (`http://freshmeat.net`) maintains the Internet's largest index of Unix and cross-platform software.

Situations where this might not apply include working environments where there are security or licensing issues with using open source software or when you're trying to learn a new language and the wheel reinvention is just a means to an end. And, OK, sometimes you're just in it for the fun. Never let it be said that I have anything against fun.

■ ■ ■

## CHAPTER 2

Centralizing Your Network: Kerberos, LDAP, and NFS

A basic rule is to centralize whenever you can. A prime candidate for centralization is your authentication and identity setup, and the best way to do this (as discussed at the start of recipe 2-1) is to combine LDAP for directory information and Kerberos for authentication. Most of this chapter deals with setting up LDAP and Kerberos, including showing how to script your interactions with LDAP and how to set up backup (slave) servers for both Kerberos and LDAP so that a master server failure won't be disastrous. You can also set up NFS to use LDAP to store automount maps, so the final recipes in the chapter cover how to do that, as well as giving a couple of other useful NFS tips.

2-1. Setting Up Kerberos Authentication

Linux offers plenty of options for authentication. The most basic is, of course, just to use the /etc/password and /etc/shadow files, but if you're running any sort of centralized system, that's not a solution that is that easy to maintain. NIS or NIS+ is another old option that is still in use in some places, but Sun is no longer developing or recommending it, since Sun is in favor of LDAP.

LDAP is currently the most popular option for both directory lookup and authentication (the Microsoft Active Directory software uses LDAP for its directory services), but although LDAP is excellent as a directory solution (storing information about your machines and users), it's not so secure for authentication. You can increase its security with TLS, but it still won't provide the same level of auth security that Kerberos does.

Kerberos, on the other hand, is explicitly designed to handle authentication and only authentication, of both users and machines. The good news is that Kerberos and LDAP work very nicely together. If you're starting from scratch, it's easiest to set up Kerberos first (covered in this recipe) and then LDAP (covered in the next). If you already have LDAP running, you should be able to follow the next recipe and make the appropriate changes.

How Kerberos Works

Before starting the setup, it's worth taking a quick look at how Kerberos works. When a user logs in to their machine, they request a ticket-granting ticket (TGT) from the key distribution center (KDC). The KDC is usually your main Kerberos server; you can also set up multiple slave servers to spread the load and provide backup, as described in recipe 2-9. After getting the TGT request, the KDC looks up the user (referred to as the *principal*) in its database, retrieves their key, and then sends back a TGT encrypted with that key. The client machine then uses the user's password to decrypt the TGT, thus authorizing it. The important point here is that, like PGP encryption, this is an asymmetrical process. The password doesn't get sent over the network: it's just used locally. So, it's not vulnerable to any kind of network intercept, providing a massive security boost.

After the TGT has been sent, it's stored locally, and any Kerberized service will use it to ask for a service-specific ticket. It proves who the user is, so they don't need to enter their password again until the TGT expires (usually after ten hours) or is manually deleted. So, if your entire system is Kerberos authenticated, you can log on once and then ssh to any system without having to reauthenticate. It's not only more secure but also easier to use!

The process works very similarly for services or machines—except that a locally stored key is used to authenticate nonpeople principals, instead of a password.

■ **Note** If you want more information, there's an excellent and very readable explanation of how Kerberos works at http://web.mit.edu/kerberos/www/dialogue.html.

2-1a. Server Installation and Configuration

Log into the machine you want to use as your Kerberos server—let's call it kerberos.example.com. Kerberos packages should be available for any major distribution (or you can of course compile from source, but I won't cover that here). For Debian/Ubuntu, you'd use this:

```
sudo apt-get install krb5-kdc krb5-admin-server libkrb5-dev krb5-config krb5-user↵
  krb5-clients libkadm55
```

■ **Note** This recipe uses the MIT version of Kerberos. The other main implementation available is Heimdal (originally developed as a non-U.S. version back when there were legal issues with the U.S.-based MIT version being exported, which is no longer the case). MIT's version is more widely used and slightly more active in development terms. Windows and Java also come with their own versions of Kerberos, and other free implementations are available.

During the installation of the packages, you'll be asked for a couple of pieces of information. One is the realm to use for krb5-config. This will usually be the uppercase version of the local DNS domain. So, for the example.com domain, the realm would be EXAMPLE.COM. You don't need Kerberos v4 compatibility. If asked for the hostname of your server, this should be the fully qualified domain name (FQDN) of your server, so in this example it's kerberos.example.com.

Next you need to create your new realm using the krb5_newrealm command. You'll be asked for a master password. You should use a strong passphrase, and do not forget it because if you lose both this password and the stash file that Kerberos creates with it, you can't decrypt your database again.

Note The important user who is created here is K/M@EXAMPLE.COM. Do not, when poking through your database at a later stage, think that you can't remember creating this deliberately and therefore you should delete it, because that would break the database in a permanent and fairly catastrophic way.

After this, most of the configuration is done in **/etc/krb5.conf**, which you should edit to look like this:

```
[libdefaults]
    default_realm      EXAMPLE.COM
[realms]
    EXAMPLE.COM = {
        kdc = kerberos.example.com
        admin_server = kerberos.example.com
        default_domain = example.com
    }
[domain_realm]
    .example.com = EXAMPLE.COM
    example.com = EXAMPLE.COM
[login]
    krb4_convert = false
[logging]
    kdc = FILE:/var/log/kerberos/krb5kdc.log
    admin_server = FILE:/var/log/kerberos/kadmin.log
    default = FILE:/var/log/kerberos/krb5lib.log
```

Check that the **/var/log/kerberos** directory exists, and create it if it does not (it may or may not have been created by your package install). As mentioned, your realm should match your local domain. In other words, if your domain is *.example.com, your default_realm will be EXAMPLE.COM.

Note The capitalization is required here. The realm mapping means that your DNS domain and your Kerberos domain don't need to be identical (you can, for example, use subdomains).

If you want to set up a slave Kerberos server as well as the master (see recipe 2-8), you can have multiple KDC lines within the [realms] section. The KDC responds to TGT requests; it reads the database and generates encrypted TGTs. However, you have only a single admin_server, which acts as the master KDC. This is the server that handles edits to the database (adding principals—users, machines, or services—and changing passwords, policies, and so on).

The [logging] section is optional, but it will make debugging easier, and it shouldn't affect performance.

Once you're done editing, start the Kerberos admin server and the KDC:

```
# /etc/init.d/krb5-admin-server start; /etc/init.d/krb5-kdc start
```

The admin server may take some time to start up, so don't panic!

Setting Up the Database

The next step is to create the database and populate it with your admin user(s).

Once your server is set up, you'll authenticate via Kerberos to make database changes. However, obviously you can't do this before Kerberos is available! So, instead you use kadmin.local for the initial setup—this runs locally on the master server, so it relies on you having logged in legitimately as root, instead of using Kerberos auth. After you use these commands to set up your admin user, you should use kadmin -p krbuser instead.

The commands to set up the database and an admin user are as follows (you need to be root for this):

```
kadmin.local -q "ktadd -k /etc/krb5kdc/kadm5.keytab kadmin/admin"
kadmin.local -q "ktadd -k /etc/krb5kdc/kadm5.keytab kadmin/changepw"
kadmin.local -q "addprinc krbadm@EXAMPLE.COM"
```

The first command creates your database, and the next two set up permissions for admin changes and password changes, by adding appropriate keys to the /etc/krb5kdc/kadm5.keytab keytab. A *keytab* is a file that stores various Kerberos principals and their keys; it is used by servers where a human user would use a password. The usual one is /etc/krb5.keytab. The admin server's key is, however, kept in this separate file.

■ **Note** A *principal* is the name used by Kerberos for any entity that has its own key. So, you can set up principals corresponding to users, to machines, to services, to roles (such as krbadm), and so on.

The final command creates a Kerberos admin principal, krbadm, and you'll be asked to provide a password. Obviously, your choice of username is up to you! Some sites prefer to create admin users that look like krbadm/admin@EXAMPLE.COM to make it clear which users have admin privileges.

You also need to edit the access control list (ACL), in the file /etc/krb5kdc/kadm5.acl, to grant access permissions to the database. A very basic example corresponding to the previous setup is as follows:

```
krbadm@EXAMPLE.COM          *
*/admin@EXAMPLE.COM         *
*/*@EXAMPLE.COM             i
*@EXAMPLE.COM               i
```

This gives all access (*) to the Kerberos admin user krbadm and to any /admin user, and it gives read-only access (i) to all principals in the domain. Run /etc/init.d/krb5-admin-server restart to activate the new access controls.

Note You need both */* and * here. `user/admin@EXAMPLE.COM` and `user@EXAMPLE.COM` are different, and when you set up client users and machines, you'll be using both formats.

Edit /etc/krb5kdc/kdc.conf to set EXAMPLE.COM as the realm, and ensure that the database, keytab, and ACL locations match what you set in the database creation previously. Most of these values stay as the defaults.

Note You must specify the `admin_keytab` location as `FILE:/etc/krb5kc/kadm5.keytab`, not just as the bare filename.

```
[kdcdefaults]
    kdc_ports = 750,88

[realms]
    EXAMPLE.COM = {
        database_name = /etc/krb5kdc/principal
        admin_keytab = FILE:/etc/krb5kdc/kadm5.keytab
        acl_file = /etc/krb5kdc/kadm5.acl
        key_stash_file = /etc/krb5kdc/stash
        kdc_ports = 750,88
        max_life = 10h 0m 0s
        max_renewable_life = 7d 0h 0m 0s
        master_key_type = des3-hmac-sha1
        supported_enctypes = des3-hmac-sha1:normal des-cbc-crc:normal des:normal
 des:v4 des:norealm des:onlyrealm des:afs3
        default_principal_flags = +preauth
    }
```

After editing this, the following will restart the KDC and the admin server so that the changes take effect:

```
/etc/init.d/krb5-kdc restart; /etc/init.d/krb5-admin-server restart
```

From now on, you should use this to make changes, not kadmin.local:

```
kadmin -p krbadm
```

To test that it's working (there's no need to be **root** to do this), use this:

```
> kinit krbadm
> klist
```

You should be challenged for the admin user's password after the first command. Then the second will show you a list of authorized tickets, and you'll see that you have an authorized principal **krbadm** in there.

2-1b. Kerberos Client Setup

For Debian/Ubuntu, use this:

```
sudo apt-get install krb5-user ntpdate
```

krb5-user provides the **klist** and **kinit** utilities. **ntpdate** is needed because the time on the server and client must match for the authentication to succeed (so that an attacker can't use an out-of-date request).

Edit /etc/krb5.conf to make sure that the following entries are correctly set—it should match your server setup values:

```
[libdefaults]
    default_realm = EXAMPLE.COM
[realms]
    EXAMPLE.COM = {
        kdc = kerberos.example.com
        admin_server = kerberos.example.com
    }
[domain_realm]
    example.com = EXAMPLE.COM
    .example.com = EXAMPLE.COM
```

2-2. Setting Up Kerberos SSH and Logon

This recipe explains how to set up both the server and clients to use Kerberos for console or gdm logon and for SSH logon. *Server* here refers to any machine that you're using **ssh** to connect to, and *client* refers to any machine that you're using **ssh** from. We'll use PAM to handle both **ssh** and local login. For Debian/Ubuntu, run this:

```
sudo apt-get install libpam-krb5 openssh-server libsasl2-dev ↵
libsasl2-modules-gssapi-mit
```

Edit /etc/pam.d/common-auth and /etc/pam.d/common-session to use pam_krb5.
so.1 (replace any existing lines):

```
# /etc/pam.d/common-auth
auth    sufficient  pam_krb5.so use_first_pass ignore_root forwardable
auth    required    pam_unix.so nullok_secure try_first_pass

# /etc/pam.d/common-session
session         sufficient      pam_unix.so
session         sufficient      pam_krb5.so ignore_root
```

The **sufficient** line enables local login (for example, by **root**) if necessary (for example, if there are network problems). At least one line in **common-auth** must be **required**, or you will be able to log in without a password!

The **use_first_pass** and **try_first_pass** options mean that you get asked for your password only once, whichever module is used—the second module to attempt authentication will use the already entered password. **ignore_root** means that the Kerberos module is not used for **root** login and improves security.

To set up **ssh** login, edit **/etc/ssh/sshd_config** to set the various Kerberos options (edit these lines if already present; add them if not):

```
KerberosAuthentication yes
KerberosOrLocalPasswd yes
KerberosTicketCleanup yes

UsePAM yes
AllowTcpForwarding yes

GSSAPIAuthentication yes
GSSAPICleanupCredentials yes
GssapiKeyExchange yes
```

Then edit **/etc/ssh/ssh_config** (not **sshd_config**!) to set these lines:

```
GSSAPIAuthentication yes
GSSAPIDelegateCredentials yes
```

Make these edits on both the server and the client side. (In practice, therefore, just make the edits for every machine in your network that you use **ssh** to or from.) Then restart the **ssh** server (on all machines you've edited) with **sudo /etc/init.d/sshd restart** after you've made the configuration changes.

You need to add the client host to the **keytab** on the client so that **ssh** can transfer the Kerberos credentials. From the client, run **kadmin -p krbadm**, which authenticates you to the admin server as the admin user and connects you to the admin server. Then execute these commands:

```
kadmin: addprinc -randkey host/client.example.com
kadmin: ktadd host/client.example.com
```

The **-randkey** option generates a random key rather than asking for a password, and this is preferable for a nonperson entity like a machine, meaning that the key is stored locally and used to decrypt a granted TGT, rather than a password having to be entered. The **ktadd** line adds the server key to the local default keyfile (**/etc/krb5.keytab**).

Create a test user, still using **kadmin**:

```
kadmin: addprinc test@EXAMPLE.COM
```

■ **Note** This test user must also exist on the test machine either as a local user (in other words, in /etc/passwd; use *K* in the password field in /etc/shadow in this case) or in LDAP (see recipe 2-4) or your alternative directory service.

Test the setup by logging on first with the console, then with a graphical logon (you may need to restart X first), and then via **ssh**. Once logged on to one Kerberized machine, you should be able to **ssh** to another Kerberized machine without typing your password again. (However, this will work only if you've done all the client config described here for the second machine as well!)

Troubleshooting

Here are some things to check if it doesn't work smoothly:

- Check (using **date**) that the time on the KDC and the client machine are the same or close. The default tolerance is five minutes. Daylight saving time can cause trouble!

- Check that **ping kerberos.example.com** returns successfully and that there aren't any other network problems.

- Check that the host key has the correct number by executing the following on the client:

    ```
    sudo klist -k /etc/krb5.keytab
    kinit krbadm
    kvno host/client.example.com
    ```

If the number of the host key for the client machine (**host/client.example.com**) given by **klist** is not the same as the number given by **kvno**, you need to start up **kadmin**, remove the client principal from the keytab (**ktrem**), delete it (**delprinc**), and then re-create and add it.

2-3. Setting Up an LDAP Server

Lightweight Directory Access Protocol (LDAP) is a way to define how a client and server interact with each other. An LDAP directory is a directory whose server uses this protocol. Directories contain entries (structures that hold information about an object in the form of attributes) arranged in a tree.

Schemas are used to define the syntax and structure for particular types of object and their attributes. Plenty of standard schemas are available, and you can also create your own schemas or add to existing ones. See recipe 2-12 for more information.

These are the stages of an LDAP request:

1. The client asks the server for a particular piece of information.

2. The server runs the appropriate search (for example, finds the entry for a given UID).

3. The server returns the requested information (an entry or part of an entry) to the client.

LDAP can run either securely (using SSL on port 636 as `ldaps:///` or using TLS over port 389 as `ldap:///`) or otherwise (on port 389 as `ldap:///` but without TLS). This recipe covers both, but it's best to use secure LDAP unless you have a good reason to do otherwise.

2-3a. OpenSSL

OpenSSL enables you to run a secure LDAP server. For Debian/Ubuntu, run the following to install it:

```
> sudo apt-get install libssl-dev openssl ca-certificates libssl0.9.8
```

You have two options for getting a certificate:

- Contact VeriSign or another certificate authority to sign your certificate. In this case, you'll need only step 2 of the following process; follow your certificate authority's (CA's) instructions about what to do with the request you produce.

- Generate a self-signed certificate. If you're going to use your certificate outside of your own network, it's best to get a proper CA to sign it. If it's just for local use, self-signing is fine (and free!).

To generate a self-signed certificate, follow these steps (for a CA certificate, use step 2 without the -x509 option):

1. First generate a certificate authority:

```
> cd /etc/ssl
> sudo /usr/lib/ssl/misc/CA.sh —newca
```

The script requires various inputs. You'll need a (secure) PEM passphrase (make sure you remember it!). The other important value is the common name (CN), which must match the FQDN of the certificate authority server (here, I'm using the LDAP server to be its own certificate authority, so the value is `ldapserver.example.com`):

```
Common Name (eg, YOUR name) []: ldap.example.com
```

Leave the `challenge password` attribute empty.

2. Create the certificate:

```
openssl req -new -x509 -nodes -out newreq.pem -keyout newreq.pem -days 365
```

The `-nodes` switch is important in order to create an unencrypted certificate so that it will work with LDAP. Again, when asked for the CN, it needs to be the FQDN of your server. This time it will be the LDAP server (here `ldapserver.example.com`).

If you're using an external CA, leave out the `-x509` option.

3. Sign the certificate:

```
cd /etc/ssl
/usr/lib/ssl/misc/CA.sh -signcert
```

Again, do not use a challenge password. The new certificate will be in `newcert.pem`. (Note: this script looks for the file `newreq.pem` and signs that; if you have used another file in the certificate creation, you will need to rename or copy it.)

Remember where these files are—you'll need to move them into the LDAP directory in the next recipe.

2-3b. LDAP Server

For Debian/Ubuntu, run this:

```
sudo apt-get install libldap2 slapd ldap-utils libdb3-dev libdb3
```

`slapd` is the LDAP server; `libdb3-dev` and `libdb3` provide the BerkeleyDB database back end. You can use other databases, but BerkeleyDB is straightforward to deal with and is strongly recommended by the OpenLDAP team. Set the admin password when asked during `dpkg-configure`.

To use SSL (as per the certificate generated earlier), you need to put the certificates generated earlier in the correct places:

```
mv /etc/ssl/newcert.pem /etc/ldap/servercrt.pem
mv /etc/ssl/newreq.pem /etc/ldap/serverkey.pem
mv /etc/ssl/demoCA/cacert.pem /etc/ldap/cacert.pem
chmod go-r /etc/ldap/serverkey.pem
chown openldap /etc/ldap/serverkey.pem
chmod a+r /etc/ldap/servercrt.pem
```

Edit `/etc/default/slapd` to include these lines (this provides LDAP both using TLS over port 389 and using LDAPS on port 636):

```
SLAPD_SERVICES="ldap:/// ldaps:///"
SLAPD_OPTIONS="4"
```

As discussed at the start of this chapter, using LDAP with Kerberos provides more secure password management. To use LDAP with Kerberos, you need to get a copy of `krb5-kdc.schema` (available from `http://www.stanford.edu/services/directory/openldap/configuration/krb5-kdc.schema` or from the `/usr/share/doc/krb5-kdc-ldap/kerberos.schema.gz` file included in the `krb5-kdc-ldap` package). Then put it in the `/etc/ldap/schema/` directory.

```
cd /etc/ldap/schema/
wget http://www.stanford.edu/services/directory/openldap/configuration/krb5-↵
kdc.schema
```

Edit /etc/ldap/slapd.conf. This is a long file, so I've included just the changes or additions you need to make here:

```
include         /etc/ldap/schema/krb5-kdc.schema
include         /etc/ldap/schema/openldap.schema

# ... other things that can stay as provided by default...

TLSCACertificateFile    /etc/ldap/cacert.pem
TLSCertificateFile      /etc/ldap/servercrt.pem
TLSCertificateKeyFile   /etc/ldap/serverkey.pem

# ... other things that can stay as provided by default...

# this section rewrites principals as needed for Kerberos authentication
authz-policy from
authz-regexp
    uid=(.*),cn=example.com,cn=GSSAPI,cn=auth
    uid=$1,ou=people,dc=example,dc=com
sasl-realm      EXAMPLE.COM
sasl-host       ldapserver.example.com


# ... rest of file ...
```

The authz section is important for setting up LDAP with Kerberos. The authz-policy line allows a user to authorize as someone else, if this is permitted in the second user's LDAP entry. The authz-regexp line takes a Kerberos authorization request and translates it into an LDAP user identifier. $1 in the second line refers to the (.*) in the first line, which corresponds to the whole of the uid field in the Kerberos auth.

So, the Kerberos authorization for user jkemp would be as follows:

```
uid=jkemp,cn=example.com,cn=GSSAPI,cn=auth
```

and would be converted to this:

```
uid=jkemp,ou=people,dc=example,dc=com
```

The SASL information is used to complete the LDAP lookup information when using SASL.

The next step is to edit your permissions, which are also set in /etc/ldap/slapd.conf. Either find and edit as appropriate the existing access lines in your config (Debian/Ubuntu includes some basic setup) or add these lines in the main Specific Directives for Database section of the config file. The example here is a basic functional setup, in which the LDAP admin user has full write access and everyone has full read access; you can complicate it as much as you want, but be warned that it can get quite confusing!

```
# Everyone can read everything
access to dn.base="" by * read

# The admin dn has full write access
access to *
        by dn="uid=ldapadm,ou=people,dc=example,dc=com" write
        by * read

# Temporary lines to allow initial setup
rootdn "cn=admin,dc=example,dc=com"
rootpw secret
```

You'll generate the specified ldapadm user in a moment.

Note You must not have comment lines between the access and by lines in this file! This will prevent it from working.

With the standard setup as described earlier, the ACLs will apply only to a specific database. To make them apply globally (although in this setup you don't have any other databases!), put them before the database back-end definitions.

If you're using a self-signed certificate, put this line in **/etc/ldap/ldap.conf**:

```
TLS_REQCERT     allow
```

This allows clients to request the TLS server certificate from the server.

Note If you need it, there is more config information for TLS/SSL in the OpenLDAP FAQ at http://www.openldap.org/faq/data/cache/185.html. There's also an Administrator's Guide at http://www.openldap.org/doc/admin24/.

To separate the slapd logs from the general systems logging, add this line to **/etc/syslog.conf**:

```
local4.*        /var/log/slapd.log
```

2-4. Finishing the LDAP Setup: Authenticating with Kerberos

Add the LDAP admin user and the LDAP server to Kerberos by running kadmin -p krbadm from the LDAP host and executing these commands:

```
addprinc ldapadm@EXAMPLE.COM
addprinc -randkey ldap/server.example.com
ktadd -k /etc/ldap/ldap.keytab ldap/server.example.com
```

The first command creates the admin user. You'll be asked for a password. Call this user whatever you like, but it should match what you set in the access controls. You should extract the server key to a keytab other than the system one at /etc/krb5.keytab (the -k flag specifies this alternate keytab), since the LDAP keytab must be owned by the LDAP user, and you don't want the main keytab to be owned by the LDAP user:

```
chown openldap:openldap /etc/ldap/ldap.keytab
```

To ensure that slapd is looking at this keytab, add the following line to /etc/default/slapd:

```
export KRB5_KTNAME=/etc/ldap/ldap.keytab
```

Restart slapd:

```
/etc/init.d/slapd restart
```

Note If there are problems with startup, change the log level in /etc/ldap/slapd.conf to 16383 to get verbose logging in the log file. Change it back before you go into production, though, because it makes the server very slow.

Setting Up the Database

To set up the database, you first use the authentication in the rootdn and rootpw directives to add the root entry, the People group, and an admin user. You should have added the admin user when you set up Kerberos as in recipe 2-1. Here it's ldapadm.

For this you need to create a "setup" LDIF file (setup.ldif). Your base domain will depend on your organization. It is a good idea to use a base domain that is related to your Kerberos domain and also to your IP domain. Here we use dc=example,dc=com (matching example.com).

```
# setup.ldif
dn: dc=example,dc=com
objectclass: organization
objectclass: dcObject
objectclass: top
o: Example Company
dc: example
description: root entry
```

```
dn: ou=people,dc=example,dc=com
objectclass: organizationalUnit
ou: people
description: Users
dn: uid=ldapadm,ou=people,dc=example,dc=com
objectClass: inetOrgPerson
objectClass: posixAccount
objectClass: shadowAccount
cn: LDAP admin account
uid: ldapadm
uidNumber: 1002
gidNumber: 100
homeDirectory: /etc/ldap
loginShell: /bin/false
```

Note The LDAP user cannot log in directly, because the login shell is set to /bin/false. This is a security measure. Alternatively, you could make objectClass be simpleSecurityObject instead of posixAccount.

To add this file, use ldapadd:

```
ldapadd -x -D "cn=admin,dc=example,dc=com" -W -f setup.ldif
```

-W is the flag that causes the password to be demanded; -x uses an anonymous bind, because you're not set up yet to use Kerberos. -ZZ would invoke TLS, which works on all the LDAP admin commands (ldapadd, ldapsearch, and so on).

After this, edit /etc/ldap/slapd.conf again to remove (or comment out) the **rootdn** and **rootpw** entries. From now on, to add, delete, or modify entries, you can authenticate via Kerberos using kinit ldapadm.

Restart slapd with /etc/init.d/slapd restart.

Testing!

Before you fully populate the database, check that it works! Try the following, first from the server. Once that's working, set up a client and try it from there.

- ldapsearch -x -H ldaps://server.example.com (-x gives simple bind)

- ldapsearch -x -H ldap://server.example.com -ZZ (to test TLS startup)

- ldapsearch -x -H ldaps://server.example.com -ZZ -TLS

- kinit username; ldapsearch -H ldaps://server.example.com (to test Kerberos auth)

Troubleshooting

Here are some things to look for if it doesn't work:

- Check the permissions on **/etc/ldap/cacert.pem**. They need to be world-readable.

- Check **/etc/hosts** if the hostname is resolving incorrectly. This will show up in the debugging output. Your client must be trying **server.example.com**, not just **server**, because it must match what's in the certificate.

- If you get the error "Key version for principal in keytable is incorrect," there is a mismatch between the Kerberos keytab and the master server. On the LDAP host, run **kadmin -p krbadm**, and execute the following:

```
ktrem ldap/server.example.com
delprinc ldap/server.example.com
addprinc -randkey ldap/server.example.com
ktadd ldap/server.example.com
```

- If you get the error "GSSAPI Error: Miscellaneous failure (Permission denied)," check that the LDAP keytab is readable by the LDAP user (**openldap**) and that **slapd** is looking at the correct keytab. You can test this quickly by also adding **ldap/server.example.com** to the system keytab at **/etc/krb5.keytab** and making that world-readable:

```
kadmin -p krbadm -q "ktadd -k /etc/krb5.keytab ldap/server.example.com"
chmod a+r /etc/krb5.keytab
```

If that starts things working, then your keytab may be the problem. Remember to change /etc/krb5.keytab back to root-only afterward:

```
chmod go-r /etc/krb5.keytab
```

and remove the **ldap/server.example.com** entry from your main keytab:

```
kadmin -p krbadm -q "ktrem -k /etc/krb5.keytab ldap/server.example.com"
```

- Add **-d 16383** to the **ldapsearch** line to enable copious debugging output. However, having high levels of debugging will slow things down hugely. That's fine when setting up but not good for a production server. Turn debugging off or down (set **loglevel** in **/etc/ldap/slapd.conf** to 0 or 1) once things are working. If you are not getting errors but **ldapsearch** appears to be hanging, try reducing the log levels in **/etc/ldap/slapd.conf** and restarting **slapd**.

2-5. Populating the LDAP Database

There are many options to populate the database. If you already have users, you'll want to migrate your data. Use the **migrationtools** package on Debian. This works fine for regular Unix setup (**/etc/passwd**, **/etc/shadow**, **/etc/groups**) and also for NIS. With some adjustment, it will also work for NIS+. You'll need to take a look at your NIS+ files and the **migrationtools** scripts and edit them as necessary. You will, however, need to migrate your passwords to Kerberos by hand. This may be a good moment to make everyone change their passwords!

To import an existing LDAP database, run this:

```
/etc/init.d/slapd stop
slapadd -l existing_database.ldif
/etc/init.d/slapd start
```

where `existing_database.ldif` is an LDIF dump of an existing database, obtained by the following, run from the machine where the existing database and LDAP server lives:

```
 /etc/init.d/slapd stop; /usr/sbin/slapcat -l existing_database.ldif; ↵
/etc/init.d/slapd start
```

You may need to empty the target database first, if you've been experimenting with it.

Remove the `rootdn` and `rootpw` entries from `/etc/ldap/slapd.conf`. They're just used to get you started (after which you should be using Kerberos to handle admin).

```
/etc/init.d/slapd start
/etc/init.d/slapd stop
```

Now import the database as earlier.

If you have startup problems, check that the database directory is owned by the LDAP user (`openldap` on Debian).

Finally, you need to make sure that there are no password references in your user database. Kerberos will be handling passwords for you, and the easiest way to make this happen is simply to remove all password references from LDAP.

Use `ldapsearch` to get the attributes for any user:

```
kinit ldapadm
ldapsearch ("uid=jkemp")Look for any password attributes.
dn: uid=jkemp,ou=People,dc=example.com
uid: jkemp
cn: Juliet Kemp
objectClass: account
objectClass: posixAccount
objectClass: top
objectClass: shadowAccount
userPassword: HASH
shadowLastChange: 13166
shadowMax: 99999
shadowWarning: 7
uidNumber: 444
gidNumber: 2222
homeDirectory: /home/jkemp
gecos: Juliet Kemp
loginShell: /bin/bash
```

Here the field is `userPassword`. Depending on where you got your database from, your setup may have a slightly different field name.

Then for any individual user, you can create the following **ldapmodify** file:

```
dn: cn=username,ou=People,dc=example,dc=com
changetype: modify
delete: userPassword
```

Make sure to replace **userPassword** with whatever field showed up in your query. Then run this:

```
kinit ldapadm; ldapmodify -f modifyfile
```

You can put multiple users in the same file. Use the previous syntax, but separate each instance with a blank line. To generate a modify file with just the DN of all your users, use this search:

```
ldapsearch ("userPassword=*") dn > modifyfile
```

You'll need to edit it a bit to remove the extraneous query information. On a single-user database, the output looks like this:

```
# extended LDIF
#
# LDAPv3
# base <> with scope subtree
# filter: (uid=jkemp)
# requesting: dn
#

# jkemp, People, example.com
dn: uid=jkemp,ou=People,dc=example,dc=com

# search result
search: 5
result: 0 Success

# numResponses: 2
# numEntries: 1
```

All you want is the **dn: uid=jkemp,ou=People,dc=example,dc=com** line. In vim, the following command line:

```
:%s/^#.*\n//
```

will remove all the lines beginning with #, leaving only the search result section to delete by hand.

Then add this after each **dn** line in the file:

```
changetype: modify
delete: userPassword
```

In vim, the following command line will do this:

```
:%s/\(^dn:.*\n\)/\1changetype: modify\rdelete: userPassword/
```

Then apply the file to your database:

```
kinit ldapadm; ldapmodify -f modifyfile
```

Alternatively, you can of course edit any data migration tool so it doesn't take the password data.

2-6. Setting Up the LDAP Client

On your client, install the required packages:

```
sudo apt-get install ldap_utils libnss-ldap autofs-ldap nscd
```

■ **Note** You need `autofs-ldap` only if you use automount. See recipe 2-14.

Edit `/etc/nsswitch.conf`:

```
passwd:     compat files ldap
shadow:     compat files
group:      compat files ldap

hosts:      files dns

services:   db files ldap [NOTFOUND=return]
networks:   db files ldap [NOTFOUND=return]
protocols:  db files ldap [NOTFOUND=return]
rpc:        db files ldap [NOTFOUND=return]
ethers:     db files ldap [NOTFOUND=return]

automount:  files
```

It is important that `compat` and `files` entries appear before `ldap` for `passwd/shadow/group`. Otherwise, if your LDAP server fails (or the client connection to it does), you won't be able to log in at all. You can use `ldap` for hosts as well if you prefer.

Edit `/etc/libnss-ldap.conf` (on Ubuntu this is `/etc/ldap.conf`—not to be confused with `/etc/ldap/ldap.conf`!) so that the only lines uncommented are as follows:

```
base dc=example,dc=com
uri ldaps://ldapserver.example.com
ldap_version 3
```

Edit `/etc/ldap/ldap.conf`:

```
BASE    dc=example,dc=com
URI     ldaps://ldapserver.example.com
```

Note If you're using TLS over the standard LDAP port, the URI line will be the URI `ldap://ldapserver.example.com`.

If you're using a self-signed certificate, you can add this line to enable the client to request the server's certificate:

```
TLS_REQCERT allow
```

Otherwise, copy the certificate to the client, and set the location with the following:

```
TLS_CACERT /path/to/file
```

If you're using a proper CA, you should be able to use this:

```
TLS_CACERTDIR /usr/share/ca-certificates/
```

to point to the directory where the **ca-certificates** package stores certificates; if this causes problems, use the `TLS_CACERT` option instead.

To set up automount to read from LDAP, see recipe 2-14.

To test your setup, try the following on the client:

```
ldapsearch -d 1 -x
```

You should see the TLS information at the top and bottom of the debug output (generated with the `-d 1` flag). If you have any problems, try specifying the server with `-H ldaps://ldapserver.example.com`. If this works, check that the values in `/etc/ldap/ldap.conf` match your setup.

Finally, test that Kerberos auth is working by typing `kinit` and then `ldapsearch` (in other words, without the `-x` simple bind flag).

You're there!

Troubleshooting

If your secure LDAP connection isn't working, check that you're definitely using SSL rather than TLS. You may need to add the following to your `/etc/libnss-ldap.conf` (`/etc/ldap.conf` on Ubuntu) file:

```
ssl on
```

If you use PAM and LDAP together, you should also add it to `pam_ldap.conf`. Some versions default to TLS, and some to SSL, which forces SSL being used. At time of writing, this was a known bug with Debian lenny.

If `slapd` won't start and there's an "unstable alock" message in the logs (increase logging in `/etc/ldap/slapd.conf` to 1 to get better error messages), move `/var/lib/ldap/alock` out of the way and restart. (`/var/lib/ldap` is where the various database files live. You shouldn't need to interact with this very often.) Note that you may need to restart a couple of times and/or allow time for the restart to check the database, because the problem that this message indicates is that the database is or might be corrupt.

2-7. Using LDAP

The basic LDAP commands are `ldapadd`, `ldapmodify`, and `ldapdelete`. Run `kinit ldapadm` before any of these to authenticate yourself if you're using LDAP with Kerberos (replace `ldapadm` with your LDAP admin user if it's different). If using non-Kerberos authentication, use the `-D` and `-W` options:

```
ldapadd -D cn=ldapadm,ou=admin,dc=example,dc=com -W
```

`-D` specifies the distinguished name (DN) to use to bind to the server. This should be the DN of your local admin or another user with appropriate privileges.

`-W` will prompt you for the password, which is more secure than using the `-w password` option on the command line. The same options are valid for the other LDAP commands.

■ **Note** See recipe 2-11 for how to use LDAP with Perl in a script.

---

ldapsearch

To find a specific entry, use `ldapsearch`:

```
ldapsearch "(uid=jkemp)"
```

This uses a search filter in an LDAP-specific format. This example would search for an entry with the `uid` value exactly equal to `jkemp`. To search for a value that ends with `kemp`, you could use the following:

```
ldapsearch "(uid=*kemp)"
```

It's important to get the double quotes and the brackets in the correct order! (The quotes go on the outside.) You can also use AND and OR arguments, and other mathematical operators are supported. The following would search for a user who had a group ID greater than or equal to 1005 and a `tcsh` shell:

```
ldapsearch "(&(gidNumber>=1005)(loginShell=*tcsh))"
```

The AND is given by the `&` at the start of the filter (note the use of brackets). To exclude a particular user from this, you can use `!`. The following would return all users with a group ID >= 1005 and a `tcsh` shell, except for the user `jkemp`:

```
ldapsearch "(&(gidNumber>=1005)(loginShell=*tcsh)(!uid=jkemp))"
```

You can string as many of these together as you like. You can also specify which attributes should be returned. The following would return all users with a login shell of zsh *or* bash but would return only their uid and cn:

```
ldapsearch "(|(loginShell=*bash)(loginShell=*zsh))" uid cn
```

The | character at the start of the filter specifies OR. You can list as many attributes at the end of the line as you want to return.

ldapadd

To add an entry from the command line, you use the command **ldapadd**. This takes an LDIF file as an argument:

```
ldapadd -f newuser.ldif
```

The LDIF file specifies the entry or entries to add. You can also do this on the command line, but you can edit a file if you make a mistake when typing and can edit and reuse it if you need to add other similar entries. The following is a sample **newuser.ldif** file, which would create a user entry and an entry for the **autofs** map for their home directory (see recipe 2-13):

```
dn: uid=jkemp,ou=People,dc=example,dc=comuid: jkempobjectClass: account
objectClass: posixAccount
objectClass: top
objectClass: shadowAccount
loginShell: /bin/bash
uidNumber: 439
gidNumber: 1005
homeDirectory: /home/jkemp
gecos: Juliet Kemp
cn: Juliet Kemp

dn: cn=jkemp,ou=auto.home,dc=example,dc=com
objectClass: automount
cn: jkemp
automountInformation: -fstype=nfs,rw server1:/export/home/jkemp
automountMapName: auto_home
```

Use a blank line to separate entries in the LDIF file, as shown here.

ldapmodify

To modify an existing entry, use **ldapmodify.** Like **ldapadd**, the best way to use this is with an LDIF file as an argument:

```
ldapmodify -f modify_file
```

This `modify_file` would changes the user's login shell to **bash**:

```
dn: uid=jkemp,ou=People,dc=example,dc=com
changetype: modify
replace: loginShell
loginShell: /bin/bash
```

The `changetype` is specified as `modify`, and the field to replace is given before the replacement value is given on the last line.

This file would add an `emailAddress` field to the specified user, with the value given in the last line:

```
dn: uid=jkemp,ou=People,dc=example,dc=com
changetype: addadd: emailAddress
emailAddress: user@example.com
```

Note the different `changetype`. You're adding a field rather than modifying it, but again you specify the field to add and then the value to add in much the same way as the replacement was specified in the previous file.

ldapdelete

Finally, use `ldapdelete` to delete an existing entry. All you need to specify for this is the DN of the entry you want to delete:

```
ldapdelete "cn=isis,ou=Hosts,dc=example,dc=com"
```

You can also use `ldapdelete -f file`, where `file` contains a list of DNs in the same format, one per line, all of which will be deleted in turn.

2-8. Setting Up a Slave LDAP Server

You can run with just a single LDAP server, but it's a far better idea to have at least two. That way, first, you can spread the request load if need be, and second, you have a backup so that if something goes wrong with your master server, users can still access the LDAP database (and thus log on and work!) while you're fixing the problem.

You can set up a slave LDAP server fairly easily. The slave server will handle any requests for information but will automatically pass any change requests to the master server. This means that the database has to be replicated in only one direction and avoids the possibility of conflicting changes being made on different servers.

For authentication, we'll use **rep_adm** as the replication admin user (which will need to operate automatically) and **ldapadm** as the regular interactive admin user (which therefore authenticates with a password).

Note This used to be handled by `slurpd`, but this has been deprecated now in favor of `syncrepl`.

In the `/etc/ldap/slapd.conf` file on your master server, add this section in the `Specific Directives for database #1` section of the file:

```
overlay syncprov
syncprov-checkpoint 100 10
syncprov-sessionlog 200
index objectClass,entryUUID eq
```

This will perform a checkpoint every 100 operations or 10 minutes (the second line) and will record 200 lines of session log (the third line). The final line sets up indexing. The session log (which is used for LDAP Sync searches) searches on `entryUUID`, so setting an index on this attribute speeds up these searches.

Set up your slave server with the same basic configuration as the master, but instead of the `syncprov` section used earlier for the master, use these lines:

```
        access to *
                by dn="uid=ldapadm,ou=people,dc=example, dc=com" write
                by dn="uid=rep_adm,ou=people,dc=example, dc=com" write
                by * read
index objectClass,entryUUID eq

syncrepl rid=450
    provider=ldaps://ldapserver.example.com:636
    type=refreshAndPersist
    searchbase="dc=example,dc=com"
    schemachecking=off
    bindmethod=sasl
    saslmech=GSSAPI
    binddn="uid=rep_adm,ou=people,dc=example,dc=com"
```

Here both `ldapadm` and `rep_adm` have access to write to the database.

Note If your master server doesn't have universal read access (which is the setup used in recipes 2-3 and 2-4 and so what I assume here), you'll need to give read access to `rep_adm` on the master server:

```
access to *
    by dn="uid=rep_adm,ou=people,dc=example, dc=com" read
```

The `syncrepl` section will perform a synchronization check on the whole database once every four hours (set by the interval line). The provider is the main LDAP server. The `refreshAndPersist` type means that the slave server will continue listening for any changes, which will be updated immediately (the less-useful alternative is `refreshOnly`, which just checks at the given interval and then signs off, so any changes won't be replicated until the next check. If you use this, you'll need to set an interval value—see the LDAP syncrepl docs).

You shouldn't need to restart the master server (the provider). Just start the slave server up, and it should automatically pick up the master server database.

For this setup to work, you need to be able to have a Kerberos ticket for both ldapadm and rep_adm alive at the same time (see the alternative configuration later in this recipe if you're not using Kerberos). Otherwise, you'd set up your authentication as rep_adm on the master machine, and that would work great until you authenticated as ldapadm to make a change to the DB, at which point it would fail. This is particularly not great given that it's precisely when you're making changes that you want replication to work!

■ **Note** If you do have this problem, you'll see this in the .rej file in /var/lib/ldap/:

```
ERROR: Referral
```

If you increase the logging of the slave, you'll also see slurpd changing users.

What you need is to set up k5start to manage more than one ticket. Set up your slapd init script (which also starts slurpd and k5start) to include this:

```
KRB5CCNAME="FILE:/tmp/ldap_replicator.tkt"
export KRB5CCNAME

.....

start_slurpd() {
    if [ "$SLURPD_START" != yes ]; then
        return 0
    fi
    echo -n " slurpd"
    reason="`start-stop-daemon --start --quiet --oknodo \
        --exec /usr/sbin/slurpd -- $SLURPD_OPTIONS 2>&1`"
    echo -n " k5start"
    # Start kstart in order to manage replication
    reason_kstart="`start-stop-daemon --start --pidfile \
        /var/run/k5start.pid \
        --exec /usr/bin/k5start -- -b -K 10 \
        -k /tmp/ldap_replicator.tkt \
        -p /var/run/k5start.pid \
        -f /etc/ldap/slurpd.keytab rep_adm`"
}
```

reason and reason_kstart are caught separately elsewhere in the script so that a failure of kstart won't cause the total failure of the LDAP server. To do this, add this section to the start of report_failure:

```
report_failure() {
        if [ -n "$reason" ]; then
                echo " - failed: "
                echo "$reason"
        else
                if [ -n "$reason_kstart" ]; then
                        echo " kstart failed: "
                        echo "$reason_kstart"
                        echo " - failed."
                else
                        cat <<EOF
}
```

Note Extracting a user to a keytab then prevents one from being able to `kinit` as that user with the normal password. This is a good reason to set up "service" principals, which can be extracted to keytabs and don't interfere with the user space.

If you're not using Kerberos replication, you can instead use this configuration for the slave server (you'll also need the access and index sections as given in the previous slave server configuration example):

```
syncrepl rid=450
            provider=ldaps://ldapserver.example.com:636
            type=refreshAndPersist
            searchbase="dc=example,dc=com"
            schemachecking=off
            bindmethod=simple
            binddn="uid=rep_adm,ou=people,dc=example,dc=com"
            credentials=mypassword
```

This does a simple bind using the given DN and the given password. Note that this is not very secure, because the password is in plain text in the configuration file!

Troubleshooting

The one problem with this setup is that it can hide problems with the master server, because everything keeps working. (You should of course be monitoring the server. See Chapter 3 for more information on monitoring.)

If your master server is down but the slaves are OK, **ldapsearch** and other lookups will work fine. But if you try to modify the database (for example with **ldapadd**), you'll get this kind of error message:

```
ldap_add: Referral (10)
      referrals:
      ldaps://masterldap.example.com/uid=test,ou=People,
dc=example,dc=com
```

Slave servers can't modify the database, so it tries to redirect to the master and fails. If you now use ldapsearch to look for your new entry, you will not find it.

You can confirm this diagnosis by trying ldapsearch -H ldaps://masterldap.example.com to force a bind to the master server.

The next stage is to find out what's causing the problem. Set the log level in /etc/ldap/slapd.conf to 1, and then restart slapd and check the logs.

These are two common problems:

- An old slapd process that hasn't been killed off properly. Check with ps and kill it if necessary.

- An alock problem, which looks like this in the log:

```
slapd[27069]: bdb_db_open: alock package is unstable
slapd[27069]: backend_startup_one: bi_db_open failed! (-1)
```

To resolve this, stop the server, delete the old alock file, and restart the server:

```
/etc/init.d/slapd stop
rm /var/lib/ldap/alock
/etc/init.d/slapd start
```

slapd may take a little while to recover the database after this and may also need to be restarted again. It's probably wise to run a database dump before doing this. Again, this is something that you should be doing regularly anyway.

Remember to return the log level to normal afterward, or the server will be very slow.

If slurpd isn't working properly, stop slapd, check the output of ps -A for old slapd processes and kill them if necessary, and then restart slapd. Check ps -A again to confirm that slapd is running.

If the slave server is missing some entries (for example, if entries were added to the main database that relied on new schemas that weren't available on the slave, which means that the slave will ignore the changes):

1. Stop slapd on the slave.

2. On the master server, run the following:

   ```
   /usr/sbin/slapcat -l backupdb.ldif
   ```

3. Copy backupdb.ldif onto the slave server.

4. slapcat -c -l backupdb.ldif on the slave. Ignore any errors regarding duplicate entries.

5. Restart slapd on the slave server.

When you are troubleshooting, bear in mind that the replog file is expected to be empty, because slurpd truncates it immediately on read. In other words, if you see an empty replog, this is not on its own an indication of or a source of any problems! However, the truncation happens whether a full successful replication has been completed, because the file is truncated immediately on read. If you have a problem with replication, you'll usually lose the replication data from the replog file, though the correct data will still be in the master database. This means that when you do get replication working again, the new data will never be transferred. To resolve this problem, use the method mentioned previously.

2-9. Setting Up Kerberos Replication

Just as with LDAP, it's a good idea to configure a second Kerberos server for backup purposes. With Kerberos, more than one server can act as a KDC and respond to auth requests, but only one can manage changes to the database (the admin server).

First of all, configure your second server as a Kerberos client (see recipes 2-1 and 2-2). Next, install `krb5-kdc` and `libkrb5-dev` (not admin server).

Edit `/etc/krb.conf` to include the following in the `[realms]` section under the relevant realm:

```
kdc = krb_slave.example.com
```

Also add a logging section:

```
[logging]
        kdc = FILE:/var/log/kerberos/krb5kdc.log
        default = FILE:/var/log/kerberos/krb5lib.log
```

Edit `/etc/krb5kdc/kpropd.acl` to include names of both master and slave servers:

```
host/kerberos.example.com@EXAMPLE.COM
host/krb_slave.example.com@EXAMPLE.COM
```

Extract the host keys to the appropriate servers:

- On the slave server:

  ```
  klist -k /etc/krb5.keytab
  ```

- Ensure that it includes an entry for `host/krb5_slave.example.com`. If it's missing, still from the slave server, run the following:

  ```
  kadmin -p krbadm
  ```

- Check that there is a `host/krb5_slave.example.com` principal present in the database. If not, run this:

  ```
  kadmin: addprinc -randkey host/krb5_slave.example.com
  ```

- Extract the slave server's key to the keytab:

  ```
  kadmin: ktadd host/krb5_slave.example.com
  ```

- On the master server:

  ```
  klist -k /etc/krb5.keytab
  ```

- Check that there is an entry for `host/kerberos.example.com`, and if not, create it as shown earlier.

Next, you need to set up `kpropd` to run on the slave server. This can be done via `inetd` by uncommenting the following line in `/etc/inetd.conf` and then restarting `inetd`:

```
krb5_prop    stream    tcp    nowait    root    /usr/sbin/kpropd    kpropd
```

Alternatively, you can start **kpropd** stand-alone from the command line with **/usr/sbin/kpropd -S**, in which case you will need to write an init script specifically for **kpropd** in order to start it at boot.

Transfer the database from the master server:

```
/usr/sbin/kdb5_util dump slave_transfer
/usr/sbin/kprop -f slave_transfer server2.example.com
```

Re-create the stash file (the file generated from the database password) on the slave server:

```
kdb5_util -m stash
```

Enter the password you used when creating the database on your master server.

Start **krb5-kdc** on the slave server, and check the logs for errors. To confirm that it's working, add the slave entry, remove the master entry from **/etc/krb5.conf** on one of your clients, and check that **kdestroy; kinit** works.

Troubleshooting

Here are some things to check if you get an error message:

"Key table entry not found":

a. Check the logs. Is **localhost** being used instead of **hostname**?

b. If so, edit **/etc/hosts** appropriately.

"Key number mismatch":

a. Compare **kvno host/server.example.com** and **klist -k /etc/krb5.keytab** on both servers.

b. If they mismatch, you may need to destroy and re-create principals.

c. In this instance, run **kdestroy; kinit** before trying again to clear cached key numbers.

"Cannot find KDC":

a. This may be a host resolve problem. Test this by replacing the name with the IP address in **/etc/krb5.keytab**.

b. If this solves the problem, check **/etc/hosts** for the wrong **localhost** entries.

The final step is to run **kpropd** regularly to propagate any changes in information from the master to the slave. This is usually done with a two-line script (dump to file and propagate the file across), which runs from **/etc/crontab** with the output directed to **/dev/null**.

The downside to this is that while you don't want to get the **SUCCEEDED** message e-mailed to you every time it propagates successfully, you *do* want to know about it in the event of failure. This slightly improved script handles that:

```
#!/bin/sh
# Script to run automatic Kerberos dump & transfer to slave server


DUMPFILE=/etc/krb5kdc/slave_dump_file
RESULT=/etc/krb5kdc/slave_dump_result
SLAVE=server2.example.com
MAIL=sysadmin@example.com

/usr/sbin/kdb5_util dump $DUMPFILE
/usr/sbin/kprop -f $DUMPFILE $SLAVE > $RESULT

if grep -vq SUCCEEDED $RESULT ; then
        mail -s "Kerberos replication problem" $MAIL < $RESULT
fi
```

Put this in the /etc/cron.hourly directory. If you want to run it more often, add a line to /etc/ crontab at whatever interval you prefer; you'll probably want to keep the file in /etc/cron.d/ in this case.

2-10. Adding a New User to LDAP with a Script

LDIF is a format used to make changes to the LDAP database, and it's perfectly possible to add, delete, and modify records just by writing LDIF files and using ldapadd, ldapmodify, and ldapdelete. In fact, sometimes that's the best option. However, it's useful to be able to script those interactions.

perl-ldap is a very useful collection of Perl modules providing an OO interface to LDAP servers. To install the Debian/Ubuntu package, run this:

```
sudo apt-get install libnet-ldap-perl
```

Or you can install it from CPAN by running this as **root**:

```
perl -m CPAN -e "install perl-ldap"
```

The following script will add a new user, with parameters taken from the command line. You would need to authenticate as the LDAP admin user before running it in full (the parts that just search should work as any user).

Net::LDAP and Net::LDAPS are the modules that handle connecting and talking to the server. Net::LDAP deals with regular LDAP connections, and Net::LDAPS deals with LDAPS (secure) connections (although Net::LDAP also has options to force an ldaps:/// connection and to handle TLS with the start_tls() method).

The following code connects to an LDAP server, makes an anonymous bind, performs a search to look for the new username (to see whether it already exists), adds the user, and takes the session down:

```
01 #!/usr/bin/perl -w
02 use strict;
03
04 # Use whichever module matches your server
05 #use Net::LDAP;
06 use Net::LDAPS;
```

```
07
08 die "Usage is adduser.pl [username] ["realname"]\n" if length(@ARGV) != 1;
09
10 my $username = $ARGV[0];
11 my $realname = $ARGV[1];
12
13 # Plain LDAP version if you prefer this to the LDAPS version
14 # my $ldap = Net::LDAP->new( 'ldapserver.example.com');
15 my $ldap = Net::LDAPS->new( 'ldapserver.example.com',
16                             verify => 'optional',
17                             cafile => '/etc/ldap/cacert.pem' ) or die $@;
18   my $mesg = $ldap->bind;
1920 $mesg = $ldap->search( base    => "ou=people,dc=example,dc=com",
21                        filter  => "(uid=$username)",
22           );
23 $mesg->code && die $mesg->error;
24
25 my $searchResults = $mesg->count;
26 die "Error! Username already exists!" unless $searchResults == 0;
27
28 $mesg = $ldap->search ( base    => "ou=people,dc=example,dc=com",
29                          attrs  => [ 'uidNumber' ],
30                        );
31 my @entries = $mesg->sorted('uidNumber');
32 my $entry = pop @entries;
33 my $newuid = $entry->get_value( 'uidNumber' );
34 $newuid++;
35
36 my  $result = $ldap->add("uid=$username,ou=people,dc=example,dc=com",
37              attr => [ 'cn'             => $realname,
38                        'uid'            => $userid,
39                        'uidNumber'      => $newuid,
40                        'mail'           => '$username@example.com',
41                        'homeDirectory' => '/home/$username',
42                        'objectclass'    => [ 'person', 'inetOrgPerson',
43                                              'posixAccount' ]
44                      ]
45         );
46
47 $mesg = $ldap->unbind;
```

If using ldaps:///, you will need the CA certificate for the CA that signed your server's certificate. For a proper CA (as opposed to self-signed), you should be able to use the **capath** (rather than **cafile**) attribute to set the directory where CA certificates live rather than needing to give a specific file.

Line 17 performs an anonymous bind. If you want to bind with a specific DN (for example, to authenticate as your admin user, if you're not using Kerberos), you can provide extra options:

```
my $adminuser = "cn=root,dc=example,dc=com"
my $password = "mypasswd";
$mesg = $ldap->bind( $adminuser, password => $password );
```

Or you can use an SASL mechanism by giving an Authen::SASL object as an argument:

```
$mesg = $ldap->bind( "cn=root,dc=example,dc=com", sasl => $sasl );
```

Lines 19–25 search the directory for an existing user with the given UID. Net::LDAP::Search acts as a container for the results of an LDAP search, and there is a Net::LDAP::Entry for each individual result.

In this example, you're checking to make sure that the username doesn't already exist, so all you need do is to find the number of entries returned. If it's 0, the username is free. Line 24 handles this: the count method gives the number of entries returned. $mesg here is a Net::LDAP::Search object.

■ **Note** Numerous other methods are available for interacting with a Net::LDAP::Search object. You can retrieve an entry by number from the Net::LDAP::Search container, sort the entries, pop off an entry at a time, or return an array of all the Net::LDAP::Entry objects found by the search.

The search method will accept attribute specifications, just as ldapsearch will (see recipe 2-7):

```
$mesg = $ldap->search(  filter => "(uid=jkemp)",
                        base   =>"ou=people,dc=example,dc=com",
                        attrs  => ['uid', 'cn', 'homeDirectory'] );
```

This will return the uid, cn, and homeDirectory of the user jkemp.

To look at the entries returned, you use the Net::LDAP::Entries methods. Lines 27–33 look for the next free user ID to allocate to our user. All the users are returned, as a Net::LDAP::Search object (a container of Net::LDAP::Entries objects), and then are sorted by uidNumber and dumped into an array of Net::LDAP::Entry objects (line 30). Line 31 pops the highest one off the stack. Our next free uidNumber is the value for that entry, plus one.

■ **Note** There are also methods to return the nth entry from a search; but in this case we don't use them because the order of our results matters (we want to get the highest existing userID and then add one), so we have to sort the results first.

Line 35–44 use the $ldap->add method (the most straightforward option) to add an entry of a user with attributes set in that hash. Attributes with multiple values (as with objectclass) use a list.

Alternatively, you could use the Net::LDAP::Entry object to write directly to the LDAP directory:

```
my $entry = Net::LDAP::Entry->new();

# set DN
$entry->dn("uid=$userid,ou=people,dc=example,dc=com");

# You can add attributes all at once, or in as many operations as you like
```

```
$entry->add (
    'cn'            => $realname,
    'uid'           => $userid,
    'uidNumber'     => $newuid,
    'mail'          => '$userid@example.com',
    'homeDirectory' => '/home/$userid',
    'objectclass'   => [ 'person', 'inetOrgPerson',
                         'posixAccount' ]
);

# Then update the LDAP server
$entry->update( $ldap );
```

Finally, the unbind operation in line 46 takes down the session when you're finished. This should always be the last thing you do with the LDAP server.

Note See the documentation available on the project web site at `http://ldap.perl.org/` for full details of this set of modules and further examples.

2-11. Modifying and Deleting Using LDAP Scripts

You can also modify entries with `Net::LDAP`. This script will change all the email addresses in the database from `userid@mail.example.com` to `userid@example.com`.

Note This doesn't check that the existing e-mail address is of the standard format, which in practice you would almost certainly want to do. If you just want to check that the address was of the format `userid@mail.example.com`, you could change line 17–18 to these lines:

```
my $email = $entry->get_value('mail');
if ($email =~ /\w+\@mail.example.com/) {
    $mesg = $ldap->modify( $entry, replace => { 'mail' => ↵
'$uid@mail.example.com' } );
    }
```

This assumes that the first part of all addresses consist only of word characters (alphabetic plus underscore) but can obviously be altered.

If you want to check e-mail address validity more generally, there are various modules that will do this, including `Mail::Verify`, `Email::Valid`, `RFC::RFC822::Address`, and `Mail::RFC822::Address`.

```
01 #!/usr/bin/perl -w
02 use strict;
03 use Net::LDAPS;
04
05 my $ldap = Net::LDAPS->new( 'ldapserver.example.com',
06                              verify => 'optional',
07                               cafile => '/etc/ldap/cacert.pem' ) or die $@;
08 my $mesg = $ldap->bind;
09
10 $mesg = $ldap->search( base    => "ou=people,dc=example,dc=com",
11                         filter => "mail=*",
12                          attrs  => [ 'uid', 'mail' ],
13                        );
14 my @entries = $mesg->entries;
15
16 foreach my $entry ( @entries ) {
17        $mesg = $ldap->modify( $entry, replace => { 'mail' => '$uid@mail.example.com'
18 } );
19 }
20
21 $mesg = ldap->unbind
```

Alternatively, you could use the Net::LDAP::Entry replace method at lines 16–19:

```
foreach my $entry ( @entries ) {
      $entry->replace(
            mail => "$uid\@mail.example.com",
      );
      $entry->update( $ldap );
}
```

Here you need to explicitly call the update method—without this, changes remain local and aren't actually passed to the server. You don't need to do this with the first method.

Deleting Entries

In the same way, you can delete an entry by DN. So, either of these two scripts would work:

```
01  #!/usr/bin/perl -w
02  use strict;
03  use Net::LDAPS;
04
05  die "Usage is deluser.pl [username] if length(@ARGV) != 0;
06
07  my $username = $ARGV[0];

08
09  my $ldap = Net::LDAPS->new( 'ldapserver.example.com',
10                               verify => 'optional',
11                               cafile => '/etc/ldap/cacert.pem' ) or die $@;
```

```
12  my $mesg = $ldap->bind;
13
14  $mesg = $ldap->delete("uid=$username,ou=people,dc=example,dc=com");
15
16  $mesg = $ldap->unbind;

01  #!/usr/bin/perl -w
02  use strict;
03  use Net::LDAPS;
04
05 die "Usage is deluser.pl [username]\n" if length(@ARGV) != 0;
06
07 my $username = $ARGV[0];
08
09  my $ldap = Net::LDAPS->new( 'ldapserver.example.com',
10                              verify => 'optional',
11                              cafile => '/etc/ldap/cacert.pem' ) or die $@;
12  my $mesg = $ldap->bind;
13
14  my $entry = Net::LDAP::Entry->new;
15  # Need to specify the DN of the entry
16  $entry->dn("uid=$username,ou=people,dc=example,dc=com");
17  $entry->delete;
18  $entry->update( $ldap );
19  $mesg = $ldap->unbind;
```

It may be easier, however, to use LDIF in this situation. For example, you might want to read in from an LDIF file a list of entries to be deleted. Net::LDAP::LDIF will read LDIF files and generate Net::LDAP::Entry objects. This script reads in entries from a file, checks for errors in the reading process, and then deletes the entries:

```
01  #!/usr/bin/perl -w
02  use strict;
03  use Net::LDAP::LDIF;
04
05  # Open a file for reading from - the r option
06  my $ldif = Net::LDAP::LDIF->new( "file.ldif", "r");
07
08  my $ldap = Net::LDAPS->new( 'ldapserver.example.com',
09                              verify => 'optional',
10                              cafile => '/etc/ldap/cacert.pem' ) or die $@;
11  my $mesg = $ldap->bind;
12
13  while( not $ldif->eof ( ) ) {
14      $entry = $ldif->read_entry ( );
15      if ( $ldif->error ( ) ) {
16              print "Error msg: ", $ldif->error ( ), "\n";
17              print "Error lines:\n", $ldif->error_lines ( ), "\n";
18      } else {
19              $mesg = $ldap->delete($entry);
20      }
```

```
21   }
22   $mesg = $ldap->unbind;
```

Net::LDAP::LDIF will also write to an LDIF file from a set of Net::LDAP::Entry objects. So, here's another approach to your new user creation script:

```
01   #!/usr/bin/perl -w
02   use strict;
03   use Net::LDAP::LDIF;
04
05   die "Usage is adduser.pl [username] [$newuid] ["realname"]\n" if length(@ARGV) != 2;
06
07   my $username = $ARGV[0];
08   my $newuid     = $ARGV[1];
09   my $realname   = $ARGV[2];
10
11   # Open a file for writing to - the w option
12   my $ldif = Net::LDAP::LDIF->new( "file.ldif", "w");
13
14   my $entry = Net::LDAP::Entry->new();
15
16   # set DN
17   $entry->dn("uid=$userid,ou=people,dc=example,dc=com");
18   # You can add attributes all at once, or in as many operations as you like
19   $entry->add (
20       'cn'            => $realname,
21       'uid'           => $userid,
22       'uidNumber'     => $newuid,
23       'mail'          => "$userid@example.com",
24       'homeDirectory' => "/home/$userid",
25       'objectclass'   => [ 'person', 'inetOrgPerson',
26                            'posixAccount' ]
27   );
28
28   # Write the entry to the LDIF file
29   $ldif->write_entry($entry);
```

After this, you could use the following at the command line to make the change to the server or move the file to another LDAP directory:

```
ldapmodify -f file.ldif
```

2-12. Querying LDAP with a Script

This script queries the LDAP database to find out which disks are available via NFS for a given machine name (see recipes 2-13 to 2-15 for more NFS information). Note that the attributes looked at here are 'automountInformation' and 'automountMap'. If your LDAP information was imported from NIS, the NFS mappings may have different names, and you may need to adjust the search filter and the attributes to return.

```
01  #!/usr/bin/perl -w
02
03  use strict;
04  use Net::LDAPS;
05
06  die "Usage: showdisks machinename\n"
unless (@ARGV == 1);
07
08  # Get & set values
09  my ($search) = @ARGV;
10  my $server    = "ldaps://ldap.example.com";
11  my $cert      = "/etc/ldap/servercert.pem";
12  my $base      = "dc=example,dc=com";
13
14  my $ldap = Net::LDAPS->new( $server,
15                              verify => 'optional',
16                              cafile => $cert ) or die $@;
17  my $mesg = $ldap->bind;
18
19  my $filter = "(automountInformation=*$search*)";
20
21  $mesg = $ldap->search(  base   => $base,
22                          filter => $filter,
23                          attr   => ['cn', 'automountInformation'],
24                       );
25
26  $mesg->code && die $mesg->error;
27
28  my @entries = $mesg->sorted('cn');
29
30  foreach my $entry ( @entries ) {
31      my $location  = $entry->get_value( 'automountInformation' );

32      my $name         = $entry->get_value( 'cn' );
33
34      if ($cn) {
35          my ($options, $path)= split $automount;
36          print "$name : $path ($options) \n";
37      }
38  }
39
40  $mesg = $ldap->unbind;
```

See recipe 2-9 for an in-depth discussion of the **Net::LDAPS** or **Net::LDAP** Perl modules (see line 04) and for how to use them to add an entry. Recipe 2-10 tackles how to modify and delete entries. Line 06 checks that there's only one argument (the machine name to look for) being passed in. Lines 08–12 set up your values, including the search value **$search** (the machine name that was passed in from the command line). Lines 14–17 connect to the LDAP server (you can if you prefer use **Net::LDAP**; see recipe 2-9).

The filter is set up on line 19 to look for **$search** anywhere in the automountInformation value. See recipe 2-13 for more on this, but your automountInformation lines will look a bit like this:

```
automountInformation: -fstype=nfs,rw mymachine:/local/data
```

Lines 21–26 set up and then run the search, returning only the cn and automountInformation attributes (line 23). Line 28 sorts the returned values by their cn.

Lines 30–38 go over the set of returned entries one by one. Lines 31 and 32 get the cn and automountInformation back. The if on line 34 is to take care of the garbage from the first couple of lines of the LDAP return (otherwise you'll get warnings in the output). You look for automount information to output only if a directory name (**$cn**) has been obtained on line 33. Line 35 splits the automountInformation value on whitespace, so the options and the machine and directory location are stored separately. In the previous example line, you'd get these values set:

```
$options = "-fstype=nfs,rw"
$path    = "mymachine:/local/data"
```

This is then output neatly on line 36:

```
mymachine_data: mymachine:/local/data (-fstype=nfs,rw)
```

Finally, line 40 disconnects from the server.

▓ **Note** The most likely problem that you'll run into with this is that your automount information doesn't quite match this format. Use ldapsearch on the command line (see recipe 2-6) to output the data so you can take a look at it and make the appropriate adjustments to the script.

2-13. Adding Your Own Fields to LDAP

You might sometimes want to create additional fields to hold information within LDAP, such as if you want to keep a record of which user has which desktop machine. (This is helpful when they contact you with a problem but forget to mention their machine name, which will be 90 percent of the time.)

One way to do this would be to create an extra objectclass called localDesktop, which can possess an attribute called localUser (which you must also create). An example of this follows: put this into a file in your /etc/ldap/schema/ directory (for example, local.schema).

```
# These OIDs are all fake.  No guarantees there won't be conflicts.
# $Id$

attributetype ( 1.2.3.1 NAME 'localUser'
        DESC 'User of desktop'
        EQUALITY caseIgnoreIA5Match
        SYNTAX 1.3.6.1.4.1.1466.115.121.1.26 )
```

```
objectclass ( 1.2.3.2 NAME 'localDesktop' SUP top AUXILIARY
    DESC 'Desktop objectclass'
    MAY ( localUser ))
```

First, then, let's talk about that warning at the top. Every object in an LDAP schema has to have an object identifier (OID). All the ones in the schemas you've already grabbed will have been officially allocated; you have the choice, when creating your own, of contacting ICANN or another registry authority to get a number range or of just making one up that doesn't clash with anything you're using locally. The former is obviously the correct way to do it! But it may not always be worth the hassle if you will use this only locally. If you do get an OID allocated, you can create anything you like underneath it. So, if you did get 1.2.3, you could also use 1.2.3.1, 1.2.3.2.2.3.1, or anything else beginning 1.2.3.

Note Check out http://www.alvestrand.no/objectid/ to see the tree of existing OIDs.

So, the rest of that first line gives the attribute a name (no spaces). DESC is a human-readable description string. EQUALITY defines how the attribute will behave in a search; this uses IA5 strings and ignores case when searching. SYNTAX defines the data type:; this one is an IA5 string.

SUP indicates that the object class has a parent. In this case, the parent is 'top', which is a special class that is the highest level of all object classes. AUXILIARY is its structural type and means that this class can be used within an entry but can't form an entry all by itself (so you can't have an object that is *just* a localDesktop).

MAY(icUser) states that an object of this type may (but does not have to) have the icUser attribute that we defined earlier.

You'll then need to add this line to your /etc/ldap/slapd.conf file, after the other schema lines:

```
include         /etc/ldap/schema/local.schema
```

and restart slapd.

Of course, just adding the schema doesn't automatically make any of your objects be of the new class or have the new attribute. You'll need to set up an LDIF file for that, with an entry like this for each machine you want to change:

```
dn: cn=client1,ou=Hosts,dc=example,dc=com
changetype: modify
add: objectClass
objectClass: icDesktop
-
add: icUser
icUser: user1
```

Leave a blank line in the file between each host that you're changing, with no blank lines around the – line (this separates modifications to be done on the same host). Then use ldapmodify -f file.ldif to make the changes. Remember to authenticate as the correct user first.

2-14. Using NFS and automount

A basic NFS shared directory is usually very straightforward to set up. To share the `/local/` directory to any other machine in the `10.1.0.*` subnet, edit the `/etc/exports` file on the machine that the source drive is on (let's call it `server1`):

```
/local  10.1.0.*     rw
```

Then restart the NFS server (`/etc/init.d/nfs-kernel-server restart`). Next mount the drive from any other machine in that subnet, on that machine's `/mnt` directory, with this:

```
mount server1:/local /mnt
```

To set this up to mount automatically on boot, add it to `/etc/fstab`:

```
/mnt            server1:/local           nfs    defaults        0 2
```

However, a more flexible approach than manual mounting is to use automount. With this, drives are automatically mounted on request, rather than being mounted all the time (as with the previous setup).

You can set up a central home disk on your server and have that automounted on request. The advantages to a central home disk are fairly obvious: anyone can work on any machine, and backups are made easier. If it's automounted, then it won't affect the bootup procedure if there's a problem of some sort with the server.

Install the package on the client:

```
apt-get install autofs
```

Then edit the `/etc/auto.master` file on the client to have this line:

```
/home           -rw              server1:/export/home
```

Restart `autofs`, and then type `cd /mnt/server`. The directory should appear and list correctly.

Automounting really comes into its own if you get your automount maps from your LDAP server. Partly, this has the usual centralization advantage that if a mapping changes, you need to change it only once, in one place, not on all your machines. But it also means that you can set up home directory mappings individually (per directory) rather than the home directory as a whole, but without having to have unwieldy swathes of mappings.

Install the `autofs-ldap` package, and edit your `/etc/auto.master` file to read as follows:

```
/home    ldap:automountMap=auto.home,dc=ph,dc=ic,dc=ac,dc=uk
```

Then log into the LDAP server. You'll need to add one parent map entry, for the directory map as a whole, and then individual per-user maps. The LDIF file here describes the parent map and one user map:

```
dn: ou=auto.home,dc=example,dc=com
objectClass: top
objectClass: automountMap
ou: auto.home
```

```
dn: cn=jkemp,ou=auto.home,dc=example,dc=com
objectClass: automount
cn: jkemp
automountInformation: -fstype=nfs,rw server1:/export/home/jkemp
automountMapName: auto_home
```

Authenticate as the LDAP admin user (`kinit ldapadm` if you're using Kerberos), and add these entries to the database:

```
ldapadd < automount.ldif
```

You should now be able to automount /home/jkemp from your client. Repeat this for your other users.

2-15. Connecting Macs to a Linux NFS Server

If you have Macs on your network that want to be able to connect to an NFS server, you will run into the problem that Linux NFS expects clients to use a privileged network port (less than 1024); while Mac (and other OpenBSD-based systems) use a port above 1024 for NFS requests.

There are two ways of solving this. The first is to add the **insecure** parameter to the **/etc/exports** file on the server:

```
/local  10.1.0.*     rw,insecure
```

If you prefer and you have only one or two Macs, you could do this for only them in particular:

```
/local  10.1.0.17           rw,insecure
/local  10.1.0.*            rw
```

The other option is to fix it at the client end. This is probably neater but may cause you more problems with users, depending on your setup. You need to add -P to the command line (one of the user problems here is that you can't do this from the Finder).
```
mount -P server:/local /mnt
```

2-16. Improving NFS Performance

If you're experiencing performance problems, you can look at **/proc/net/rpc/nfsd** for some diagnostic information. For example, the th line in that file indicates the number of seconds during which the thread usage was at the maximum allowable. If this is a large number, you may want to increase the number of NFS instances available (that is, the number of servers running). The standard default is 8, but more heavily used servers may benefit from having more. This is specified with the **RPCNFSDCOUNT** value, which is given in the init script (**/etc/init.d/nfs-kernel-server** on Debian/Ubuntu).

Note If you're using a system on which the file `/etc/default/nfs-kernel-server` exists (for example, Debian/Ubuntu), then you'll also need to set the new `RPCNFSDCOUNT` value in this file.

If you're experiencing load or performance issues, you can also increase the memory queue limits. These are frequently low by default, especially on 2.4 kernels, and because the memory queue is shared between all the server instances, it's probably a good idea to increase the memory queue if you increase the number of servers. The limits are set using **proc**. Use `/proc/sys/net/core/rmem_default` and `/proc/sys/net/core/rmem_max` for the read limits, and use `/proc/sys/net/core/wmem_default` and `/proc/sys/net/core/wmem_max` for the read limits. Reset them to 256k as follows:

```
# echo 262144 > /proc/sys/net/core/rmem_default
# echo 262144 > /proc/sys/net/core/rmem_max
# echo 262144 > /proc/sys/net/core/wmem_default
# echo 262144 > /proc/sys/net/core/wmem_max
```

Then restart the NFS server with `/etc/init.d/nfs-kernel-server`.

Note There are some reports of problems generated in other systems if these values are left unchanged for long periods of time. You can reset them after you've restarted the NFS server (using the same lines as shown previously, but substitute `65536` for `262144`). However, bear in mind that in this case, the new values will be discarded the next time you have to restart NFS. Perhaps better is to watch for problems and reset the values if they arise.

`nfsstat -s` (on the server) and `nfsstat -c` (on the client) may also be helpful. These both show NFS statistics. In particular, if `badcalls` is greater than zero, you may have network problems, and if `writes` is greater than 10 percent, it may be worth looking into write caching to speed up operation.

`nfsstat -m` from the client provides server information from the client's point of view. The `srtt` gives a smoothed round-trip time value. If this is greater than 50ms, the mount point is slow. `cur` gives the timeout value. If `cur > 80ms` for lookups, `cur > 150ms` for reads, and/or `cur > 250ms` for writes, then the requests are taking too long.

■ ■ ■

## CHAPTER 3

Monitoring and Updating

As mentioned in the previous chapter, centralization will make your life easier. This also extends to centralizing your system/network monitoring and centralizing as much as possible of the setup and later management of individual machines. Various tools are available to help you do this; this chapter looks at Nagios for monitoring, Puppet for centralized configuration management, and another useful tool, ClusterSSH, for repeating commands across your network simultaneously. All three tools are great ways to save yourself some time and effort!

3-1. Nagios: Setting Up Centralized Monitoring

It's embarrassing when the first time you hear about a problem with one of your servers or a desktop machine is when someone comes to you to complain about it. Far better is to set up some kind of monitoring, and Nagios is an excellent tool for this. The setup can be a little complicated, but once Nagios is up and running, it gives you a web-based interface providing oversight of all your machines and a fair amount of control and information, and it's very low maintenance.

Nagios is centralized: you set up a server, which then collects and displays information on any client machines that you tell it to monitor. You can get basic service accessibility information on the monitored machines (whether they're pingable, whether SSH is OK, whether HTTP/LDAP/NFS is OK, and so on) without needing to install any software on them; the Nagios server does all the work. With a little more setup, you can get more information than this from the monitored machine (CPU information, for example), as described in recipe 3-7. The server can react to alert situations (with alert thresholds set by you) by sending e-mail or text to inform a human or by running any script you provide.

■ **Note** For lots more information on Nagios and how to set it up, check out *Pro Nagios 2.0* by James Turnbull (Apress, 2006). This book refers to Nagios 2 rather than Nagios 3, but largely the information will carry over.

As usual, you can install from source from the web site, or there should be a package available for your system. For Debian/Ubuntu, the current stable version is Nagios 3, which can be installed with the following:

```
sudo apt-get install nagios3 nagios-plugins
```

See recipe 3-7 for a discussion of plug-ins: these provide a way of getting more information from clients.

During the setup, it'll ask you for the admin password. Remember this! You can reply "no" to the question about version 1 backward compatibility.

You'll also need to install apache2 if you don't already have it installed. (Nagios will also work with Apache if you're already running that; if you're installing from scratch, then use apache2.) The Debian install will automatically create a symlink from /etc/apache2/conf.d/nagios3.conf to /etc/nagios3/apache2.conf, thus including the config provided with the Nagios package in your web server config. If your distro doesn't do that, you can create the symlink yourself or copy the contents of the /etc/nagios3/apache.conf file into your apache2 config file. This default configuration will provide a basic setup that should work with the default Nagios install to get the web reporting working. If you've personalized your apache2 or Nagios install or moved any files around, you'll need to check that the various directives and aliases are pointing to the correct places. Restart apache2 with /etc/init.d/apache2 force-reload, and that's the setup for the web interface; however, currently there's no data being collected for it, so there's nothing much to show.

■ **Note** All files or directories referred to here live in /etc/nagios3 unless otherwise stated.

The Debian configuration setup (which I'd recommend as an approach worth taking even if you're installing from another system or from source) is to create a conf.d directory in which the majority of the config files are put. Within this directory, configuration can be broken out into separate files as much as you like, since all the files in the directory will automatically be included in the configuration. This is far more manageable and maintainable than using one enormous file, because it means that when you go to change the setup for a particular machine or a particular service, you can immediately locate the file matching that service, rather than having to page or grep through one huge single file.

Within the main config file, nagios.cfg, you include this directory with this line:

```
cfg_dir=/etc/nagios3/conf.d
```

You can add any other directories with a similar line.

Note By default, some of the files in this directory (when installing from the version in Debian stable at the time of this writing, which was 3.0.6-4) still have names that end with nagios2, despite the version of the software as a whole being Nagios 3. Feel free to change the file names if you prefer; here I'll refer to them by the default names that the Debian package uses.

For the basic server setup, monitoring only the server itself (localhost) from a package install, most of the default settings should be OK. All you need to do is to edit the conf.d/contacts_nagios2.cfg file to put your e-mail address in as the value of the email parameter under the first defined contact:

```
# comments must start with # with no whitespace in front
define contact{
        contact_name                    root
        alias                           Root
        service_notification_period     24x7
        host_notification_period        24x7
        service_notification_options    w,u,c,r
        host_notification_options       d,r
        service_notification_commands   notify-by-email
        host_notification_commands      host-notify-by-email
        email                           myself@example.com
        }
```

This means that if an alert is triggered (see recipe 3-5 for alert setup), you'll be e-mailed.

Note It's a good idea to use Subversion to keep track of changes in config files; see Chapter 1.

A good habit to get into is that of checking the config syntax whenever you make a change; you can do so with this:

```
nagios3 -v /etc/nagios3/nagios.cmd
```

Once you've checked the config, reload Nagios with /etc/init.d/nagios3 reload, and go look at http://server.example.com/nagios3 (you'll be asked for that nagiosadmin password that you set at install). From the welcome page, click Tactical Overview in the left menu, and the report screen will come up, as shown in Figure 3-1.

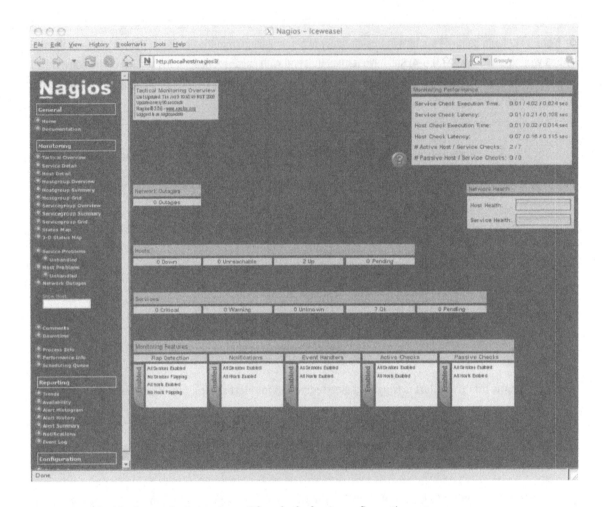

Figure 3-1. The Nagios tactical overview with only the basic configuration set up

The tactical overview shows an overview of hosts, services, and their states. For Nagios, hosts and services can be in one of several states:

- Pending means that it's not done checking yet.

- OK (shown in green) means that all is well.

- There are several levels of not-OK states: yellow for Warning and red for Critical.

You can set the detail of when these levels should be triggered in the config files. If you click a service, you'll be taken to a detailed page of information about that service (or host). There are numerous other ways provided of looking at the information; click around a bit to try them.

■ **Note** To make the front page of the Nagios web interface more useful, you can set it to go straight to the tactical overview rather than to a home page. Edit /usr/share/nagios3/htdocs/index.html, and replace this line:

```
<FRAME SRC="main.html" NAME="main">
```

with this one:

```
<FRAME SRC="/cgi-bin/nagios2/tac.cgi" NAME="main">
```

3-2. Adding Another Host to Nagios

So far, Nagios is monitoring the Nagios server machine itself and that one default gateway. Next, you need to add a host, that is, another machine that you're monitoring. The best way to do this is to create a conf.d/host-hostname.cfg file, named for the machine you want to monitor (here **cepheus**, so the file will be conf.d/host-cepheus.cfg):

```
define host{
        use            generic-host
        host_name      cepheus
        address        10.0.0.2
        }
```

As you can see, this can be very basic; almost all the information is taken from the host template (see recipe 3-3 for more information about templates). Reload Nagios:

```
/etc/init.d/nagios3 reload
```

It will take maybe a minute to run the various checks before the data shows up on the web page, so be patient.

That's your first very basic Nagios setup done. The server now checks itself and an external client and will alert you to any problems.

3-3. Using Templates in Nagios

Nagios provides templates as a way of saving yourself work. The previous recipe used one of these: take a look at the defaults defined for the localhost in conf.d/localhost_nagios2.cfg. The host definition and the first service definition should look a bit like this:

```
define host{
        use             generic-host
        host_name       localhost
        alias           localhost
        address         127.0.0.1
        }
# Define a service to check the disk space of the root partition
# Warning if < 20% free, critical if < 10% free space on partition.
define service{
        use                 generic-service
        host_name           localhost
        service_description Disk Space
        check_command       check_all_disks!20%!10%
        }
```

The use keyword is used in the definition to refer to a template. Templates mean that you can set your service or host defaults in a single place rather than having to retype them constantly. Config reuse, like any other code reuse, is always a good idea—less hassle and more maintainability! You can think of the Nagios configuration as effectively object-oriented. It treats both services and hosts as objects and then sets up relationships between them. As with OO code, objects (hosts or services) can inherit things from a "parent" object, which is the generic-host or generic-service template in this case. (You can also set up other templates and call them anything you like, of course!)

The generic-host template lives in the conf.d/generic-host_nagios2.cfg file. It sets a bunch of defaults, including notification enablement, various aspects of dealing with notifications and events, and so on. However, in the individual host definition, you can override any of these simply by specifying them.

generic-service works as a per-service (rather than per-host) template in the same way. Take a look at conf.d/generic-service_nagios2.cfg to see what this looks like and what defaults are set.

check_command is a command in the file /etc/nagios-plugins/config/disk.cfg. The plug-in directory at /etc/nagios-plugins/config/ contains all the commands for checking various services, and there are an enormous number of plug-ins that you can add on top of the ones that a default package install will give you (if installing from source, you may need to get more of these by hand). See recipe 3-7 for more on plug-ins.

3-4. Using Hostgroups and Services in Nagios

From the setup in the previous recipes, Nagios can see the monitored machine (cepheus in recipe 3-2) and check that it's up, but there aren't any specific service or status checks defined for it. You could add them individually to the host config file in the same way that checks are defined in the localhost config file that I covered initially. However, it would be a lot of hassle to have to go through this for every host. As with the templates, you want to type things once only. This means using *hostgroups*, which are exactly what the name says—they're groups of hosts, allowing you then to define a service per hostgroup rather than per host.

Edit conf.d/hostgroups_nagios2.cfg to add the short name of the host to the relevant groups. You can, if you want to, create a new group. For example, here's how to create a server hostgroup:

```
define hostgroup {
        hostgroup_name   debian-servers
        alias            Debian GNU/Linux Servers
        members          localhost,webserver,ldapserver
        }
```

Since all you're really doing with a hostgroup is collecting machines together, there aren't many options to set: you should use the templates (see recipe 3-3 for template information) to set your default or standard options. What hostgroups do mean is that you can create as many basic host config files as you like; I prefer to keep them in separate files, named by the machine name, but it's not obligatory. Then you add them easily to hostgroups and use the hostgroups to define your service monitoring. This enables you to split machines up by their usage, operating system, or any other criteria you like. Machines can belong to more than one hostgroup.

So, you have your client host, and you've added it to a webgroup; let's call the group debian-servers, as per the previous code snippet. Now, edit the conf.d/services_nagios2.cfg file to set up a couple of service checks for that hostgroup. Let's set up checks to establish whether these hosts will return a ping and whether they're accessible via SSH:

```
define service {
        hostgroup_name            debian-servers
        service_description       SSH
        check_command             check_ssh
        use                       generic-service
        notification_interval     0
}

define service {
        hostgroup_name            debian-servers
        service_description       PING
        check_command             check_ping!100.0,20%!500.0,60%
        use                       generic-service
        notification_interval     0
}
```

In fact, what you will probably want is to define a group of machines that you expect to be SSH-accessible and a group that you expect to be ping-accessible, and these two don't have to be the same. For example, the default setup expects the gateway to be pingable, but you don't necessarily expect it to be accessible via SSH. But here I'll just use the single group, because I currently have only one nonserver machine.

Nagios will now check the machines in those groups for the services in the check_command statement with the generic-service settings, and it will complain if it finds a problem.

3-5. Setting Up Nagios Alerts

The Nagios web page is useful to have, but it's not ideal to have to check the web page constantly for problems. Instead, you can set up an alert, such as to your e-mail, to let you know about any problems.

In recipe 3-1, you set up your contacts_nagios2.cfg file. This file also defines an admin contact group—using contact groups rather than individual users increases maintainability. If there's a personnel change, you need to change only the group membership, not any other references.

The generic service definition is useful again here. I'll show how to set up the default to be for any service that has errors to send an e-mail. In the `conf.d/generic-service_nagios2.cfg` file, add the following to the service definition:

```
notification_interval       1440
is_volatile                 0
check_period                24x7
normal_check_interval       5
retry_check_interval        1
max_check_attempts          10
notification_period         24x7
notification_options        c,r
contact_groups              admins
```

The notification interval defines how often you get reminded (in minutes). **1440** minutes means every 24 hours. `check_period` defines when the service is expected to run—here, it's all the time. Time periods such as **24x7** are defined in `conf.d/timeperiods_nagios2.cfg` and can be edited or added to if they don't meet your needs. The `normal_check_interval` and `retry_check_interval` are also in minutes. The service here is set to be checked every five minutes, but if an answer isn't forthcoming and a retry is made, the retry should happen every minute. Ten retry attempts will be made before it is concluded that there's something wrong with the service, and again, you can change this number.

`notification_period` sets when alerts should be sent (all the time), and `notification_options` sets when you should receive an alert. For hosts, **d** = notify on down states, **u** = notify on unreachable states, **r** = notify on host recoveries, and **f** = notify when host starts and stops flapping. For services, **w** = notify on warning states, **u** = unknown states, **c** = critical states, **r** = recovery, and **f** = start/stop of flapping. Finally, `contact_groups` defines who to contact when a notification is required.

■ **Note** *Flapping* refers to when a service or host changes state too frequently, resulting in a large number of problem/recovery alerts. This can indicate config problems or real network problems.

Once you have all that in place, reload Nagios, and then try turning off SSH on your test client. You should receive a message to the address you set in the contacts file, telling you that the client is not SSH accessible. Turn it back on, and you'll get another alert telling you it's OK again.

■ **Note** The default From line in the e-mail alerts is the `nagios` user; this may not be good if you have a mail server that wants a registered address before it will send. If you're using `exim4`, you need to set the "untrusted user" option and then add the following to the end of the `host-notify-by-email` and `notify-by-email` commands in `commands.cfg`:

```
-- -f address@example.com
```

3-6. Defining Nagios Commands

If the existing Nagios commands don't meet your needs, it's possible to define new ones. For example, say you are running more than one domain on a single web server. If you just want to check that a web server is responding to HTTP requests, the existing check_http command is fine. However, this won't check that all your web sites are actually responding OK. To do this, first edit commands.cfg and add the following lines:

```
define command{
    command_name    check_http-website1
    command_line    /usr/lib/nagios/plugins/check_http -H website1.example.com
}
```

Create similar commands for as many web sites as you have. Then edit the web server's host config file (for example, conf.d/host-webserver.cfg) to include service for each command:

```
define service{
    host_name               webserver
    service_description     website1
    check_command           check_http-website1
    use                     generic-service
    notification_interval   1440
}
```

This can go in any file; I find it neatest to keep it with the web server configuration. Restart Nagios, and you're done.

3-7. Writing a Nagios Plug-In

Nagios has a plug-in system to make it easily extensible in a variety of ways. Check out http://nagiosplugins.org/ for a repository of plug-ins that are user-supplied and available for you to download.

Note Running /usr/lib/nagios/plugins/plugin_name -h will get you help output for a particular plug-in.

It's also pretty straightforward to write your own plug-in. Plug-ins live in /usr/lib/nagios/plugins/, and the file /usr/lib/nagios/plugins/utils.sh provides a few useful functions and fixed variables for you to use. This is a generalized plug-in that takes a single argument (see the next recipe for one way of using plug-ins like this) and checks to see whether the process named by the argument is running:

```
01  #! /bin/sh
02
03  PATH=/bin:/sbin:/usr/bin:/usr/sbin:/usr/local/bin:/usr/local/sbin
04
```

```
05   PROGNAME=`basename $0`
06   PROGPATH=`echo $0 | sed -e 's,[\\/][^\\/][^\\/]*$,,'`
07   REVISION=`echo '$Revision: 1 $' | sed -e 's/[^0-9.]//g'`
08
09   process=$1
10
11   . $PROGPATH/utils.sh
12
13   print_usage() {
14           echo "Usage: $PROGNAME process-to-check"
15   }
16
17   print_help() {
18           print_revision $PROGNAME $REVISION
19           echo ""
20           print_usage
21           echo ""
22           echo "This plugin checks if the given process ↵
                     is running, using ps and grep."
23           echo ""
24           support
25           exit 0
26   }
27
28   case "$process" in
29       --help)
30                   print_help
31                 exit 0
32                   ;;
33       -h)
34                   print_help
35                 exit 0
36                   ;;
37       --version)
38       print_revision $PROGNAME $REVISION
39                 exit 0
40                   ;;
41       -V)
42                 print_revision $PROGNAME $REVISION
43                 exit 0
44                 ;;
45       *)
46                 processdata=`ps -A | grep $process 2>&1`
47                 status=$?
48                 if test ${status} -ne 0 ; then
49                         echo Process not found
50                         exit 2
51                 fi
52                 else
53                         echo Process running
54                         exit 0
```

```
55                  fi
56                  ;;
57  esac
```

Lines 01 to 27 set up assorted variables, source the routines in `utils.sh`, and set up usage and help subroutines, as well as (in line 09) assign the command-line argument to `$process`. Lines 29 to 44 check to see whether the argument passed in is a request for help information or for the version number. Lines 45 to 55 are the ones that actually do the work: line 46 checks for the process, and line 47 gets the exit value. If this is other than 0, then the process has not been found, and the script returns 2. Otherwise, the process is there, and we return 0.

Plug-ins can return 2 (for alert), 1 (for warning), or 0 (for success). In this case, we don't bother returning a warning.

3-8. Setting Up the NRPE Plug-in for Nagios

The NRPE plug-in allows you to monitor disk usage, CPU usage, and other similar things on remote hosts. Without something like this on your remote/client hosts, Nagios allows you to monitor only whether the hosts are up and providing whatever services you expect them to provide. It would be even more useful to monitor whether they're about to run out of disk space or whether the mail delivery is down. NRPE makes this possible.

Install the NRPE plug-in on your central Nagios server (the `nagios-nrpe-plug-in` package on Debian), and install the NRPE server (the `nagios-nrpe-server` package on Debian) on the remote host you want to monitor.

■ **Note** The terminology can be a bit confusing here! The *Nagios* server is the machine that you're running Nagios on, as per the setup in recipe 3-1. However, the NRPE plug-in, which you install on the Nagios server, wants to talk to an *NRPE* server on every machine that it monitors. The NRPE server is therefore installed on each monitored machine (so it would be installed on the machine `cepheus` that was set up in recipe 3-2). The NRPE server will collect information from this machine and pass it on to the plug-in when it is contacted by the main server.

To test the communication between the server and the monitored machine, run the following on the server once you've installed the packages on both machines:

```
/usr/lib/nagios/plugins/check_nrpe -H cepheus -c check_users
```

It should tell you how many users are logged into the machine `cepheus`.

Next, check `/etc/nagios-plugins/config/check_nrpe.cfg` on the server. It should look like this, defining generic checking commands:

```
# this command runs a program $ARG1$ with one argument, $ARG2$, passed to $ARG1$
define command {
        command_name    check_nrpe
        command_line    /usr/lib/nagios/plugins/check_nrpe -H ↵
                        $HOSTADDRESS$ -c $ ARG1$ -a $ARG2$
}
# this command runs a program $ARG1$ without any argument passed in to it
define command {
        command_name    check_nrpe_1arg
        command_line    /usr/lib/nagios/plugins/check_nrpe -H ↵
                        $HOSTADDRESS$ -c $ ARG1$
}
```

Edit /etc/nagios/conf.d/services_nagios3.cfg on the monitored machine (cepheus in this example) to add the services you want to monitor:

```
# SMTP doesn't need any arguments passed into the check_smtp
# program, so we use check_nrpe_1arg
define service {
        service_description     SMTP
        use                     generic-service
        hostgroup_name          nrpe
        check_command           check_nrpe_1arg!check_smtp
}

define service {
        service_description     LOAD
        use                     generic-service
        hostgroup_name          nrpe
        check_command           check_nrpe_1arg!check_load
}

# check_disk takes an argument, /, so we use check_nrpe
define service {
        service_description     DISK
        use                     generic-service
        hostgroup_name          nrpe
        check_command           check_nrpe!check_disk!/
}
```

■ **Note** This requires an nrpe hostgroup to be set up on the server.

Commands that take only one argument—the service to check—use the check_nrpe_1arg command (see /etc/nagios-plugins/config/check_nrpe.cfg).

If you want to give further arguments to commands, you need to edit /etc/nagios/nrpe.cfg on the client machine so that the dont_blame_nrpe keyword has the value 1. Then use the check_nrpe command. In the previous code, I use it to pass the disk mount point to be checked.

■ **Note** Setting `dont_blame_nrpe` to 1 is a security hole. The arguments passed to NRPE aren't thoroughly checked/sanitized, so it is possible for an attacker to run arbitrary evil commands via the `check_nrpe` command. It's up to you how you assess risk in your own setup and with the specific command that you're using. You should certainly at least understand what the command you're passing in to `check_nrpe` will do with the options you provide. In the previous example, `check_nrpe!check_disk` will just run the `check_disk` command without any arguments on the monitored machine, with whatever disk is hard-coded in that command to be checked. `check_nrpe!check_disk!/` will pass the third argument (here /) to `check_disk`, and `check_disk` will operate on that argument. If your `check_disk` command involved, say, an echo line, and the argument was, instead of a disk mount point, some malicious code, then the malicious code could be echoed and thus run.

Restart Nagios, and you should be able to start seeing information from your monitored machine.

■ **Note** Instead of editing `/etc/nagios/nrpe.cfg` on the monitored machine, you can instead edit `/etc/nagios/nrpe-local.cfg`. NRPE will check both files (`/etc/nagios/nrpe.cfg` and `/etc/nagios/nrpe-local.cfg`), but if there is a conflict, `/etc/nagios/nrpe-local.cfg` will win. This has the advantage of keeping your local changes separate from the package files, so if the package is updated, there's no risk of your changes being overwritten. Similarly, you can keep files in `/etc/nagios/nrpe.d/`.

Possible commands are at `/usr/lib/nagios/plugins` on the client—or you can create your own in `/etc/nagios/nrpe-local.cfg`. Try these commands, added to `/etc/nagios/nrpe-local.cfg`:

```
command[check_disk]=/usr/lib/nagios/plugins/check_disk -w 10% -c 5% -p $ARG1$
command[check_smtp]=/usr/lib/nagios/plugins/check_smtp -w 1 -c 2
```

The first one means that I can check whichever local disk I want, rather than being restricted to / as with the default `check_disk` command; the second checks that SMTP is OK. Use them by adding this section to `conf.d/services-nagios2.cfg`:

```
define service {
    use                     generic-service
    hostgroup_name          disk-local
    service_description     DISK-LOCAL2
    check_command           check_nrpe!check_disk!/local
}
```

```
define service {
    hostgroup_name          nrpe
    service_description      SMTP
    check_command           check_nrpe_1arg!check_smtp
    use                     generic-service
}
```

Then set up which hosts have these checks by defining a hostgroup in **conf.d/hostgroups_nagios2.cfg**:

```
define hostgroup {
        hostgroup_name   disk-local
        alias            Hosts with /local
        members          client1, client2
    }
define hostgroup {
        hostgroup_name   smtp
        alias            Hosts with SMTP
        members          client1, client2, server1
    }
```

Restart Nagios, and you're done!

■ **Note** One gotcha to watch out for is that the check_disk command takes percentage arguments, and it warns on percentage free, rather than percentage used. Mine is set to warn at 10 percent and to be critical at 5 percent.

3-9. Enabling External Commands in Nagios

Enabling external commands means that you can do various things from the web interface, such as restarting services. To turn them on, first you need to stop Nagios (**/etc/init.d/nagios3 stop**). Edit **nagios.cfg**, and set the **check_external_commands** value to 1.

Next, if you're using Debian, you need to set the permissions on **/var/lib/nagios2/rw** correctly. To make that directory read-writeable by your **apache2** user (on Debian this is **www-data**), use these commands:

```
dpkg-statoverride --update --add nagios www-data 2710 /var/lib/nagios2/rw
dpkg-statoverride --update --add nagios nagios 751 /var/lib/nagios2
```

This will override the package defaults to set the **rw** directory to be owned by the **www-data** group and to be group-executable. It also sets the setgid bit so that files created within this directory will also be owned by **www-data** rather than by the user who created the file. The permissions on the parent directory (**/var/lib/nagios2**) are changed similarly, but by using the **nagios** group rather than **www-data** and without the setgid bit.

Now restart Nagios (`/etc/init.d/nagios3 start`), and you should be able to use commands. Test this by clicking the Service Detail link in the sidebar, and then pick one of the services. Figure 3-2 shows the screen for the HTTP service on `localhost`; the commands are in the box on the right of the screen. An easy test is to click "Re-schedule the next check of this service." You'll be given the opportunity to set the time for the next check.

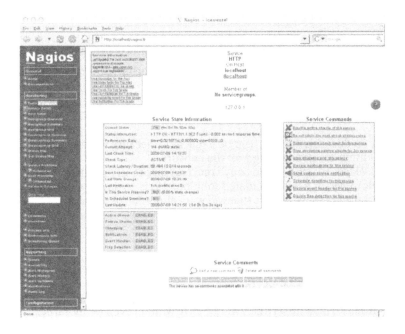

Figure 3-2. *State information for the HTTP service on localhost. Note the external commands in the box at right.*

It's also useful with external commands to be able to temporarily turn off checks or notifications of a service or host (for example, if you are aware that it's down and don't want to keep being told!).

You can also restart Nagios itself from the web interface (using the Process Info page) if you're logged in as `nagiosadmin`. To restart it as any other user, you'll need to edit `/etc/nagios3/cgi.cfg` to add the username to the `authorized_for_system_commands` line.

■ **Note** You can find a list of all available external commands at `http://www.nagios.org/developerinfo/externalcommands/commandlist.php`.

3-10. Synchronizing Your Root Setup

If you're working on lots of machines, it can be enormously frustrating to realize that a shortcut or alias that you're used to while working on machine A isn't there on machine B. For your own personal setup, this is one of the reasons why centralized login and NFS-mounted directories are useful—your settings, aliases, preferences, and whatever else will follow you around from machine to machine.

■ **Note** Puppet (see recipe 3-11) is another centralization option. If you're centralizing a lot of files, it's likely to be a better idea to use Puppet. However, if it's just one or two, a method like this can be appropriate (avoiding the use of the proverbial nut-cracking sledgehammer).

Unfortunately, you can't directly do this with the **root** user on a machine, because you need to be able to log in as **root** even when something has gone wrong with the network.

One possibility is to use ClusterSSH (see recipe 3-17) to copy **/root/.bashrc** to all the other machines every time you change it. However, as a nonautomated solution, this is obviously suboptimal.

Another option is to set up a centralized **/root/.bashrc** that will work almost all of the time.

```
source /shared/config/root.bashrc
```

Make sure this is owned by **root** and readable only by **root**!

```
chown root:root /shared/config/root.bashrc; chmod og-rw /shared/config/root.bashrc
```

There will probably be a few vital aliases or settings that you can't live without even temporarily; these will need to go in the main **/root/.bashrc** file on each machine.

If you don't like the possibility of being without *any* of your aliases, you could set up a cronjob so a central file is copied out to the file on each machine at regular intervals.

One final hack that will work either with the roll-your-own centralization or with Puppet (see the next recipe) is automatically copying any changes you make locally to the central file for propagation. This script, run regularly on each machine as a cronjob, will back up the old file with the name of the machine from which the new file is taken and the date/time and then put the new file in its place. It'll need to run as **root** for the permissions to be correct.

```
01  #!/bin/bash
02  export PATH=/usr/bin;/usr/sbin;/bin;/sbin
03  hostname=`hostname`
04  date=`date +%Y%m%d-%H%M`
05  local="/root/.bashrc"
06  central="/shared/config/root.bashrc"
07  diff=`diff -q $local $central`
08  if [ $diff != "" ] ; then
09     cp $central $central.$date.$hostname
10     cp $local $central
11  fi
```

> **Note** You need the quotes surrounding the `diff` command in line 7 because if the files are different, `diff` returns a multiword string. Without the quotes, `bash` gets confused by this.

3-11. Setting Up Puppet

One of the biggest sysadmin centralization problems is getting your configuration set up the same way across all your machines. Even if you have centralized install set up, configuration is changed over time, and eventually you end up with some machines working and some not, and you have little real idea why the difference is and where to look for a cause.

Puppet is a centralized configuration management system, which helps you avoid this and other similar problems. A central Puppet server—the *puppetmaster*—keeps track of the configuration files and options for all its client machines in a cross-platform language. On the client, you run a daemon that checks in with the puppetmaster at intervals and copies over any changes to the client.

> **Note** Remember that if you're using Puppet and you make a change manually on a client machine, the next time the daemon checks in with the puppetmaster, the change will be reverted. To make the change permanent, you need to remember to make the changes centrally every time. If you need to test a change locally first, you can either set up a "testing" machine configuration within Puppet or just turn off the Puppet daemon on the client machine when you're testing. Remember to turn it back on when you're done! Setting up a testing sandbox is probably the more correct option, and if you have your Puppet files checked into Subversion, you have an automatic backup you can revert to, but it is more time-consuming when bug fixing.

Anything Puppet will manage is called a *resource,* and resources are categorized into the following types:

- Files (ownership, mode, content, and existence can all be managed)
- Users and groups
- Packages
- Services
- Commands and scripts (Puppet can execute these under particular conditions)
- Crontabs
- Mounts

Puppet is under very active development, and people are regularly adding more types—or you can create your own.

To install Puppet on Debian/Ubuntu, use this:

```
sudo apt-get install puppetmaster
```

This will also install a set of Ruby packages. Puppet is also available for other distros or can be compiled from source. Because it's still moving quite fast, for once installing from source may actually be preferable to using the packaged version, especially if you run into any problems. Note that (at the time of this writing), the current package in Debian stable and Ubuntu is 0.24.5-3, while the current source release is 0.24.7.

The main configuration file is at /etc/puppet/puppetmaster.conf:

```
[puppetmasterd]
# Make sure all log messages are sent to the right directory
# This directory must be writable by the puppet user
logdir=/var/log/puppet
vardir=/var/lib/puppet
rundir=/var/run
```

The Puppet user is **puppet**, so to check directory ownership, use the following:

```
chown puppet { /var/log/puppet, /var/lib/puppet }
```

You almost certainly want to be able to store file content, for which you need a basic file server configuration file at /etc/puppet/fileserver.conf:

```
[files]
  path /etc/puppet/files
  allow *.example.com
```

This specifies where files will be stored on the puppetmaster and allows access to all machines in example.com. You can also ban specific machines or domains and can specify by IP address if preferred:

```
deny *.evil.example.com
allow 192.168.0.0/24
```

The first time you run the **puppetmaster** daemon, use the **mkusers** and **nonodes** flags to create the daemon user and to avoid it complaining that you haven't set up any nodes yet:

```
/usr/bin/puppetmasterd --mkusers --nonodes
```

Setting Up a Client

On Debian/Ubuntu, install with the following:

```
sudo apt-get install puppet.
```

Edit /etc/puppet/puppetd.conf to set the server name for your site:

```
server = puppetserver.example.com
```

However, don't run it until there's something to run it on: this requires setting up the site manifest.

Setting Up Your Site Manifest

The site manifest is the main or initial source of information for the puppetmaster, and anything in this file will run on all clients. It's at /etc/puppet/manifests/site.pp. This recipe gives the /etc/sudoers file on all client machines the properties specified here:

```
file { "/etc/sudoers":
    owner => "root",
    group => "root",
    mode => "440"
}
```

■ **Note** When testing, it's best to run your puppetmaster as puppetmasterd --verbose. This sends output to the screen rather than to logs so you can immediately tell what's happening. Also, run the client with puppetd --test, again to see more output (and to run the job once and once only, rather than at intervals).

Change something about the /etc/sudoers file on the client—for example, the modes or owner of—so that they differ from what you've set in site.pp on the puppetmaster. On the server, run this:

```
puppetmasterd --verbose
```

Then run the client for the first time:

```
puppetd --waitforcert 60 --test
```

Clients are authenticated by a certificate request to the puppetmaster. You will see the client complain about the lack of certificate and pause. You need to tell the puppetmaster to sign the client's certificate by running this on the puppetmaster machine:

```
puppetca --sign client.example.com
```

After 60 seconds, the client will pick up the signed certificate and will then run. The **test** flag makes the client run in verbose mode, one time through only.

■ **Note** puppetca --list on the puppetmaster shows the list of clients waiting for a signature. puppetca --sign --all will sign all the waiting certificates.

After the run finishes, check **/etc/sudoers**; the modes should have changed to be as you set on the puppetmaster!

Puppet can manage file content as well as attributes. Create a sample **sudoers** file, and put it in /etc/puppet/files/sudoers. Then edit **site.pp** again:

```
file { "/etc/sudoers":
    owner => "root",
    group => "root",
    mode => 440,
    source => "puppet://puppetserver.example.com/files/sudoers",
}
```

Edit the file on the client so it looks in some way different from this sample file (for example, add a test comment line), and run Puppet on the client again with **puppetd --test**. The file content will change!

■ **Note** Having file content in one place also makes it very easy to use Subversion (or another version control system). I strongly recommend that you do so! The ability to roll back changes is very helpful.

When managing files, you can also ensure that softlinks exist or that directories exist. This config snippet also shows how you can use a single `file { }` container for multiple file resources. Note the semicolon at the end of each resource specification.

```
file {
    "/star":
        ensure => link,
        target => "/soft9/star";

    "/test/dir":
        ensure => directory;
}
```

You can set up defaults for any resource. For example, if most of your files are owned by root and have chmod value 644, this snippet will set these values as the default for all files:

```
File {
    owner => "root",
    group => "root".
    mode  => "644"
}
```

You can override this default by specifying a different value for any of these within a particular resource. Whatever you specify for the resource will override the default.

> ■ **Note** Defaults apply only to their own scope (class) and any class beneath that. If you want them to apply globally, you should set them outside any class, for example, in `site.pp`.

3-12. Creating Puppet and Resource Dependencies

Resources interact with each other—certain packages are required for certain services, or you may want a service to restart or to reload automatically when a particular file is changed. Puppet has dependencies, notably **require** and **subscribe**, so that you can set up these interactions.

This example uses the **service** type, which you can use for **exim**, Apache, or any other daemons that you want to keep running. Here it's **slapd**:

```
service { "slapd":
    ensure     => running,
    hasrestart => true,
    require    => Package["slapd"],
    subscribe  => [File["ldap.conf"], File["/etc/ldap/schema"]],
}
```

The `hasrestart` option lets Puppet know whether to restart service with **stop/start** or with **restart**. There are two varieties of dependency:

- **require** guarantees that the specified resource (here the **slapd** package) will be set up before this resource. All types support this.

- **subscribe** is a reactive dependency. If the specified resources change, then the resource will refresh. The types **exec**, **service**, and **mount** support this.

Puppet resources are specified in dependencies using the type name capitalized and giving the name of the resource. An error will be generated if the resource referred to doesn't exist as a resource definition.

3-13. Puppet: Managing Other Types

Puppet can manage numerous types; here are some more examples. For a full list, see the Puppet web site,[1] or see *Pulling Strings with Puppet: Configuration Management Made Easy* by James Turnbull (Apress, 2008).

---

[1] `http://reductivelabs.com/trac/puppet/wiki/TypeReference`

- *Packages:* Puppet interacts with most of the major packaging systems and can ensure that particular packages are installed. This is particularly useful when setting up a new machine. You can set up your default nodes (see recipe 3-13) to have the standard packages you want to have installed using this syntax:

```
package {   "slapd":    ensure => installed; }
```

- *Exec:* This executes internal commands. The subscribe command is very useful here. This snippet updates exim4 when the exim4 config file is changed:

```
exec { "exim4-update":
    command    => "/usr/sbin/update-exim4.conf",
    user       => "root",
    subscribe  => File["update-exim4"],
    refreshonly => true,
}
```

- *Users and groups:* This is mostly intended for managing system users, rather than normal users. It is possible to manage the home directory (for example, to create it) as well as other user attributes:

```
user { "manager":
    ensure     => present,
    home       => "/local/manager",
    managehome => true,
    gid        => "systemusers",
}
```

- *Cron:* Manages cronjobs. You can use this to restart Puppet on clients if it fails:

```
cron { restart-puppet:
    command => 'if [ -e /var/run/puppetd.pid ];
                then ps uw -p `cat /var/run/puppetd.pid`
            | grep -q ' ruby /usr/sbin/puppetd'
            || (rm /var/run/puppetd.pid; /etc/init.d/puppet start); fi',
    user => root,
    minute => '0',
}
```

- The command is given here on multiple lines for printing purposes, but in fact it must all be on a single line. The hour and day that the cronjob is to be run at can also be set, and the user who the cronjob should run as can be set (as shown in the previous example). The command is added to the relevant user's crontab.

- *Mount:* Mount paths that should be present. If the ensure parameter is set to present, the filesystem will be in the table but not mounted. If it's set to mounted, it will be put in the table and mounted. If it's set to absent, it will be removed from the table.

Various networking attributes are also available: hosts, interfaces, mail lists, mail aliases, and SSH host keys.

New types are also being developed all the time, but you may need to update to the latest version of Puppet to use them.

3-14. Setting Up Nodes in Puppet

The previous recipes have all been using the `site.pp` file, which means they will be applied to every single client. This almost certainly isn't what you want in most cases. Different machines can have very different requirements.

Before you start setting up anything complicated, you should consider how you organize your files and manifests. There are various suggestions for best practices on the Puppet web site—whatever system you use, make sure it is comprehensible and easily updatable. My system looks like Figure 3-3.

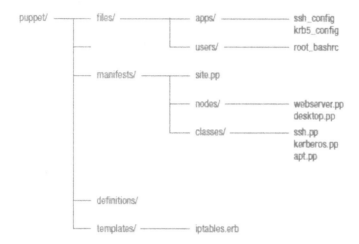

Figure 3-3. *The directory structure of the Puppet files on my puppetmaster*

The subdirectories all contain class files (as discussed in a couple of paragraphs' time), and in order to include these, `site.pp` looks like this:

```
import "classes/*"

import "definitions/*"
import "nodes/*"
import "users/*"
```

So far, I've shown the configuration for just a single machine. But, of course, Puppet really comes into its own when you have multiple machines. If they're all identical, you need to set up only one configuration—the default one that has been set up in the previous recipes, which will then run on any Puppet client connecting to this puppetmaster.

```
# site.pp
default {
    include sudo
}
```

You can also have configurations that differ for each machine. Or you can set up base configurations and then either inherit from or include them in the node configuration.

You may have a basic server config that differs from your desktop config, and both may inherit from a base or default config. This could look like this:

```
class base {
    # Various basic things
    include autofs
    include cron
    include puppet
    include ssh
    # and so on
}

class desktop inherits base {
    # Everything in the base class will automatically be included here
    # Then you can also
    include latex
    include gnome
    # and so on
}

class server inherits base {
    # Again, everything from the base class will automatically be included
    # Then some other server-only things
    include nfs
    # and so on
}
```

Classes can be specified either in a single file or in a file per class. So here, you could have all the previous setup in a single file **classes.pp**, or you could separate it into **base.pp**, **desktop.pp**, and **server.pp** (see the suggested directory structure in Figure 3-3). I recommend the latter to make configuration management easier, because it means that you can easily find the node or application whose configuration you want to edit.

3-15. Defining Your Puppet Nodes in LDAP

Instead of defining your nodes in **site.pp**, you can keep them in LDAP as the **puppetclass** attribute. This enables you to automatically set up the type of Puppet node that a machine should be set up as when you first add it to the directory. You can have as many of these **puppetclass** attributes per host as you like—for example, my web server has **webserver**, **ftpserver**, and **server** as **puppetclass** attributes.

site.pp therefore has only import statements, not node definitions. Your class definitions are set in **/etc/puppet/manifests/classes**, as described in the previous recipe, and you import them in **site.pp** (again, as in the previous recipe).

Note Find more information about this at http://reductivelabs.com/trac/puppet/wiki/LDAPNodes or in *Deploying OpenLDAP* by Tom Jackiewicz (Apress, 2004).

A reasonable setup to start with is to have the **base.pp**, **desktop.pp**, and **server.pp** classes, as mentioned in the previous recipe (with **server.pp** and **desktop.pp** inheriting from **base.pp**). You can then add further **puppetclass** attributes (for example, **webserver** and **nfsserver**) as required for your setup.

Install **libldap-ruby1.8** on the Puppet server (Debian package).

Add the Puppet schema to your LDAP schema directory (/etc/ldap/schema/). See recipe 2-12 for a discussion of LDAP schemas and object identifiers (OIDs). Or just put the following in as /etc/ldap/schema/puppet.schema:

```
# These OIDs are all fake.  No guarantees there won't be conflicts.
# $Id$

attributetype ( 1.1.3.10 NAME 'puppetclass'
        DESC 'Puppet Node Class'
        EQUALITY caseIgnoreIA5Match
        SYNTAX 1.3.6.1.4.1.1466.115.121.1.26 )

attributetype ( 1.1.3.9 NAME 'parentnode'
        DESC 'Puppet Parent Node'
        EQUALITY caseIgnoreIA5Match
        SYNTAX 1.3.6.1.4.1.1466.115.121.1.26 )

objectclass ( 1.1.1.2 NAME 'puppetClient' SUP top AUXILIARY
        DESC 'Puppet Client objectclass'
        MAY ( puppetclass $ parentnode ))
```

Add a schema line to /etc/ldap/slapd.conf:

```
include          /etc/ldap/schema/puppet.schema
```

Restart **slapd**:

```
/etc/init.d/slapd restart
```

Your **server.pp** and **desktop.pp** classes will now correspond to a **puppetclass** attribute in the LDAP tables. To modify a host, you can use an LDIF file that looks like this (this one updates the server **server1** and the desktop **desktop1**):

```
dn: cn=server1,ou=Hosts,dc=example,dc=com
add: objectClass
objectClass: puppetClient
-
add: puppetclass
puppetclass: server

dn: cn=desktop1,ou=Hosts,dc=example,dc=com
add: objectClass
objectClass: puppetClient
-
add: puppetclass
puppetclass: desktop
```

Add all the other hosts you want to use with this system. Authenticate as the LDAP admin user, and run the modification:

```
kinit ldapadm; ldapmodify -f puppet.ldif
```

Finally, in /etc/puppet/puppetmasterd.conf on the Puppet server, add the following:

```
[ldap]
ldapnodes = true
ldapserver = ldapserver.example.com
ldapbase = dc=example,dc=com
```

and restart the puppetmaster.

■ **Note** If you're changing the puppetmaster config or any other Puppet setup stuff, it can be useful to stop the running puppetmaster process and restart it interactively with the verbose option: `puppetmasterd --verbose`. This helps a lot with debugging.

3-16. Puppet: Using Facter and Templates

Another useful aspect of Puppet is that it works together with a piece of software called Facter. Facter sets up per-host variables (such as hostname, IP address, and operating system) automatically. So, you can apply types, configure resources, and make specific changes according to these facts, or you can create your own facts.

To see the full lists of the facts provided by default, type **facter** at the command line.

You can refer to these facts within Puppet with `$factname`. There are two important uses for these facts:

- To create conditional structures

- To use in templates

There are three types of conditionals in Puppet:

- Selectors, which are used within a statement:

```
package {
    "krb-clients":
        ensure => $operatingsystem ? {
            ubuntu  => absent,
            debian  => installed,
            default => undef
        };
}
```

  Here, if the $operatingsystem fact is set to ubuntu, the package is not installed; if
  it's set to debian, it is installed. The default is to not do anything at all. Note the
  lack of comma on the final line.

- case statements provide a way of conditionally applying classes:

```
case $operatingsystem {
    ubuntu:  { include ubuntu }
    debian:  { include debian }
    default: { include basic }
}
```

  In this snippet, the class specific to each operating system is included depending
  again on the value of the $operatingsystem fact. Multiple conditions can be
  specified using a comma.

- A simple if/else structure:

```
if $needexample {
    file { "/usr/local/example": ensure => present }
}
else {
    file { "/usr/local/test": ensure => present }
}
```

  Currently it is possible to determine only whether the variable is or is not set, not
  to distinguish between particular values of a variable—for that, you must use the
  case or selector statements.

A template uses Ruby to put variables into a source file. In other words, it's like providing a central
file that can vary machine by machine.

A good example of using a fact in a template is to set an ipchains policy. The following file,
iptables.erb (ERB is the Ruby template syntax), uses $ipaddress:

```
*filter
:INPUT DROP [0:0]
:FORWARD DROP [0:0]
:OUTPUT ACCEPT [0:0]
-A INPUT -d 127.0.0.0/255.0.0.0 -i ! lo -p tcp -j DROP
-A INPUT -d <%= ipaddress %> -m state --state RELATED,ESTABLISHED -j ACCEPT
-A INPUT -i lo -j ACCEPT
```

```
-A INPUT -s 104.198.153.0/255.255.255.0 -d <%= ipaddress %> -j ACCEPT
-A INPUT -d <%= ipaddress %> -p tcp -m tcp --dport 22 -j ↵
    LOG --log-prefix "ssh:"-A INPUT -d <%= ipaddress %> ↵
    -p tcp -m tcp --dport 22 -j ACCEPT
COMMIT
```

You can then refer to this template as follows:

```
file { "iptables_config":
    name    => "/etc/sysconfig/iptables",
    content => template("/etc/puppet/templates/iptables.erb"),
}
```

Note that although files need the **puppet://puppetserver.example.com** syntax, templates do not.

Custom Facts

The default facts are available on all clients automatically. However, if you write custom facts, you will want to keep them on the puppetmaster and then set up the clients to synchronize their facts with the server. To do this, first add a section to **/etc/puppet/fileserver.conf** on the puppetmaster:

```
[facts]
  path /etc/puppet/facts
  allow *.example.com
```

Then, on each client, add a line to **/etc/puppet/puppetd.conf**:

```
factsync = true
```

Restart **puppetmasterd** on the server and **puppetd** on the clients. Now you can put any custom facts in **/etc/puppet/facts** and have them propagated. For example, to set up a fact that sets the **$home** fact to the **$HOME** environment variable, create this **/etc/puppet/facts/home.rb** file:

```
Facter.add("home") do
    setcode do
        ENV['HOME']
    end
end
```

The next time Puppet runs on your clients, this fact will be synchronized and can then be used in any of your recipes.

Other Variables

You can also use variables in other situations. A variable set in **site.pp** will be available to all other manifests or classes. So, for example, if you have a standard set of users who are allowed to log into your servers and you want to edit **/etc/ssh/sshd_config** accordingly, this snippet and template will work well:

```
# in site.pp
$server_ssh_users = "root jkemp admin"

# in ssh.pp or wherever else you want to keep it
file { "sshd_config":
    name => "/etc/ssh/sshd_config",
    allow_users => 'AllowUsers $server_ssh_users',
    template => "/etc/puppet/templates/sshd_config.erb",
}
# relevant snippet of sshd_config.erb
LoginGraceTime 600
PermitRootLogin without-password
StrictModes yes

<%= allow_users %>
```

Setting the file server via a variable is also a good idea. That way, if your server ever changes, you won't have to edit every file that refers to the Puppet server. So, you could edit site.pp and sudo.pp as follows:

```
# line to add in site.pp
$fileserver = "puppet://puppetserver.example.com/files"
#section in sudo.pp
file { "/etc/sudoers":
    owner => "root",
    group => "root",
    mode => 440,
    source => '$fileserver/sudoers',
}
```

3-17. Using ClusterSSH

If you're administering a large number of machines, sometimes you'll want to execute the same command on all of them (even when you have a centralized config solution like Puppet set up—see the previous recipes).

ClusterSSH (cssh) allows you to set up "sets" (clusters) of hosts and to log into them all at once via SSH. Then, whatever you type in the main cssh window will be replicated in all the hosts. Since an xterm is shown for each connection, it's easy to keep track of what's going on. If you click any individual xterm, you are connected directly to that host and can issue commands just for that.

■ **Note** Be very, very careful with this! If you type something wrong, you could hose not just one system but all the systems you're connected to. However, used carefully, it can be incredibly useful. Just check twice (maybe even three times in some cases...) before you hit Enter.

It's available as a package for Debian/Ubuntu:

```
sudo apt-get install clusterssh
```

or can be installed from source (`http://sourceforge.net/projects/clusterssh/`).

Generate a default global config file with this:

```
cssh -u > /etc/csshrc
```

Then, to set up a system-wide cluster definition, edit the `/etc/clusters` file to look something like this:

```
servers server1 server2 server3
```

This creates a group called **servers**, with members **server1**, **server2**, and **server3**. If you now type this:

```
cssh servers
```

you'll see three SSH windows opening, one to each of the servers.

■ **Note** You can also generate a personal config file with this:

```
cssh -u > /$HOME/.csshrc
```

and can add cluster definitions to this with the same syntax as with the `/etc/clusters` file. Any cluster definitions in here will of course exist only for you, rather than being system-wide.

With this setup, though, you'll be logging on as whatever user you're currently logged in as. To set it up so that you log in as a specific user (say, as **root**), you can use this syntax in the cluster tag:

```
servers root@server1 root@server2 root@server3
```

It becomes even more useful if you have login via SSH key set up; see recipe 6-1 for more on this.

■ **Note** You can also stick clusters together. If you set up these cluster definitions (tags):

```
servers server1 server2 server3
desktops desktop1 desktop2 desktop3
all servers desktops
```

then cssh all will connect to all six machines at once.

CHAPTER 4

■■■

Taking Backups
and Managing Data

A backup of some sort is absolutely essential for any system—whether it's just your own laptop or several hundred (or more) machines across an entire organization. It's possible to roll your own backup system using tools such as `rsync` (see recipe 4-6 for situations where `rsync` may be very useful), but in general, that will rapidly become difficult to maintain as your system grows beyond more than three or four machines.

Note Mirrored RAID is not a reliable backup. Disks will tend to fail at very similar times. And if the machine gets fried, both disks are likely to fry simultaneously.

Instead, it's far better to use an existing software solution. The options are many; they include the following:

- Bacula (free)

- Amanda (free)

- Mondo (free)

- BackupEdge (not free)

Whichever software solution you choose, you'll also need to pick a media solution (that is, what you'll use to store the backups) and a backup policy. In terms of media, disks are increasingly cheap and therefore a possibility, but tapes still have the advantage that you can change them (and thus keep previous weeks' copies in a fireproof box or even ship them off-site once a week, which is an important part of a reliable backup strategy because it provides at least some disaster proofing). Currently, tapes are still cheaper per gigabyte than a similarly sized disk, although the difference is steadily coming down as disks become cheaper.

I won't go into the details of setting up any of the specific backup solutions, but here are some general factors to consider when you're working out your backup policy:

- How much data do you need to store? See recipe 4-1 for a script to calculate your current total disk size and actual current usage.

- How often do your files change? Recipe 4-2 has a script to establish this.

- What is the purpose of your backups? Do you want a long-term archive of file history or just a backup so that if someone accidentally types `rm -rf .` in their home directory, you can restore their files for them?

- Related to the previous point, how long do you want to archive your data for, and how long do you want to give users to realize that they've accidentally deleted their Important Directory? Often this is going to be dictated either by company policy or by finances.

- How important is it that you are able to restore fast? You can usually choose, when backing up, either to do a full backup dump or to do a diff backup. The former takes up more space and takes longer to do but is quicker to restore from. Chances are you want somewhere between the two.

Once you've considered all this information, you can start pricing various options. For example, if you want a full backup weekly and then a diff backup nightly, use the information from the first two bullets to calculate how much space you want (and how much space you might want if all your disks fill up) for the full backup and then for each day's incremental change. That's your weekly data requirement. Based on that, how many weeks can you afford tapes for before you have to rotate? What about adding an extra archive copy per month?

You also need to consider how long each backup will take—how fast does data move over your local network, and how fast can your preferred backup media be written to? (Remember that tapes are faster than disk.) As a rule, you probably don't want backups running during the day if you can avoid it, so you need to think about how much you can back up every night.

Finally, if you're pricing a new backup solution, think about the future. You should allow for *at least* a 100 percent increase in the quantity of data you need to back up over the life of the system, and preferably more. Many systems now are modular, so you can buy more drives or libraries to extend your setup in the future for less than the cost of a whole new system.

■ **Note** Your backups are only as good as your last restore check. Confirm that restores are working OK (and therefore that the backups are working OK) weekly by running a test restore from your backup software.

4-1. Calculating Your Network's Total Disk Size and Current Usage

To establish what backup policy you need, one of the things to find out is the total potential size of your disks and what your current usage is. The following script can calculate this for all the machines in your network:

```perl
01  #!/usr/bin/perl -w
02  # Script to tally up total disk space available and used in local network
03  # JK 25.03.2009
04
05  use strict;
06  use Net::LDAPS;
07
08  die "Usage: dfscript\n" unless @ARGV == 0;
09
10  my ($search) = @ARGV;
11  my $server   = "ldaps://ldap.example.com";
12  my $cert     = "/etc/ldap/servercert.pem";
13  my $base     = "dc=example,dc=com";
14  my $total    = 0;
15  my $used     = 0;
16
17  my $ldap = Net::LDAPS->new( $server,
18                              verify => 'optional',
19                              cafile => $cert ) or die $@;
20  my $mesg = $ldap->bind;
21  my $filter = "(objectClass=ipHost)";
22  $mesg = $ldap->search(  base   => $base,
23                          filter => $filter,
24                          attr   => ['cn'],
25                       );
26  $mesg->code && die $mesg->error;
27
28  my @entries = $mesg->sorted('cn');
29
30  foreach my $entry ( @entries ) {
31      my $machine      = $entry->get_value( 'cn' );
32      if ( $machine ) {
33          open my $info, '-|', "ssh $machine 'df'"
34              or warn "Can't ssh to $machine";
36          while (<$info>) {
37              if ( /^\/dev/ ) {
38                  my @list = split;
39                  $total += $list[1];
40                  $used  += $list[2];
41              }
42          }
43      }
44  }
45
46  $mesg = $ldap->unbind;
47  print "Total is: $total\nUsed is: $used\n";
```

Lines 17–28 get the list of machines on your network from the LDAP database (see Chapter 2 for a discussion of LDAP setup) and sort them by name. Lines 30–44 check each machine for the available disk and the current usage. Line 31 gets the name of the machine from the LDAP entry (retrieved from the list of LDAP entries in line 30). Line 32 checks that you received a value for the name of the machine (this allows for any garbage returned by the LDAP query); then in line 33, the script connects to the machine with ssh and runs df to get the disk information. You use open with a pipe for the system call to ssh (rather than backticks, system, or exec), because this means that the information is returned line by line, which makes it very straightforward to loop over it, which is done in the while loop (lines 36–42).

Line 37 checks the output of df for /dev/ (which will indicate a local hard disk). Note that this will include any currently connected external disks but won't pick up on unmounted ones. The df line is then split (on whitespace, which is the default if you don't give an argument to split). The second entry on each df line is the total size of that disk (line 39 adds this to our running total), and the third entry is the size of the disk that is used (line 40 adds that to the other running total).

After all the machines have been checked, the LDAP connection is shut down, and the final value of all the local disks on all the checked machines is printed. Note that it'll be in 1KB blocks, because this is the default df output.

■ **Note** If you don't use LDAP, you can use this slightly altered script:

```
01  #!/usr/bin/perl -w
02  # Script to tally up total disk space available and used in local network
03  # JK 25.03.2009
04
05  use strict;
06
07  die "Usage: dfscript\n" unless @ARGV == 0;
08
09  my $total   = 0;
10  my $used    = 0;
11  my @machines = qw/ client1 client2 server1 server2 /;
12
13  foreach my $machine ( @machines ) {
14          open my $info, '-|', "ssh $machine 'df'"
15              or warn "Can't ssh to $machine";
16          while (<$info>) {
17              if ( /^\/dev/ ) {
18                  my @list = split;
19                  $total += $list[1];
20                  $used  += $list[2];
```

```
21                }
22            }
24  }
25
26  print "Total is: $total\nUsed is: $used\n";
```

You'll need to edit line 11 to have the names of all the machines you want to check. The main section of the script (lines 13–24) works exactly as described earlier.

Lines 30–45 ssh into each machine in turn, get the disk information from df, and then parse it and add the values to the running totals.

You may be able to reduce this total if you usually have a separate root partition that contains only a standard install, and if you need to restore, you can do another standard reinstall rather than restoring from backup. However, since as discussed earlier you need to allow room for expansion, it's probably better to overestimate than to underestimate your requirements.

■ **Note** If you do decide not to back up /, be aware that you may want to back up /root, especially if you have a tendency to keep useful scripts or other information there. You should also check where database and web information is kept (this is often in /var) and ensure that this is being backed up. If you're not using centralized config management (see Chapter 3), /etc may be another candidate for backup.

4-2. Finding Out How Often Your Files Change

Again, to create your backup policy, it's useful to know how often your files change. Here's a script you can run daily on each machine to find out:

```
01  #!/bin/bash
02  # Script to find and mail total size of files altered in the last 24 hrs
03  # JK 25.03.2009
04
05  TOTAL=0
06  HOST=`hostname`
07  EMAIL="juliet@example.com"
08  for FILE in `find / -mount -mtime -1`; do
09      SIZE=`stat -c %s $FILE`
10      TOTAL=$(($TOTAL+$SIZE))
11  done
```

```
12   MESSAGE="/tmp/changemsg.txt"
13   echo "Size of files changed in last 24 hrs: $TOTAL bytes" > $MESSAGE
14   /usr/bin/mail -s "Filechange on $HOST" "$EMAIL" < $MESSAGE
15   rm $MESSAGE
```

Save this script as **/etc/cron.daily/filechange** on each of your machines, and leave it there for a week or so. You'll get a daily e-mail from each machine telling you how much change there has been. Line 08 looks for files changed in the past 24 hours (`-mtime -x` checks for files that have been modified in the last $x \times 24$ hours); line 09 calls **stat** to get the size information in bytes. Lines 12–14 handle the mail sending.

4-3. Backing Up Your Wiki

If you're using MediaWiki (see recipe 1-4), then your wiki information is kept in a database in MySQL. You should of course be backing up your databases as part of your regular backup strategy (see recipe 4-4 for information on backing up MySQL), so from that point of view, your wiki and therefore your information are safe.

However, if something goes wrong with your MySQL server or with your Apache server, you may temporarily not be able to get at the wiki, which is not much good if it contains your notes on how to resolve problems with MySQL and/or Apache! So, it's a good idea to also have a static mirror.

■ **Note** If you're using a text-based wiki (for example, moinmoin) rather than a database-based one, this is less of a problem, because you can access the files manually and read them with a text editor if need be. However, it's probably still a good idea to have a copy of the wiki files on a second machine (other than your web server), created either with httrack as described here or with a cronjob and cp.

A good tool for this is **httrack**, which is a website-mirroring tool. (It's available as the **httrack** package for Debian/Ubuntu or from **http://www.httrack.com**.)

For a standard MediaWiki install living at **http://wiki.example.com**, this is the command to run from the command line:

```
httrack "http://wiki.example.com/" -O "/home/jkemp/wikibackup" \
    "+*.example.com/*" "-*oldid*" -v
```

To run an update daily, edit your crontab with **crontab -e**, and add a line that looks like this:

```
5 4 * * *    httrack –update "http://wiki.example.com/" ↵
-O "/home/jkemp/wikibackup" "+*.example.com/*" "-*oldid*"
```

> ■ **Note** Alternatively, you can create a two-line script:

```
#!/bin/bash
/usr/bin/httrack "http://wiki.example.com/" .
-O "/home/jkemp/wikibackup" "+*.example.com/*" "-*oldid*" -v
```

> and save it as /etc/cron.daily/wikimirror. Note that in Debian/Ubuntu, run-parts (which handles
> /etc/cron.*/ files) will not run any file that has any extension, so don't call this wikimirror.sh!

The first command will store a copy of the wiki at **/home/jkemp/wikibackup/** (the **-O** output option).
The **-v** option at the end means verbose; you may want to remove this once you've run the command to
check that it works. The **cron** entry runs an update daily at 4:05 a.m.; the **--update** option means that
httrack won't ask whether it's OK to overwrite your existing mirror.

The **+*.example.com/*** and **-*oldid*** options are filters. The first one limits the mirror to pages
within the **example.com** domain, ensuring that any links to external pages won't be mirrored. (That is
what you want; if you need those pages, you can get them from the external sites!) **+regexp** means that
the backup should include only the links that match this regexp.

The **-*oldid*** part is MediaWiki-specific; if you're using another wiki, check what convention it uses
for its history pages. MediaWiki keeps a history of all the changes to a page. This is great, but if you
mirror every single version of a page, it's going to take a long time and take up a lot of space. Remember,
this mirror doesn't need to be a full backup of your wiki. The standard backup of your database back end
takes care of that. This is just for emergency reference. History pages and links to a diff between the old
version and the current one in MediaWiki are referred to in the following format:

```
http://wiki.example.com/index.php?title=Main_Page&oldid=5253
http://wiki.example.com/index.php?title=Main_Page&diff=5249&oldid=5238
```

So, by using the **-regexp** notation, which means "exclude links that match this regexp," you exclude
all the history records.

> ■ **Note** If you have a link to an external page with information about what to do when your Internet access
> breaks, you may want to copy that information onto your wiki and add a note about where it came from. Or, keep
> the bookmark on your phone or other data device.

Once you've run this command, looked at the mirror produced at **/home/jkemp/**
wikibackup/, and confirmed that it has done what you want, you can add it to your crontab.

4-4. Backing Up MySQL

To back up a MySQL database, you can use the `mysqldump` command:

```
mysqldump -u root -pPASSWORD --single-transaction ↩
    --all-databases > databasesbackup.sql
```

This will back up all available databases on that server to the file **databasesbackup.sql**; to specify a particular database, use the database name in place of **-all-databases**. If you're doing this by hand, you can leave out **PASSWORD**; the **-p** option with no argument will ask for the password on the command line.

■ **Note** `--single-transaction` works for transactional tables (such as InnoDB and BDB), because it will dump the state of the database when the command was issued. MyISAM or MEMORY tables, however, could still change state. For these types of tables, you can instead use the `--lock-tables` option. Bear in mind that tables for different databases are locked separately, so there could be inconsistencies between databases (if something changed in database 2 while database 1 was locked, for example). For MyISAM tables, another option is to use the `mysqlhotcopy` utility, which is the fastest backup option.

However, as with all backups, what you want is to automate it. Save the following script as `/etc/cron.daily/mysqlbackup`:

```
01  #!/bin/bash
02  dir="/usr/local/backups/"
03  remotedir="/shared/raid/server_backups"
04  mysqldir="${dir}ldap"
05  filename="databases_"
06  num=`date +%Y%m%d`
07  mysqldump -u root -pPASSWORD --single-transaction -all-databases ↩
        > ${mysqldir}${filename}${num}.ldif
08  find $mysqldir -mtime +14 | xargs rm --
09  cp $mysqldir/* $remotedir
```

This script saves a dump of the database in a local directory (`${mysqldir}`, line 07) and then copies it to a remote directory as well (line 09). The call to **date** on line 06 will produce files named for the date created, such as **/var/backups/databasesbackup_20090711.sql**, which means that you keep a history of database backups; line 08 clears out any backups older than two weeks so that you don't end up overrun with them.

One obvious problem with this is that your MySQL root password is right there in plain text in the file. Not very secure! A better bet is to create a user with minimal privileges (you can use **SELECT**, which effectively allows the user to view everything, and you can use **LOCK TABLES** so that the tables can be locked if need be) just for the purposes of backing up. Connect to your MySQL server as **root** (mysql -u root -p), and issue this command:

```
mysql> grant SELECT,LOCK TABLES on *.* to backupuser@localhost ↵
       identified by 'password';
```

Then replace the username and password in line 07 of the previous script with the backup user's username and password.

To restore from one of these files, use the following command, which will ask for your **root** password on the command line:

```
mysql -u root -p databasename < databasesbackup_20090711.sql
```

You'll need to do this for each database.

4-5. Backing Up Kerberos and LDAP

It's important to back up your Kerberos and LDAP databases. A full regular backup should of course include the files that Kerberos and LDAP use for their databases, but it's also a good idea to keep a regularly updated dump of the databases elsewhere. This means that if you have corruption problems or a server goes down (although see recipes 2-7 and 2-8 for setting up slave/backup servers for LDAP and Kerberos!), you can reload the information straightaway.

This is exactly the sort of thing that **cron** is useful for. For LDAP, save this script as /etc/cron.daily/ldapbackup:

```
01  #!/bin/bash
02  dir="/usr/local/backups/"
03  remotedir="/shared/raid/server_backups"
04  dbdir="/var/lib/ldap/"
05  ldap="ldap/"
06  ldapdir="$dir$ldap"
07  filename="database"
08  num=`date +%Y%m%d`
09  /etc/init.d/slapd stop > /dev/null
10  cp -r $dbdir $dir
11  /usr/sbin/slapcat -l ${ldapdir}${filename}${num}.ldif
12  /etc/init.d/slapd start > /dev/null
13  find $ldapdir -mtime +14 | xargs rm --
14  cp $ldapdir/* $remotedir
```

Lines 02–08 set up the directory and the variables for the file names. The dump files will be saved with names in the format **database20090321.ldif** in the **/usr/local/backups/ldap/** directory. (Feel free to change this to whatever you prefer.)

Lines 09–12 stop LDAP to avoid problems with database inconsistencies, copy the contents of the LDAP database directory (**/var/lib/ldap/**) to the backup directory, and then dump the database as an LDIF file using **slapcat**. Then LDAP is restarted. (This should take only a second or two all told.)

■ **Note** If you don't want to have LDAP offline, you can use a slave server (see recipe 2-7) and either run the backup off that or rely on the slave to pick up any LDAP requests that come in the interim.

Finally, line 13 deletes any files in the backup directory that are more than 14 days old, which prevents you from ending up with enormous stacks of old LDIF files. Line 14 copies the backup directory to a shared directory on a different machine (here mounted as **/shared/raid/server_backups**). Thus, if your LDAP machine crashes altogether, you don't lose the backup directory as well.

Putting the script in **/etc/cron.daily/** means it will automatically be run once a day (the default is for this to happen overnight). Make sure it's **root**-owned and executable (note also that the name needs to have no extension, as shown here, or it won't be run by **run-parts**):

```
chown root:root /etc/cron.daily/ldapbackup
chmod u+rx /etc/cron.daily/ldapbackup
```

For Kerberos backup, save this script as **/etc/cron.daily/krbbackup**:

```
01  #!/bin/sh
02  dir="/usr/local/backups/kerberos/"
03  file="kerbdumpfile"
04  server="raidserver:/raid"
05  mntdir="/mnt/"
06  remotedir="server_backups/"
07  mount -t nfs $server $mnt
08  kdb5_util dump $dir$file
09  cp $dir$file $mntdir$remotedir
10  umount $mntdir
```

Again, lines 02–06 set up the variables. Line 07 mounts the remote server. You can use this method if you don't want the NFS remote directory to be permanently mounted, or automounted, on the Kerberos server. (You can make a similar change to the earlier LDAP backup script, if you prefer.)

Line 08 dumps the Kerberos database using **kdb5_util dump**, and lines 09–10 copy the dump file across to the remote server and then unmount it.

Again, make sure the script is **root**-owned and executable:

```
chown root:root /etc/cron.daily/krbbackup
chmod u+rx /etc/cron.daily/krbbackup
```

4-6. Performing a Rapid Restore with Automated rsync

One problem with a tape backup solution is that in the event of some kind of catastrophic data loss (machine or drive failure, for example), tapes can take quite some time to restore, especially for large drives.

It's therefore a good idea to have, as well as your tape backups, some kind of mirror of important directories. Obviously, if you have a RAID 0 machine, you have this automatically, but if you don't (or if you would prefer that your mirror be on another machine or even at another site), you can set up your own mirroring with rsync.

In this case, let's look at the case of a shared home directory at homeserver:/shared/home.

The basic rsync command is as follows:

```
rsync /dir/source /dir/destination
```

This compares the two directories and copies across any files in /dir/source that are newer than those in /dir/destination. So, the first time it's run, it will copy everything (and may take some time); thereafter, it copies only what has changed, thus saving both time and network capacity.

That basic command synchronizes from one local directory to another local directory, but in fact /dir/destination can be on another machine:

```
rsync /dir/source machinename.example.com:/dir/destination
```

■ **Note** You can also reverse this:

```
rsync machinename.example.com:/dir/source /dir/destination
```

which is useful for restore.

---

rsync has numerous options, but these are the most useful ones:

- -a: Archive, which both recurses over the directory structure and keeps file attributes (ownership, permissions, edit times, and so on) intact.

- -u: Update, which does not update any files that are newer on the destination directory than on the source.

- -z: Compress, which compresses during the transfer.

- -v: Verbose, so you can follow what's happening.

- -L: Follow symlinks, copying the files that they point to in full, rather than using the default option of recording them as symlinks.

- --delete: Deletes from the destination directory files that no longer exist on the source directory.

- -n: Does a dummy run but doesn't actually transfer any files (useful with -v when testing).

So, if you have a backup drive available at backupserver:/shared/backuphome, you can back up your shared home directory like this, logged in as root on homeserver:

```
rsync -avuz /shared/home backupserver:/shared/backuphome
```

■ **Note** This will use `ssh` to `backupserver` as `root`, which may or may not be permitted on your system. If `backupserver` isn't on your local network, you'll need to specify its address in full: `backupserver.example.com`.

`rsyncd` must be running on **backupserver**. To set this up, install the relevant package for your distro (in Debian/Ubuntu it's `rsyncd`), then edit `/etc/default/rsync` to set RSYNC_ENABLE to `true`, and finally run `/etc/init.d/rsync start`.

You'll be challenged for your **ssh** password (see recipe 6-3 for how to avoid this), and then `rsync` will log a message to the screen that it is building the file list. This means that it is working out what files to copy. In this case, it'll copy all of them, because this is a first backup. Once the list is built, the copying will start, and using the `-v` switch means there'll be a message logged to the screen for each file.

Once `rsync` has finished, your backed-up files will be in `/shared/backuphome` on `backupserver.example.com`.

■ **Note** `rsync`'s treatment of directories differs depending on whether there is a trailing slash at the end of the source directory. The following:

`rsync /test/one /backup`

will transfer all the files in `/test/one` to `/backup/one`. In other words, it copies the whole directory (and its contents) by name. By contrast, the following, with the trailing slash on the source directory:

`rsync /test/one/ /backup`

will copy all the files in `/test/one` to `/backup`. In other words, it copies only the contents, not the directory itself. Most of the time, you'll want to use the first version because it is tidier in the sense that it keeps all the files within the copied directory rather than scattered into your parent backup directory.

Once your first run has finished, try changing a single file and running the same command again. You'll see that only a single file is copied this time.

To avoid the **ssh** password challenge, you could also use `mount` to mount the shared backup directory over NFS. This script, run from **homeserver**, will mount the directory, run the `rsync`, and unmount the directory; it doesn't use the `-v` (verbose) option to `rsync` so that output is reduced. Save it as `/etc/cron.d/home-backup-script`.

```
mount -t nfs backupserver:/shared/backuphome /mnt
rsync -avuz /shared/home /mnt
umount /mnt
```

Make it executable with chmod u+x /etc/cron.d/home-backup-script.

Finally, you need to automate this. Type crontab -e, and add this line to your crontab file:

```
5 0 * * * /etc/cron.d/backupscript
```

The numbers at the start of the crontab entry mean that this will run at five (5) minutes past midnight (0) every day (check the crontab man 5 page for more details).

■ **Note** One issue with this setup is that you have only one day's version, so if something happens to your disk overnight, the "bad" version may be written as the backup.

To avoid this, you could set up a cronjob on your backup machine that runs just before the scheduled rsync and copies your existing backup directory elsewhere. For example, this line in your crontab would do the job:

```
5 23 * * * rsync -auz --delete /home/user/backup /home/user/backup2
```

This runs at 11:05 p.m. daily. It would keep only one extra day's worth of data, but that might be enough for you. You could extend this to keep more backups, but this has a high disk space penalty (although disk these days is cheap), and there quickly comes a point where you are better off relying on your tape backups.

If you do have a disaster, you can now just rewrite your LDAP NFS maps (see recipe 2-13) to use backupserver:/shared/homebackup rather than homeserver:/shared/home, and everyone can access their files again (albeit with possibly up to 24 hours lost) while you fix the problem. This script will rewrite the LDAP maps for you:

```perl
01  #!/usr/bin/perl -w
02  use strict;
03  use Net::LDAPS;
04
05  my $ldapserver = 'ldapserver.example.com';
06  my $base       = 'ou=people,dc=example,dc=com';
06  my $oldhome  = 'homeserver:/homedisk/';
07  my $newhome = 'newserver:/newhome/';
08
09  my $ldap = Net::LDAPS->new( $ldapserver,
10                              verify => 'optional',
11                              cafile => '/etc/ldap/cacert.pem' ) or die $@;
12  my $mesg = $ldap->bind;
13
14  $mesg = $ldap->search( base    => $base,
15                         filter  => "automountInformation=*$oldhome*",
```

```
16                                    attrs   => [ 'dn', 'cn', 'automountInformation' ],
17                               );
18   my @entries = $mesg->entries;
19
20    foreach my $entry ( @entries ) {
21            my $cn = $entry->get_value( 'cn' );
22            $mesg = $ldap->modify( $entry, ↵
                        replace => { 'automountInformation' =>
                                     '-fstype=nfs,rw $newhome$cn'  } );
23   }
24
25   $mesg = ldap->unbind
```

Lines 05–08 set up the names for your old and new servers and the directories; edit this as appropriate for your network. Lines 09–12 open the connection to the LDAP server (see recipe 2-9 for more details on the Net::LDAPS Perl module). Lines 14–18 search for any automount entries with the old server name.

Lines 20–23 are the ones that do the work. For each entry, the value of the directory name is retrieved ($cn; this would be jkemp for user jkemp, for example), and then the map is modified to change homeserver:/homedisk/jkemp to newserver:/new/ home/jkemp for each entry. See recipe 2-13 for a discussion of the other options in the automountInformation line. Line 25 tidies up the LDAP connection when you're done.

After this, log in to newserver, and check that /etc/exports has this line:

```
/new/home               *.example.com(rw)
```

Then restart the NFS server on that machine with sudo /etc/init.d/nfs-kernel-server restart, and restart autofs on all other machines across the network (sudo /etc/init.d/autofs restart). ClusterSSH (see recipe 3-20) may be useful for this. All should be well again. You can now fix homeserver in a bit less of a rush, since everyone can carry on working while you do it!

4-7. Using rsync with SSH Keys

You can use the method in the previous recipe for off-site backup, as well, if you have shell access to an off-site machine. Simply give the machine's full name:

```
rsync -avuz /dir/to/backup offsite.example2.com:/shared/backupdir
```

Note This is probably not something you want to do for your full-site home directory, unless you have a very fast connection to the off-site machine. However, it may be useful for some key directories.

However, at this point, it still requires an ssh password, which is no good from an automation point of view. The final stage is to set up a password-free ssh key.

■ **Note** See recipe 6-1 for further discussion of `ssh` and keys.

To create your private key, enter this into a terminal window on your home machine:

```
ssh-keygen -t rsa -f ~/.ssh/rsync
```

This will generate an RSA key and save it in `~/.ssh/rsync`.

■ **Note** You can also generate DSA keys. DSA is a slightly older standard than RSA. It's quicker for some operations (notably for key generation), but RSA is quicker overall. It's sometimes suggested that RSA is stronger than DSA, but there's some debate about the details of this. The default key length for RSA is 2,048 bits, whereas DSA keys must be 1,024 bits long. Since longer keys are in general stronger, this is a significant advantage for RSA, which is also more flexible. Unless you have a specific reason for using DSA, stick with RSA.

You will be prompted for a passphrase. Hit Enter to leave this blank. You will now have files `rsync` and `rsync.pub` in your `~/.ssh` directory.

With a passworded key, all you would need to do here is add the contents of `~/.ssh/rsync.pub` to the file `~/.ssh/authorized_keys2` on **offsite.example.com**. However, with a passphraseless key, that's a bad idea, since then if an attacker gained access to your home machine, they would also immediately have unlimited access to your account on **offsite.example.com**.

Instead, it's possible to reduce the security risk by restricting what this particular key can do. In this case, let's restrict it to a single command, using the `~/.ssh/authorized_keys2` file on **offsite.example.com**

Copy `~/.ssh/rsync.pub` to `tmpfile`, and edit `tmpfile` so that it's a single line (this single line is the public half of your key, which will look like a big block of random characters, with an English identifier at the end). Then add this at the start of that line:

```
command="rsync -avuz -e "ssh -i /home/user/.ssh/rsync" ↵
/test user@offsite.example.com:/home/user/backup", ↵
no-port-forwarding,no-X11-forwarding,no-agent-forwarding ↵
```

■ **Note** There are line breaks here for printing reasons only; your version should not include any line breaks. It must be a single line, including both the previous code and your private key.

Now add the contents of `tmpfile` to `~/.ssh/authorized_keys2` on **offsite.example.com** (using cut and paste, or `cat`). Again, ensure that it remains as a single line.

To specify which key the **rsync** command should use, run the following:

```
rsync -avuz -e "ssh -i /home/user/.ssh/rsync" /test \
    user@offsite.example.com:/home/user/backup
```

This line must match the command you put in the previous `~/.ssh/authorized_keys2` file, or `offsite.example.com` will refuse your access. You should see output indicating **rsync** connecting via **ssh** without a password prompt, building the `filelist`, and then updating with any changes.

4-8. Creating an Off-Site Backup via E-mail

Another option for the off-site backup of a limited number of files is to use e-mail. In particular, at the time of this writing, Gmail offered 7GB of storage for free and was prepared to sell you further space; you may even have access to your own off-site e-mail server. You can set up a Perl script to e-mail a given set of files to your Gmail account and then run it automatically every night with **cron**.

■ **Note** There are size limitations with this! Most e-mail servers will limit the size of mail message that they are prepared to accept, because very large e-mails are a nuisance and can cause network slowdown. So, this method is really useful only for small numbers of smallish files. Text files tend to be small, so it may be reasonable to e-mail yourself a backup of your script directories or even of the dump of your wiki as described in recipe 4-3. It's not a good solution for an entire home directory, however.

The Perl modules **Net::SMTP**, **File::Find**, **Mime::Lite**, **Archive::Tar**, and **IO::Zlib** are required for this script. In Debian, the first two of these are a default part of the regular Perl install; install the others with the following:

```
sudo apt-get install libmime-lite-perl libarchive-tar-perl libio-zlib-perl
```

Alternatively, you can install them using CPAN (see the appendix for notes on CPAN and Perl modules):

```
perl -MCPAN -e "install Net::SMTP"
perl -MCPAN -e "install File::Find"
perl -MCPAN -e "install Mime::Lite"
perl -MCPAN -e "install Archive::Tar"
```

The script looks like this:

```
01  #!/usr/bin/perl -w
02
03  use strict;
04  use Archive::Tar;
05  use File::Find;
```

```
06  use MIME::Lite;
07  use Net::SMTP;
08
09  sub sendmail();
10  sub wanted();
11
12  my $email       = 'my.name@gmail.com';
13  my $from        = 'my.address@example.com';
14  my $smtpserver  = "smtp.example.com";
15  my @archive_list;
16  my $backup_dir  = "/home/jkemp/personal/";
17  my $tarfile     = "/home/jkemp/gmailtar.tgz";
18
19  find ( \&wanted, $backup_dir );
20  Archive::Tar->create_archive($tarfile, "1", @archive_list);
21  sendmail();
22
23  sub wanted() {
24      return unless -f $File::Find::name;
25      push @archive_list, $File::Find::name;
26  }
27
28  sub sendmail() {
29      my $msg = MIME::Lite->new(To   => $email,
30                  From => $from,
31                              Subject => "Backup email",
32                              Type    => "multipart/mixed");
33      $msg->attach(Type  => "application/gzip",
34                   Path  => $tarfile,
35                   Filename  => "gmailtar.tgz");
36      $msg->send('smtp', $smtpserver);
37  }
```

Before you run it, change the permissions:

```
chmod u+x gmail.pl
```

Lines 04–10 import the other required modules and declare the subroutines that come later in the code. Lines 12–16 set your variables up, which is another good coding practice.

Line 18 uses the find command from File::Find to recurse over the directory you want to back up (here /home/jkemp/personal/). It calls the wanted subroutine (defined in lines 22–25) to check that the name that has been passed in (here /home/jkemp/personal corresponds to an existing file and, if so, adds the file to the array of files to be archived).

■ **Note** When using subroutines, you must either define them before they are first used or declare them first and define them at the end. I've done the latter here.

Line 19 does all the heavy lifting. It creates a tar archive called $tarfile from the files in @archivelist. Line 20 sends the e-mail. Having this as a subroutine makes testing easier. You can quickly comment out the e-mail sending step while you're checking that the archive is being correctly generated. If you do run it like this, you should see the gmailtar.tgz file in the directory you ran the script from. Check its contents with this:

```
mkdir test
mv gmailtar.tgz test/
cd test/
tar zxf gmailtar.tgz
ls test/*
```

The sendmail() subroutine in lines 27–34 is straightforward. It creates a new MIME message, attaches the gzipped backup file, and sends it as a message.

As it stands, the script will leave the tar file it creates on your machine. To delete this, add an extra line after line 20:

```
unlink $tarfile;
```

If you don't do this, the tar file will simply be overwritten the next time the script runs.

■ **Note** You probably don't want to have the delete line in during testing because you may want to look at the archive file after the script has run.

To make this include more than one directory, replace line 15 with this:

```
my @backupdir = ("/dir1/", "/dir2/");
```

Replace line 18 with these three lines:

```
foreach my $dir ( @backupdir ) {
        find ( \&wanted, $dir );
}
```

Use crontab to run this daily. Run crontab -e, and then edit your crontab to look something like this:

```
13 04 * * *      /path/to/script
```

4-9. Using anacron for Laptop Backups

cron is great for servers and desktops that are always on, but if you want to schedule a backup (or indeed any other job) on a laptop or another machine that may not always be on, you're probably better off using anacron instead.

With cron, you schedule a job at a specific date and time. If at that particular time the machine is down, the job just won't run (until the next time it's scheduled). With anacron, you schedule a job to run at specific intervals, for example, daily, weekly, or monthly. anacron will try to keep as closely to this schedule as system uptime permits. So, if a job is supposed to run daily but when the computer is switched on the anacron daemon finds that it hasn't run in the last 24 hours, it will be run there and then.

The downside of anacron is that you can run it only at intervals of one or more days—unlike cron, which can run at intervals as small as one minute. For backup purposes, this probably won't be a problem because most backup schedules will run at most daily.

■ **Note** anacron can be configured only by the root user, whereas cron can be used by any user.

To set up an rsync backup for your laptop, edit the file /etc/anacrontab, as root, to add the following line:

```
1 5 backup rsync -auz -e "ssh -i /home/user/.ssh/rsync" ↵
/test user@offsite.example.com:/home/user/backup
```

This line will run the given rsync command every day (the first parameter) with a delay of five minutes (the second parameter) and identify the job in logs as backup (the third parameter). As with cron, anything after the time and log parameters is assumed to be part of the command to be run. Ensure that the whole command is on a single line.

4-10. Performing Basic Data Recovery: fsck and dd

If a filesystem or hard drive goes bad, there are some basic steps you can take with fsck and dd that may be able to solve the problem.

■ **Note** If a disk fails, the very first thing to do is to shut down the affected machine ASAP. Writing to the problem disk may cause further problems. To run any of the suggested fixes in this recipe, you'll need to boot from another hard disk or from a LiveCD of your or another distro. Rescue distributions like Knoppix (http://www.knoppix.net/) can be useful, especially if, as with Knoppix, they include the ddrescue package (see step 3).

---

1.   The first thing to try is a straightforward run of **fsck**:

     fsck /dev/sda1

     If you're lucky, this may be all you need. If this succeeds, **fsck** will probably ask
     you to confirm a few fixes. To avoid being asked this, use the **-y** option.
     However, be warned that this should be used with caution, because it means
     that **fsck** will attempt to fix any and all errors it encounters, which may cause
     data loss.

■ **Note** This is not true of all filesystems. If you're using XFS, for example, then checking is conducted on mount,
and **fsck** does nothing. **xfs_check** and **xfs_repair** may also be useful. However, **fsck** is fine with the Linux-
standard ext3 (and ext2) filesystems.

     If this does work, update your backups immediately in case it wasn't just a
     one-off failure!

2.   If you get a "bad superblock" error, you can try using an alternative block. On
     an ext2 or ext3 filesystem, the superblock contains the filesystem metadata.
     Because it's essential to the filesystem, backup copies of the superblock are
     kept, but you may need to use them explicitly.

     To get the superblock information for the problem filesystem, run the
     following:

     dumpe2fs /dev/hda2 | grep superblock

     This will work for both ext2 and ext3. Your output should look a bit like this:

     ```
     Primary superblock at 0, Group descriptors at 1-3
     Backup superblock at 32768, Group descriptors at 32769-32771
     Backup superblock at 98304, Group descriptors at 98305-98307
     Backup superblock at 163840, Group descriptors at 163841-163843
     [ etc ... ]
     ```

     Pass in one of the backup superblocks as an option to **fsck**:

     fsck -b 32768 /dev/hda2

     If this runs successfully, try mounting the filesystem with **mount**. If you still
     have problems, try passing the backup superblock into **mount** explicitly:

     mount sb=32768 /dev/hda2 /mnt

3.   The next stage, if steps 1 and 2 have both failed, is to use **dd** to generate a bit-
     for-bit copy of the failed disk. To do this, you'll need a spare drive at least as
     large as the failed one because **dd** copies even empty space over.

     For a spare drive mounted at **/mnt/recovery** (this must not be the drive you
     booted from) and a failed drive connected at **/dev/hda**, use the following:

```
sudo dd if=/dev/hda of=/mnt/recovery/hdaimage.dd
```

This may take a while to run!

By default, **dd** will abort on error. Avoid this with the **noerror** option:

```
sudo dd conv=noerror if=/dev/hda of=/mnt/recovery/hdaimage.dd
```

Another option is the GNU utility **ddrescue**, with which you can skip the dodgy areas (**dd** will keep trying to get at bad areas of disk). This is the **gddrescue** package (and the utility is called **gddrescue**) in Debian/Ubuntu. Note that this is *not* the same as the package/utility **dd_rescue**, which is a slightly less useful program.

```
gddrescue -n /dev/hda /mnt/recovery/hdaimage.raw rescued.log
```

This command will grab most of the error-free areas quickly, after which you can rerun it with **-r 1** instead of **-n** to get as much as possible of the bad patches. This is especially useful if you're worried about how long your disk will continue to spin, because you can get a copy of any good data immediately.

Once you have your bit-for-bit copy, you can run **fsck** on it:

```
fsck /mnt/recovery/hdaimage.dd
```

Next, if it's a single-partition drive, you can mount the image as a loopback device:

```
mount -o loop /mnt/recovery/hdaimage.dd /mnt/hdaimage
```

Ideally, your data will now be available at **/mnt/hdaimage**. However, if your failed disk had multiple partitions, you'll need to do a little more work. Find out where the partitions are with this:

```
fdisk -lu /mnt/recovery/hdaimage.dd
```

which will list the start and end cylinders of each partition and the units in which they're measured. If the second partition starts at cylinder 80300 and the units are 512 bytes, then that partition starts at $80300 \times 512 = 41{,}113{,}600$ bytes. In this case, the command you want looks like this:

```
mount -o loop,offset=41113600 /mnt/recover/hdaimage.raw /mnt/hdaimage
```

Finally, you can use **dd** again to write the image back onto another disk, for example, /dev/hdb:

```
dd if=/mnt/recovery/hdaimage.raw of=/dev/hdb
```

■ **Note** Another emergency rescue tip for a bad disk: put it in the freezer for a few hours (in a watertight sealed bag). This may sound odd, but cooling the disk can give it a brief lease of new life—long enough for you to grab your data from it.

4-11. Using Foremost to Retrieve Data

If `fsck` and `dd` aren't enough to retrieve your data, you'll need to try a little harder. You'll need to start looking through the raw disk data. You *can* do this manually by grepping through the disk image or using strings (see recipe 9-6), but it's very hard work and will get you somewhere only if you're lucky and if you're just looking for text files.

An easier alternative is Foremost (`http://foremost.sourceforge.net/`, available as the Debian/Ubuntu package `foremost`). This software was originally developed by the U.S. government for data recovery, and it searches through a disk image to look for file headers, file footers, and other internal data structures.

■ **Note** It's a better bet to run this on a disk image, produced with `dd` as in recipe 4-8, than on your bad disk.

The default rescue is straightforward and will output to the directory from where you ran it:

```
foremost image.dd
```

Or you can search for all defined types. These include text files; `.jpg` and other image files; `.doc` files; OLE files (a format used by PowerPoint, Excel, and so on); zipped files; media files using `.avi`, `.wmv`, and other formats; and some source code files). Then write them to a specified output directory:

```
foremost -t all -o /rescue/dir -i image.dd
```

The `-i` switch identifies the image, the `-o` switch identifies the output directory to write to, and the `-t` switch gives file types (here it's `all`). You can use the specific file type options if you're looking only for specific file types or if you want to extract and deal with different file types separately.

If Foremost works, your files will be extracted without correct ownership and permissions, so you'll need to go over the data afterward to correct that.

■ **Note** `scalpel` and `magicrescue` (both available as Debian/Ubuntu packages of the same names) do the same sort of data recovery but are a little less resource intensive. None of these will re-create your directory structure.

4-12. Rescuing Data: Autopsy

Autopsy/Sleuthkit (available at `http://www.sleuthkit.org/autopsy/` or as a package for most distros, called `autopsy` and `sleuthkit` on Debian/Ubuntu) is a Perl disk forensic browser with which you can look through a filesystem in detail. If the previous recipes haven't got you anywhere, you can try this recipe.

Note Again, you should run this on a disk image (created as in recipe 4-8) rather than on the disk itself. The more you use your damaged disk, the more you risk damaging it.

Start Autopsy, and see whether you can read your copied filesystem. It is possible that even if the filesystem itself is still unreadable, you may be able to get at some of the inode and metadata information.

In this case, you can experiment with the Sleuthkit command-line tools:

- `ils` lists inode information from the image.

- `ffind` finds the file or directory name using the inode.

- `icat` outputs the file content based on its inode number.

So, you can get inode information, use `ffind` to get the file/directory name, and then output the content with `icat` once you establish whether you're looking at a file or a directory.

As an example of this process, the Sleuthkit `fls` command will list the files and directory names in a particular image:

```
fls hdaimage.dd -r -f ext3 -i raw
```

So, you might get some output from `fls`, which includes the following line:

```
r/r * 10: myfile.txt
```

The `r/r` at the start of the line gives the directory entry type value and the file type (`r` means regular file; `d` is a directory). As a rule, these will match. `*` indicates that it's been deleted, and `10` is the inode number. The final field is of course the file name.

Use this command to retrieve the contents of this file:

```
icat -r -f ext3 -i raw hdaimage.dd 10 > myfile.txt
```

This uses file recovery techniques (`-r`) since the file has been deleted. `-f ext3` specifies the filesystem type, and `-i raw` uses the image type that you're working from. `hdaimage.dd` is the path to the image file, and `10` is the inode we want (as retrieved from the earlier `fls` command). The recovered output is piped into the file name that was retrieved from `fls`.

Note Use the `sorter` script to look for particular types of file (for example, images). To use the supplied `images.sort` file, this should work:

```
# sorter -f ext3 -C /usr/local/sleuthkit/share/sort/images.sort ↵
    -d data/sortedimages -h -s hdaimage.dd
```

This will treat the source image (using the -s option, which here is `hdaimage.dd`) as an ext3 filesystem (set with the -f option). -C specifies the config file, and -d specifies the directory to output to. If you add the -h option, thumbnails of the image files will also be created. There are other config (rules) files supplied, or you can write your own.

4-13. Securely Wiping Data

It's quite common to find yourself replacing machines that are still functional but don't match up to the specs you now need. These days, a three-year practical life span is about the best case in most environments, but a three-year-old computer should still be perfectly functional. Ideally, therefore, you should give them a new home rather than just throwing them out. Take a look for charities or recycling organizations in your area, or even offer them around to your staff!

However, before you send the machines off to begin their new life, you need to consider data security. Just deleting old data isn't enough. It's possible, if you know what you're doing, to retrieve deleted data from the disk.

DBAN (which stands for Darik's Boot And Nuke), available from `http://www.dban.org/`, is designed to fully and securely wipe your disk. It's a downloadable self-contained boot disk, available for CD/DVD, floppy disk, or USB flash drive. Boot from it, and it will look for hard disks on the system and then give you the option of deleting any or all of them by just hitting Enter.

■ **Note** For RAID arrays, you may need to manually disassemble the array first.

Several wipe methods are available, from a quick erase to a full three-pass wipe, including a couple of methods that are used by the U.S. Department of Defense! The `autonuke` option, which is the default from the first screen, will automatically run through *all* detected disks, securely wiping them, so be careful with it, and make sure that you really are done with the machine before you start.

■ **Note** A full standard disk wipe, especially on an old or slow machine, can take a long time (three to four hours is quoted as standard, but it can be much more than that on older machines). I usually leave it running overnight.

DBAN is easy to use and very secure; it uses multiple methods (including the Gutmann method and the Mersenne twister) to ensure that the data really is gone for good. It's a handy program to keep around on disk, but make sure you label it very clearly and don't end up booting from it by accident! (It won't run without input, but it's still best to be careful with anything seriously destructive.)

CHAPTER 5

■ ■ ■

Working with Filesystems

Filesystems are the backbone of a Linux system (after all, in Linux, absolutely everything is a file). This chapter discusses how to tune and make changes to the default Linux filesystems, how to resize your filesystems when you find yourself running out of space (something that seems to happen however much room you think you've given yourself!), RAID arrays, and alternative filesystems.

5-1. Changing ext2 to ext3 with tune2fs

The ext2 and ext3 filesystems, which are the filesystems that you're most likely to be using on your Linux systems, have various parameters set at the time of creation. (ext3 is the default on most modern distros now.) One of these is the journaling parameter, which is the fundamental difference between an ext2 filesystem and an ext3 filesystem. tune2fs enables you to change these parameters on the fly.

By turning an ext2 filesystem into an ext3 filesystem, you can add journaling to the filesystem on the fly. Journaling filesystems log changes to a journal area before committing them to the main disk, which avoids potential data inconsistencies in the event of a crash. In general, disk operations in Linux will require more than one write event (for example, removing a file directory entry and then also marking the space as free), so if there's a power failure or other problem when only one part of a disk operation has been completed, the filesystem will be in an inconsistent state. In a non-journaled filesystem, you run fsck or a similar tool to walk the whole filesystem looking for (and ideally fixing) inconsistencies. In a journaled filesystem, the journal is instead used to rerun all recent operations until the filesystem is consistent again. This is much quicker and more reliable.

The basic command to create a journal for an ext2 filesystem is as follows:

```
tune2fs -j /dev/hda1
```

This will create an *immutable* journal file (one whose state cannot be manually altered, so it's safe from accidental deletion) for the filesystem. On the next reboot, this file will be moved to a special inode. You may want to reboot sooner rather than later to make sure this happens (and thus that the journal file can't be accidentally lost).

■ **Note** If the filesystem you're changing is the root filesystem, you may need to boot from a LiveCD or rescue disc and then run e2fsck /dev/hda1 from there so that the journal file can be moved to its new inode. Then reboot as normal. Debian, and some other distros, have a workaround that avoids having to do this.

If your existing filesystem is too full to have space for the journal file (the normal default is about 5 percent of the filesystem size), you can use -J to set various options to work around this problem. (Or see recipe 5-5 for how to resize filesystems on the fly.) The following will create a journal of size 512MB:

```
tune2fs -j -J size=512 /dev/hda1
```

Alternatively, you can create a journal file on a different device (here, **/dev/hdb2**) with this:

```
mke2fs -O journal_dev /dev/hdb2
```

Then when you set up journaling on your overfull filesystem, you can set it to use this external journal file:

```
tune2fs -j -J device=/dev/hdb2 /dev/hda1
```

5-2. Making Changes to Automatic fsck Checking

If you're running a nonjournaled filesystem, you will be familiar with the automatic **e2fsck** check for inconsistencies that is triggered after a certain number of mounts. (Journaled filesystems don't need this because the journal is what avoids inconsistencies.) This can be irritating if it happens at bootup when you need a machine to come up quickly. Using **tune2fs**, it's possible to turn it off altogether:

```
tune2fs -c 0 /dev/hda1
```

-c 0 sets the number of mounts between checks to 0, thus turning it off.

■ **Note** This means that your filesystem will never be checked unless you do it manually! This is a problem only if you're using a non-journaled filesystem such as ext2. Journaling means that there's no need for regular automatic fscks.

More useful is setting the value to different numbers for different partitions so that they don't all get checked on the same bootup. This means that at least you'll be checking only one partition on any given boot, which will speed things up a little.

```
tune2fs -c 13 /dev/hda1
tune2fs -c  17 /dev/hda2
```

Alternatively, set the filesystem to be checked every so many days rather than every so many mounts:

```
tune2fs -i 13d /dev/hda1
```

`-i 13d` sets the interval between checks to 13 days. Use `13w` for 13 weeks, or use `13m` for 13 months. Again, you can set this to be different values for different partitions.

To force a check at the next reboot, you can set the number of mounts that the filesystem has had:

```
tune2fs -C 14 /dev/hda1
```

`-C 14` will set the mount count to 14, which if you've set the automatic check to happen every 13 mounts, means that the next time the filesystem is mounted (most likely on system reboot), it'll be checked.

5-3. Saving Space on Large Filesystems and Directories

If you have a really large filesystem, you can save some space by limiting the number of backup superblocks (see recipe 4-10 for when backup superblocks can come in handy.) However, you don't need quite as many as the default setting gives you if your directory is very large.

```
tune2fs -O sparse_super /dev/hda1
```

Similarly, for large directories, you can use hashed b-trees to speed up directory lookups:

```
tune2fs -O dir_index /dev/hda1
```

To set two `-O` options at once, use a comma and no space between the options:

```
tune2fs -O dir_index,sparse_super /dev/hda1
```

5-4. Working with Disks, UUID, and Labels

As well as the standard `/dev/hda1`, `/dev/sda2` notation that you're probably used to for referring to disks, Linux also provides universal unique identifier (UUID) notation. The major advantage of this is that, unlike the `/dev` notation, it's linked specifically to a particular piece of hardware. So, although `/dev/` notation can shift between disks depending on how they're plugged in, if you use UUID, this shouldn't happen. This avoids the possibility of a system reconfiguration causing disks to be renamed and thus causing knock-on breakage of things that reference that disk.

The first part of this is to find out the existing UUID of your disks; you can do this using the `blkid` command:

```
> blkid /dev/hda1
/dev/hda1: UUID="0ef96300-36c0-4575-8a1d-2d36ff4cd585" SEC_TYPE="ext2" TYPE="ext3"
```

■ **Note** You can also do this the other way around, starting from the UUID to find the /dev/ reference:

```
> findfs UUID=d40acb36-5f32-4832-bf1a-80c67833a618
/dev/sda5
```

Alternatively, use df to look at the devices you currently have mounted, and then look at /dev/disk/by_uuid/ to see how they match up:

```
> ls -l /dev/disk/by-uuid
total 0
lrwxrwxrwx 1 root root 10 2008-10-13 13:41 ↵
    178f2692-fef4-4485-b9c5-445c990b502e -> ../../sda2
lrwxrwxrwx 1 root root 10 2008-10-13 13:41 ↵
    5b67edaf-078d-4ac0-8b1b-f2119da85482 -> ../../sdb1
lrwxrwxrwx 1 root root 10 2008-10-13 13:41 ↵
    77cb9269-447a-45ce-b585-1c45ae3290bd -> ../../sda1
lrwxrwxrwx 1 root root 10 2008-10-13 13:41 ↵
    d40acb36-5f32-4832-bf1a-80c67833a618 -> ../../sda5
```

Once you have the UUID of a device, you can use it in your /etc/fstab by putting UUID=uuid at the start of the relevant line, instead of /dev/hdaX:

```
UUID=d40acb36-5f32-4832-bf1a-80c67833a618    /local ext3    defaults    0    2
```

A similar but more human-readable option is to give the disk a human-readable label using the tune2fs command:

```
tune2fs -L localdata /dev/hda2
```

Then edit /etc/fstab to use the label to mount the disk:

```
LABEL=localdata       /local       ext3    defaults       0       2
```

However, the advantage of using the UUID is that you can check what device name (for example, /dev/sda2) this is being translated to by looking at /dev/disk/by-uuid/ (see the earlier code snippet), whereas there's no similar list by disk label.

If you've cloned a disk, such as by using dd (see recipe 4-10), you might want to be able to mount both the original and the clone at the same time. To make sure that the UUIDs don't clash, first generate a new UUID, and then assign it to the new disk with tunefs:

```
> uuidgen
79fb806d-4350-4b8c-8bc3-f3bb0c6b56f2
> tune2fs -U 79fb806d-4350-4b8c-8bc3-f3bb0c6b56f2 /dev/sdc1
```

Now mount the new disk:

```
mount -U 79fb806d-4350-4b8c-8bc3-f3bb0c6b56f2 /mnt/clonedisk
```

■ **Note** See some of the other things you can do to filesystems on the fly with `tunefs` in recipes 5-1 to 5-3.

5-5. Resizing Partitions on the Fly

If you have old machines, you may find that you start running out of space on / after a while. It's worth checking that there's not lots of space being wasted in **/tmp** and/or **/var**. Use the `du` command to summarize disk usage in various directories. The **-s** option summarizes the disk space used by all the relevant subdirectories, and **-h** gives human-friendly output in megabytes/gigabytes rather than in kilobytes.

```
du -sh /tmp
du -sh /var/*
```

However, the bottom line is that software keeps getting bigger, as do distributions. It may be that you really do want everything you have installed in / but you're still running into the size limits imposed by whatever size you set / to originally. One way to avoid this is simply to use a single nonswap partition per disk, but that has other disadvantages; for example, separating the system/software files in / from user data (in **/home** or elsewhere) means that it's easy to reinstall a system if you start having problems with it.

Instead, it's useful to have options for resizing a partition when that becomes necessary. **parted** is a very useful utility that will resize your partition on the fly. It does have one important restriction: you can resize partitions only at their ends. You can't move the start point of a partition. This means that you can't just take space from the front of the next partition along when you need to resize a partition.

However, there is a way to get around this!

■ **Note** It is strongly recommended that you read the `parted` manual before starting to do this and also that you have backups of all your data (which you should have anyway, of course).

Let's say your disk setup looks like this (we'll ignore the swap space for the moment):

```
/dev/hda1     /           5GB     4.5GB used
/dev/hda2     /local     105GB    40GB used
```

You want to expand / by 5GB, which should give you enough breathing space for the immediate future. It requires some juggling around and may take a while (because you will need to copy large quantities of data around more than once), but this is how to do it.

Note This method will work only if the total size of your second partition is greater than ((2 × space used on 2nd partition) + desired expansion of the first partition). Here, 105GB > (2 × 40GB) + 5GB, so we're fine to go ahead. See the description of the process and Figure 5-1 for an explanation of this math, or if you don't have this much spare space, another option is described later in this recipe.

What you're going to do is as follows (it is a little complicated, but it does work!):

1. Divide the second partition (**/dev/hda2**) into two sections (**/dev/hda2** and **/dev/hda3**), each one of which is big enough to hold all the data currently in that partition (here, 40GB).

2. Move the data into the second of those two partitions (**/dev/hda3**).

3. Delete the now-smaller **/dev/hda2** to generate some free space into which **/dev/hda1** can expand.

4. Expand **/dev/hda1** as required.

5. Create a new **/dev/hda2** in the free space that's left over. (This new **/dev/hda2** needs to be at least as big as the data that's now in **/dev/hda3**).

6. Move the data from **/dev/hda3** back into the re-created **/dev/hda2**.

7. Delete **/dev/hda3**.

8. Expand **/dev/hda2** into the free space that **/dev/hda3** occupied.

Effectively you've moved the start point of **/dev/hda2** along a little to allow more room for **/dev/hda1**; but because you can't move the start point of a partition, it's necessary to do this complicated shuffling-around process (see Figure 5-1).

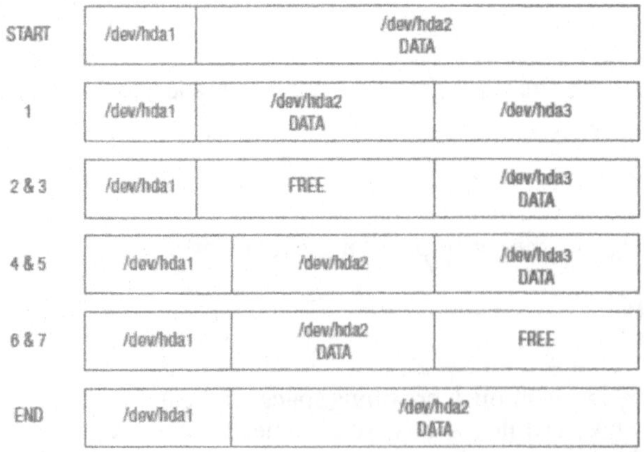

Figure 5-1. An illustration of what you're doing to your hard drive in this process

OK, then, here's how to actually go about this.

Boot from a rescue disk or LiveCD if you will be resizing your / partition at all, as in this example. If you're just resizing other partitions, then you can boot from / as normal and unmount any other partitions after bootup.

```
umount /dev/hda2
```

Use `fdisk -l` to find the start and end of the partitions:

```
> fdisk -l
Device      Boot    Start        End      Blocks    Id    System
/dev/hda1    .          1       1288    10345828    83    Linux
/dev/hda2              1289       8924    61336138    83    Linux
```

Using `parted`, shrink **/dev/hda2** to 50GB, leaving 55GB spare at the end. `parted` takes the size in megabytes, and `fdisk` gives the size in 1KB blocks, so you need to translate from the 1KB block size that `fdisk` has given you to the megabytes that `parted` needs. You can use the calculator `bc` to do this (multiply the number of 1KB blocks by 1,024 to get the total bytes, and then divide by 2^20 to get megabytes).

```
> echo "10345828*1024/(2^20)" | bc
10103
> parted resize /dev/hda2 10104 61303
```

■ **Note** That first bc line gives the megabyte size of the first partition (10103MB); add one to get the start of the next partition, and then add 50GB (51200MB) to that to get the end.

Create a third partition in that 55GB using `fdisk` and `mke2fs`:

```
> fdisk
fdisk> n
fdisk> 3
fdisk> 83
fdisk> w
> mke2fs -j /dev/hda3
> mkdir /mnt/newpart
> mount -t ext3 /dev/hda3 /mnt/newpart
```

Copy the data from **/dev/hda2** to the new partition:

```
> cp -rf /local/* /mnt/newpart
```

Delete **/dev/hda2** with **fdisk**:

```
> fdisk
fdisk> d
fdisk> 2
fdisk> w
```

Resize **/dev/hda1** to include an extra 5GB from that 50GB of space in the middle.

```
> parted resize /dev/hda1 0 10240
```

Use **fdisk** to re-create **/dev/hda2** in what's now 45GB of space:

```
> fdisk
fdisk> n
fdisk> 2
fdisk> 83
fdisk> w
> mke2fs -j /dev/hda2
> mount -t ext3 /dev/hda2 /local
```

Copy the data back across to your re-created **/local**:

```
> cp -rf /mnt/newpart/* /local
```

Delete the temporary new partition, and resize **/dev/hda2** to use all of that space again:

```
> fdisk
fdisk> d
fdisk> 3
fdisk> w
> parted resize /dev/hda2 10241 112640
```

Finally, you'll need to tidy up a bit. At least some of your partition **/dev** disk IDs (**/dev/hda1**, **/dev/hda2**, and so on) will have changed, so you'll need to edit **/etc/fstab** and possibly your boot loader, before you reboot. Use **fdisk -l** to check the current labels on your partitions, or use **tunefs** to create human-readable labels for your partitions (see recipe 5-4).

With a Nearly Full Disk

If your **/dev/hda2** partition is mostly full, you can't use the previous method. Instead, you may find that you have a swap partition of a couple of gigabytes that lives between / and **/local**. Remember earlier when you were ignoring the swap? Now you're not. For example, let's say the output of **fdisk -l** looks like this:

```
/dev/sda1   *       1      13     104391  83  Linux
/dev/sda2          14    1288  10241437+  83  Linux
/dev/sda3        1289    1543   2048287+  82  Linux swap / Solaris
/dev/sda4        1544    8924  59287851   83  Linux
```

In this setup, **/dev/sda1** is **/boot**, and **/dev/sda2** is **/**, so it's **/dev/sda2** that you want to resize. There's a couple of gigabytes available in **/dev/sda3**, the swap partition.

What you do this time is first delete **/dev/sda3** (the swap partition) with **fdisk**:

```
fdisk /dev/sda
fdisk> d
fdisk> 3
fdisk> w
```

Then resize **/dev/sda2** to use that new free space that was formerly swap:

```
> parted resize /dev/sda2 101 12103
```

■ **Note** 101 is the megabyte size obtained from 104,391 blocks (that is, the size of /dev/sda1) using bc, as explained earlier:

```
> echo "104391 * 1024 / (2^20)" | bc
101
```

12103 is the megabyte size obtained from (104,391 + 10,241,427 + 2,048,287) blocks (that is, the size of /dev/sda1 plus /dev/sda2 plus /dev/sda3, as shown in the fdisk output) translated in the same way:

```
> echo "(104391+10241427+2048287) * 1024 / (2^20)" | bc
12103
```

Resize **/dev/sda4** to free up some space at the end of the disk to put a new swap partition in. The end point should be current end – previous size of swap partition, so in this case, 59,287,851 – (10,241,438 – 104,391) = 49,150,804 blocks, which is 47,998MB:

```
> parted resize /dev/sda4 12104 47998
```

Re-create the swap partition in this new free space:

```
> fdisk
fdisk> n
fdisk> [ create partition appropriately and set as swap ]
```

Again, you'll need to tidy up afterward. As discussed earlier, check **fdisk -l** for the new partition labels, or use **tune2fs** to add human-readable labels.

■ **Note** To avoid having to do this, allow more room than you think you'll need when creating / on new machines! Disk space is cheap these days, so you can be generous with it.

5-6. Using RAID Arrays and mdadm

RAID arrays offer a way of using multiple disks underneath your filesystems. Any kind of filesystem (journaled or otherwise) that you can run on a regular disk, you can also run on a RAID array. The filesystem will see the array as a single disk space, and the RAID hardware or software (hardware vs. software RAID is discussed later in this recipe) handles the physical details of what data is written where and how it is accessed.

There are two basic options with RAID arrays: mirroring and striping. (RAID0 also offers aggregation, where you just add two disks together.) With *mirroring*, you have one disk with your content and another disk or disks providing an exact mirror of that. With *striping*, you have multiple disks acting in effect as one disk, with the content being "striped" across both of them. Striping will improve performance; mirroring may give some performance improvement if you have multiple processors. Both striping and mirroring provide increased redundancy. They both also have a disk space cost, in that you can't use all the theoretically available space on your disks because some is used for implementing the redundancy. Mirroring is more expensive in this sense than striping is. You can also combine both, which gives you the following options:

- *RAID0, aka striping only:* The data is split across multiple disks (usually two) to speed up access. In the event of one disk failing, all the data is lost because there's no fault tolerance or redundancy. The striping is optional. If you prefer, you can just concatenate multiple disks so they are seen by the filesystem as one big disk. However, without striping, there's no speed increase. The only gain is the disk size.

- *RAID1, aka mirroring only:* The data is mirrored across multiple disks (usually two). There's slight speedup if using multiple processors, and data redundancy; if one disk fails, all the data is still available from the other one.

- *RAID5, aka striped set with distributed parity:* The data is split across multiple disks, but if a single drive is lost, the missing data can be calculated from the data on the remaining drives (this is the parity), so no data is lost. A second drive failure will lose all the data, so it's important to replace a failed disk immediately.

- *RAID6, aka striped set with dual distributed parity:* Like RAID5, but you can lose up to two disks before data is lost.

- *RAID10, aka RAID1+0 or RAID0+1:* This offers striping and mirroring. In RAID0+1, you use two sets of disks, each of which are striped, with one of the striped sets mirroring the other. If drives fail only on one side, then you lose no data; if drives fail on both sides, then you lose all the data. With RAID1+0, you create a striped set from a series of mirrored drives. The fault tolerance is higher, because you can afford to lose any single disk in one of the mirrored sets *and* an entire mirrored set, before data is lost. The performance is also better than RAID5; however, you get less usable space from your total purchased disk space (losing space to both mirroring and striping).

It's important to bear in mind that RAID, of any variety, is not a backup in and of itself. In particular, if all your disks are of the same vintage (which is likely in almost all cases, because you'll probably have bought them all at the same time), the probability of more than one of them failing simultaneously is *not* independent; it's, if not likely, at least not *unlikely* that this will happen. This also means that if you do have a disk fail, you don't want to delay in replacing it, because the extra strain on the single disk may be enough to trigger another fail event.

For a small array, RAID5 is probably the best bet, because it provides both faster access than with a single non-RAID disk and fault tolerance. The larger the array, the more likely it is that two disks will fail at once, and thus the more useful RAID6 becomes. RAID6 works out to be more expensive in disk purchases, because you lose (in effect) two disks' worth of space per array. A RAID6 array of six 500GB disks will have 2TB (4 × 500GB) of useful space, while the same array setup as RAID5 will have 2.5TB (5 × 500GB) of space.

■ **Note** You can also add a hot spare disk or disks in RAID5 and RAID6 setups. In the event of a disk failure, the hot spare will automatically be swapped in, meaning that a second disk failure won't cause problems. Again, it's important to replace the failed disk ASAP, and this increases the cost further because the hot spare disk doesn't add anything to the usable capacity of the drive.

The other decision to make is hardware vs. software RAID, in other words, whether the physical data distribution is managed by a hardware controller or by a software layer sitting between the logical drives (what your filesystem sees) and the physical devices. Software RAID will be cheaper but may have slower performance; however, upgrading your server CPU can produce significant improvements in software RAID. In the event of controller failure, in a software RAID setup, disks can be moved to another server running the same OS, whereas you might well have to buy a new matching hardware controller to rescue your hardware RAID data. (You *do* have a backup as well, right?) Software RAID also enables you to create RAID arrays from partitions rather than from whole disks, so you can mix RAID levels on different disk partitions.

■ **Note** You shouldn't have two partitions on the same physical disk acting as part of the same RAID, because in the event of disk failure, this means you lose two RAID sections rather than just one.

---

mdadm

If you're using software RAID, you may well be using `mdadm` to manage it. The default setup, set in `/etc/mdadm/mdadm.conf`, should be that you'll receive warnings of any problems via email. This will probably go to **root** unless you've changed it, so make sure that you have something useful set as your **root** e-mail address in `/etc/aliases` (which is a good idea anyway!):

```
root: admin@example.com
```

If you get a notification of a problem, it's straightforward to remove the disk and rebuild the array. To check which disk has failed and what the problem is, use this:

```
mdadm --query --detail /dev/md0
```

Remove the faulty disk with the following:

```
mdadm --remove /dev/md0 /dev/sda1/
```

Run fsck on the disk:

```
fsck /dev/sda1
```

Once the problem is fixed, add the disk back into the array:

```
mdadm --add /dev/md0 /dev/sda1/
```

The array will automatically rebuild after the disk has been added back in.

It's usually worth trying fsck once to see whether this fixes the problem; disks do sometimes have minor corruptions that aren't indicative of serious hardware problems. If you have this problem repeatedly and, in particular, if it's the same disk repeatedly, it's best to replace the disk altogether.

■ **Note** To trigger a scan information e-mail, use mdadm --monitor --scan -1.

5-7. Using rsnapshot

Snapshot filesystems, which offer instant-availability backups from multiple time points, are a great idea. But migrating to a new filesystem is a major deal. rsnapshot works on an ext3 filesystem; it uses rsync and hard links to create something that looks and works like multiple instant-availability full backups (as with a snapshot system) but that takes up the space of only one full backup plus incremental changes.

That "full backup space" is of course still the gotcha—basically, you'll need a spare disk. However, external disks are increasingly cheap, and rsnapshot can be used remotely with ssh. So, you could use one large central disk to keep snapshots of your most important data from multiple clients. (See recipe 4-6 for another discussion of doing this without snapshots.)

rsnapshot is relatively easy to configure. Install the rsnapshot Debian/Ubuntu package, and then check /etc/rsnapshot.conf for the minor edits needed, making sure to uncomment the interval lines.

■ **Note** Directory names in /etc/rsnapshot.conf require a trailing slash, so it's /local/, not /local. Also, you need tabs (not spaces) between elements.

Most of the defaults should be fine. Make sure to uncomment the **cmp_cp** line because this (on a Linux system) enables **rsnapshot** to run more efficiently:

```
cmd_cp          /bin/cp
```

Set the following lines to your own specification:

```
snapshot_root          /snapshotsinterval          hourly     6
interval        daily    7
interval        weekly   4
```

snapshot_root should be the mount point of your backup disk. The `interval` value sets how many hours/days/months of snapshots are kept. (**retain** does the same thing in more recent versions of **rsnapshot**, but the current Debian and Ubuntu files use `interval`.)

■ **Note** If using removable backup media, uncomment this line:

```
no_create_root     1
```

This means that if the `snapshot_root` directory doesn't exist, it won't be created. So, if your removable media isn't plugged in when an `rsnapshot` run is due, you won't have the directory created on your existing disk and backed up into, thus potentially causing problems with space.

Set up your backup directories in this form:

```
backup   /local/  localdata/
```

This will back up the `/local/` directory to `/snapshots/hourly.0/localdata/local/`. Daily snapshots will go to `/snapshots/daily.0/localdata/local/`, and so on. The next time a snapshot is run, this will move to `/snapshots/hourly.1/localdata/local/`, although in fact hard links are used extensively to minimize space usage.

Add another line for each directory you want to back up.

To run an hourly backup from the command line (to test), use this:

```
rsnapshot hourly
```

The first run may take a while (as always with a first run of **rsync**). Subsequent runs will be much faster because the files are updated from the snapshot.

Once you've confirmed that it's working correctly, you probably want to set up a cronjob to run it automatically. The package automatically installs an **/etc/cron.d/rsnapshot** file. You can uncomment (and edit if need be) the relevant lines in this to run it automatically, or you can add these lines to your **/etc/crontab**:

```
40 */4 * * *          /usr/local/bin/rsnapshot hourly
30 02 * * *           /usr/local/bin/rsnapshot daily
20 02  * * 7          /usr/local/bin/rsnapshot weekly
```

The hourly/daily/weekly retain levels don't actually have to be at hourly/daily/weekly rates; they're just labels. You can set them to run however often you like in the cronjob. What the value in the config file does is to set how many of each are retained. So here, we're running the "hourly" snapshot every 4 hours, and thus we keep 6 past versions to make up 24 hours (at which point a "daily" snapshot will be taken and the "hourly" can restart).

■ **Note** If you get lock error messages from the "hourly" backup occasionally, it may be that the "daily" still has the lock. Increase the ten-minute interval between the two in the crontab to solve this. Here's an example:

```
50 */4 * * *          /usr/local/bin/rsnapshot hourly
```

Make sure you set **/snapshots/** to be owned by **root** so that users can't modify their own files:

```
chown root:root /snapshots; chmod og-w /snapshots
```

To set up **rsnapshot** so any user can pull their own backups, rather than relying on root access, simply give read/execute access to this directory:

```
chmod a+rx /snapshots
```

and then export it read-only over NFS, with the following line in **/etc/exports**:

```
/snapshots 192.168.0.0/255.255.0.0(ro)
```

Restart **nfs-kernel-server** (**/etc/init.d/nfs-kernel-server restart**) when you've finished editing **/etc/exports**. The files should be saved with the appropriate ownership and permissions, so any user can grab their own files but won't be able to modify them, because the share is read-only.

rsnapshot should run on nearly any Unix-type system (requiring only **perl** and **rsync**) and is available as a package for most of the major Linuxes.

5-8. Working with Other Filesystems

As well as the standard ext2 and ext3 Linux filesystems, other filesystems are available that you may want to investigate. You may have to recompile your kernel to use these (either as modules or built in to the kernel). Find out what filesystems your current kernel supports using this:

```
> cat /proc/filesystems
```

Check out /lib/modules/[kernelversion]/kernel/fs to see what further filesystem modules you have available; these should be loaded automatically by mount if needed, or you can try using insmod /path/to/module.o as root if need be.

■ **Note** Unless you have a particular reason to use ext2, you're far better off with ext3, since it has a journaling system that minimizes data loss in the event of any problems. See recipe 5-1 for how to convert ext2 to ext3 on the fly.

---

ext4

This has improvements intended to better manage large filesystems (including a doubling of the subdirectory limit, to 64,000) and improve performance with large files. The maximum filesystem size is 1EB, compared to 16TB with ext3. (But note that the standard partition table will allow only 2TB per partition, although GNU parted can be used to make larger partitions.) It also has options for persistent preallocation (where space is allotted ahead of time for files), which has benefits for media streaming and for databases. Extra timestamp bits defer the "year 2038" problem for another 500 years. It's backward compatible with ext2 and ext3, so it's easy to experiment with if you want. Switch your partition with this command:

```
umount /dev/sda1
tune2fs -O extents,uninit_bg,dir_index /dev/sda1
fsck -pf /dev/sda1
mount -t ext4 /dev/sda1
```

Edit /etc/fstab to set the partition type as ext4:

```
/dev/sda1    /local    ext4    errors=remount-ro    0 1
```

If you're doing this to a root partition, you'll need to edit /boot/grub/menu.lst as well. Add this to the end of the kernel line:

```
rootfstype=ext4
```

and then update grub:

```
sudo update-grub
```

As ever, make sure you have an up-to-date backup before you start doing this! It is designed to be a safe process and should work cleanly, but it's always possible to run into problems when messing with filesystems.

> ■ **Note** You can't convert backward from ext4 to ext3. It is possible (although complicated) to mount an ext3 filesystem as ext4 without actually using any of the new data features, in which case you would still be able to mount the filesystem as ext3 as well. But it would be a bit pointless because you'd miss the ext4 features!

XFS

XFS is a 64-bit journaling filesystem created by Silicon Graphics. It's available for nearly all mainstream Linux distros, although in general it's not possible to use it for the boot partition, because `grub` doesn't always handle it reliably. (However, you can create a small `/boot` partition as ext3 and then run the rest of your filesystems as XFS.)

Online defragmentation (that is, defragmentation while the filesystem is mounted) is available for XFS, although, like ext4, XFS uses delayed allocation and extents (a method of listing blocks that enables them to be given as a continuous list rather than named individually) to reduce fragmentation. To use the `xfs_fsr` defragmentation tool, you'll need to install the `xfsdump` package (Debian/Ubuntu).

`xfs_fsr`

Just using the command with no options will set it to spend 7,200 seconds (two hours) looping over and reorganizing the filesystems listed in `/etc/mtab`. To change this time to one hour (or substitute any other seconds value), use this:

`xfs_fsr -t 3600`

Alternatively, you can set it to defragment a particular file:

`xfs_fsr /local/mybigfile.tar.gz`

You can also use `xfs_growfs` to resize an XFS filesystem on the fly:

`xfs_growfs /filesystempath`

> ■ **Note** You will need space to grow the filesystem into! This is most often used with logical volume management setups. Or you can adapt recipe 5-5 to generate more partition space and then use `xfs_growfs` to extend the filesystem.

XFS is the fastest journaling filesystem in benchmarking tests and is reasonably low in CPU demand. Note, however, that an XFS filesystem can't be shrunk once it's created.

CHAPTER 6

■ ■ ■

Securing Your Systems

Security concerns are a fact of life for any systems, especially once you connect your machines to the Internet at large. This chapter looks at various ways to use SSH and SSH keys, at setting and enforcing password policy on your system, at options to make sudo secure, and at increasing your protection , against other attacks from the outside world.

6-1. Using and Limiting SSH Keys

The standard way of logging on with SSH is to just type your password when prompted. This does of course work, but a better way of using SSH is via SSH keys.

Using a key is more secure, because an attacker needs both the private key file and the passphrase to gain access to your account. You can also use it passphraseless (see recipe 6-3); this is less secure (relying on you keeping your private keyfile safe) but does enable unsupervised login for cronjobs and so on.

One of the big advantages is that you can use ssh-add and ssh-agent to store your SSH keys for you (see recipe 6-2), thus meaning that you need to type your password only once. (See Chapter 2 for information on setting up Kerberos and getting single sign-in across your network, but SSH keys can still be useful for logging into other networks and for logging on as another user.)

In particular, it's useful to set up a key that will allow you to log in as root on all machines on your network. Creating a key is straightforward. Enter the following in a terminal on your desktop machine. You don't need to be root; indeed, you probably don't want to be because it's more useful to be able to log in elsewhere as root while logged in as your default user on your own desktop.

```
ssh-keygen -t rsa -f ~/.ssh/root_key
```

This will generate an RSA key and save it in ~/.ssh/root_key, with the public part in ~/.ssh/root_key.pub. Make sure you enter a good passphrase. Longer is better, with a mixture of letters, numbers, and punctuation.

You can now simply cat the ~/.ssh/root_key.pub file into the /root/.ssh/authorized_keys2 or /root/.ssh/authorized_keys file on all your machines (you may have to create the /root/.ssh/ directory).

However, it's a good idea to limit the scope of this key slightly so that in order to use it, you have to start from your own desktop machine. To do this, first copy the contents of ~/.ssh/root_key.pub into tmpfile, and then add this to the start of the only line in tmpfile (note the comma at the end of the line!):

```
from="mydesktop.example.com",
```

Note To limit it to allow this key to be used within your domain only, you can use wildcard pattern matching:

```
from="*.example.com",
```

However, note that, like any domain-based access control, this is vulnerable to an attack from someone setting up reverse DNS lookup that contains your domain.

Copy the whole contents of `tmpfile` into `/root/.ssh/authorized_keys2` on every machine you want to be able to log into with this key.

Note Make sure it's a single line for each key!

Check that the permissions on `/root/.ssh/` on every machine are correct, because SSH is very picky about permissions:

```
chmod -R go-rx /root/.ssh
chown -R root:root /root/.ssh
```

Test that this works as expected by running the following from your desktop machine:

```
ssh root@test.example.com -i ~/.ssh/root_key
```

Note See recipe 6-5 for how to set your SSH options so the key is picked up automatically.

If all is well, you can edit your `/etc/ssh/sshd_config` files on all your machines to allow root login only with an SSH key:

```
PermitRootLogin          without-password
```

This doesn't mean that you can log in without specifying a password! It means that you can't use the password auth mechanism but have to use an SSH key.

See recipe 6-3 for another example of limiting an SSH key—in that case, when using `rsync` and wanting to be able to use it passphrase-free.

6-2. Managing Keys with Keychain

As discussed in the previous recipe, using SSH keys has many advantages, but one of the major ones shows up only if you use keychain to manage your keys. keychain is a small script that improves on ssh-agent. ssh-agent will cache your keys for you (so that you need to enter your passphrase only once per terminal session for each key), but by default, it won't run across shell sessions. So, if you set it to start in your ~/.bash_profile, you'll still have to type your passphrase once per new terminal session.

■ **Note** If you use GDM, ssh-agent will start by default on login. Otherwise, add this line to your ~/.xsession file:

```
ssh-agent gnome-session
```

substituting in whatever window manager you use for gnome-session. Now, to add a key, type ssh-add ~/.ssh/key_name.

---

keychain improves on ssh-agent by checking for a running ssh-agent process when you log in and either hooking into one if it exists or starting a new one up if necessary. (Some X GUI environments also have something similar available.) To set up keychain, first install the keychain and ssh-askpass packages for your system. For Debian/Ubuntu, use this:

```
sudo apt-get install keychain ssh-askpass
```

Now edit your ~/.bash_profile file to include these lines:

```
01  #!/bin/bash
02  /usr/bin/keychain ~/.ssh/id_rsa ~/.ssh/id_dsa > /dev/null
03  source ~/.keychain/hostname-sh
```

In line 02, you should include the paths to any keys that you want keychain to manage; check your ~/.ssh directory. For example, if you've used recipe 6-1, you'll have a ~/.ssh/root_key key, and line 02 will read as follows:

```
02  /usr/bin/keychain ~/.ssh/id_rsa ~/.ssh/id_dsa ~/.ssh/root_key > /dev/null
```

Route the output to /dev/null to avoid getting the agent information output to the screen every time you start a new terminal. Line 03 sources ~/.keyring/hostname-sh (which is created when keychain first runs to store ssh-agent information) to access SSH_AUTH_SOCK, which records the Unix socket that will be used to talk to ssh-agent. Obviously, you should replace hostname with the name of the host you're using.

The first time the keychain process is started up (so, the first time you log in after setting this up), you'll be asked to enter the passphrases for any keys that you've listed on line 02. These will then be passed into ssh-agent. Once you have a bash prompt, try logging into a suitable machine (that is, one where you have this key set up; see recipe 6-1) with one of these keys. You won't need to use your passphrase.

Now, log out, and then log back in again. This time, you shouldn't be challenged for your passphrases, because the ssh-agent session will still be running. Again, you should be able to log in to that suitable machine without typing your passphrase. The ssh-agent session should keep running until the next time you reboot.

■ **Note** This means that if you're away from your computer, even for just a few minutes, then someone with physical access to your machine will also be able to access any machines with keys managed by keychain/ssh-agent. Always lock your screen whenever you leave your machine! This is good security practice anyway.

This long-term running may be seen as a security issue. If someone managed to log in as you, they'd automatically be able to use your keys, as well. If you use the --clear option for keychain, then every time you log in, your passphrases will be cleared, and you will be asked for them again. Substitute this line for the earlier line 02:

```
02   /usr/bin/keychain --clear ~/.ssh/id_rsa ~/.ssh/id_dsa > /dev/null
```

■ **Note** The passphrases are cleared when you log *in*, not when you log *out*. This feature means that you can set your cronjobs, and so on, to get the passphrases via ssh-agent, and it won't matter if you've logged out overnight.

6-3. Limiting rsync Over ssh

There may be circumstances in which you want to be able to allow users to rsync to a server but not to ssh into it, but you'd still rather run rsync over ssh (which is a good security practice). In general, it's a bad idea to allow users to log on to servers. Use the AllowUsers directive in /etc/ssh/sshd_config to restrict this:

```
AllowUsers        jkemp, manager, admin
```

However, let's say you want to allow users to back up their own laptops to a RAID array or other big disk. rsync by default these days runs over ssh, which is great in many obvious ways but means that if you restrict ssh login to the machine, rsync won't work either. You could mount the disk over NFS from a gateway machine, but that would mean the user transferring their data over two connections: ssh to the gateway machine and then NFS to the RAID array.

There is a solution, however, which works like this:

1. ssh is allowed, but only for a subset of users who have asked for backup access, using the AllowUsers directive in /etc/ssh/sshd_config:

    ```
    AllowUsers        jkemp, admin, user1, user3
    ```

2. These users are then added to /etc/password, with the shell set as
   /bin/nologin (thus overriding the LDAP data):

   ```
   user1:x:3434:102:User Name:/disk/raid/userdir:/bin/nologin
   ```

   The second field points to /etc/shadow for the password; the third and fourth
   fields are the userID and groupID, which you'll need to get out of LDAP with
   ldapsearch "(uid=user1)". The sixth field sets their home directory, which in
   this case is their user directory on the RAID array (or whatever other big disk is
   being used for laptop backup purposes). The seventh field is the one that sets
   the shell to /bin/nologin.

3. They're also added to /etc/shadow, with *K* (meaning "use Kerberos") as the
   password. This avoids maintaining two sets of passwords, which is a bad idea:

   ```
   user1:*K*::::
   ```

   (Since you're getting password information from Kerberos, you can leave all
   the fields in /etc/shadow other than the username and password blank—you
   need four colons after the *K*.)

4. /bin/nologin looks like this:

   ```
   01  #!/bin/sh
   02  # Script to disallow remote login - set as shell in /etc/passwd
   03  # JK 03.04.2009
   04  command=$2
   05  if (expr "$command" : 'rsync ..server .* .raid' > /dev/null)
   06      then
   07          if (expr "$command" : '.*;' > /dev/null)
   08          then
   09              exit
   10          else
   11              /bin/sh "$@"
   12          fi
   13      else
   14          echo "********************************"
   15          echo "*        No login allowed!     *"
   16          echo "********************************"
   17          exit
   18      fi
   ```

   Lines 04 and 05 test to see whether the command being used is one that looks
   roughly like rsync directory/ server:/raid. The trick I used for finding the
   command that's being sent (which is not the same as the command that you
   type on the command line when you use rsync!) was to first set up
   /bin/nologin simply as this:

   ```
   #!/bin/sh
   echo $@ > /tmp/command
   exit
   ```

   and then examine /tmp/command on the rsync server. $2 is the second argument
   on the line in /tmp/command.

■ **Note** This script doesn't worry about looking terribly hard for shell escapes (although line 07 does look for anyone trying to pass an extra command in using ; as in `rsync directory/ "server:/data/directory/;rm -rf /"`. If you're using this in a local-access-only setup with a small number of reasonably trusted users, this is a reasonable risk. If it's a machine that's open to the world at large, you'll want to be more careful. Also, bear in mind that using the command `/usr/bin/rsync` (as opposed to `rsync`) will trip the "no login" script.

The echo statement in lines 14–17 will show up if someone tries to log in directly, but unfortunately, `rsync` doesn't handle echo statements well. So, there is no message to the user if they are misusing `rsync` (whether deliberately or accidentally). Again, depending on your setup (for example, if it's a small setup where users can contact you when there's a problem), this may well be fine.

Test by creating a test user and setting the user up in `/etc/password` and `/etc/shadow` as shown earlier. Check that you can use `rsync` and that you can't log in directly via `ssh`. Then check that you can still `ssh` in as yourself or as whatever admin user still has access in the `ssh AllowUsers` directive.

6-4. ssh Options: Keeping Your Connection Alive

There are stacks of options that you can set on SSH, and some of them can save you quite a lot of hassle. SSH options can be set on the command line (with the -o option) or by editing your `~/.ssh/config` file (to set the option for just that user) or `/etc/ssh_config` file (to set the option globally).

SSH uses the first setting that it encounters for an option. It reads command-line options, then per-user config, then the global config, and finally general/default ones at the end. So, the command line will override per user, and so on.

If you leave an SSH connection sitting open for too long but don't actually put any data through it, you may find that it drops out. This can be irritating, but it's easily fixed with the SSH config option `ServerAliveInterval`.

Add this to your `~/.ssh/config` file to turn `ServerAliveInterval` on for all SSH connections:

```
Host *
Protocol 2
ServerAliveInterval 60
```

The first two lines state that this section applies to every host (to apply only to some hosts, specify a hostname rather than *) and that an SSH v2 connection should be made. SSH v2 is significantly more secure than SSH v1, and `ServerAliveInterval` requires v2. There's virtually no reason to be running SSH v1 these days, and modern Debian/Ubuntu runs v2 only by default, so stick to v2.

Note To use this on the command line, you'd just use this:

```
ssh server.example.com -o ServerAliveInterval 60
```

ServerAliveInterval sends a package through the encrypted channel after the specified number of seconds of inactivity to the server, requesting a response. It's turned off by default, and you may need to experiment a little with the value. However, once you have the value set to work with your system, you should be able to keep your SSH sessions connected.

Note Most systems will have TCPKeepAlive on by default. This sends a TCP package after a period of idleness, usually two hours. This is often too long an interval to prevent disconnection. Also, TCPKeepAlive packets can be spoofed, whereas ServerAliveInterval ones can't.

6-5. ssh Options: Minimizing Typing

Another useful option to set is IdentityFile. SSH keys, ssh-agent, and keychain are useful to minimize password typing (see recipe 6-2). But you don't necessarily want to use the same key for all the machines you log onto, which means that you need to specify -i keyfile on the command line. Alternatively, you can set the identify file per host with a section like this in your ~/.ssh/config file:

```
Host ssh.example.com
IdentityFile ~/.ssh/example_id_rsa
```

You can also use the ~/.ssh/config file to set hostname abbreviations and usernames. This is useful if you regularly log into a particular machine that has an inconveniently long name or for which you have a different username. Here's an example:

```
Host longname.machine.example.com
HostName lmach
User julietkemp-longname
```

This, put in your ~/.ssh/config file, will enable you to log in to that machine simply by typing ssh lmach rather than ssh julietkemp-longname@longname.machine.example.com. You could do something similar with a bash alias; however, since scp will also use settings from the .ssh/config file, editing this file is a more generalized solution and therefore superior.

The -X and -Y command-line options enable X11 forwarding and trusted X11 forwarding, respectively. If you always want to forward X11 but want trusted X11 for a particular machine only, try this:

```
Host desktop.example.com
ForwardX11Trusted yes

Host *
ForwardX11 yes
```

Since `ssh` picks up the first option it encounters, for `desktop.example.com` that first setting will be used, while all other hosts will fall through to the second setting.

6-6. Transferring Files Over an Existing ssh Connection

`ssh` is an excellent and essential tool, but it does have one major lack: the inability to transfer files within a session. Of course, you can use `scp` for this job, but it's a nuisance to have to fire up another connection for the transfer when you're already connected to that machine!

A possible solution is `ssh-xfer`, which uses the local SSH agent to transfer files using an existing connection. It can also do this over multiple connections, which means that if you've ssh'd into desktop A and then through that to server B, `ssh-xfer` will allow you to transfer a file directly from server B to your local machine.

■ **Note** `ssh-xfer` is limited in that, at least currently, you can transfer files only from the remote machine to the local machine, not vice versa.

Unfortunately, currently `ssh-xfer` isn't a standard part of the `ssh` setup, so you'll need to patch your `ssh-agent` locally and install the `ssh-xfer` binary remotely. However, you can put the binary in your own directory on the remote server, so you don't need root access to that machine.

To get this set up, you'll need the OpenSSH source code locally so you can apply the patch and build the `ssh-xfer` binary. Download the OpenSSH patch from the `ssh-xfer` web site at http://matt.ucc.asn. au/ssh-xfer/, and save it to the OpenSSH source directory. Then run the following

```
patch -p0 < patch-file-name
```

Next, build the `ssh-xfer` binary, in the same directory, with this:

```
./configure; make ssh-xfer
```

Finally, you must transfer the `ssh-xfer` binary to the remote server:

```
scp ssh-xfer myuser@remote.server.example.com:bin/ssh-xfer
```

Now, run a bash shell via the new agent on your local machine:

```
ssh-agent-xfer bash
```

This will open a new shell, running with the patched `ssh-agent`. Then open a connection to the remote server with agent forwarding enabled (the -A option):

```
ssh -A myuser@remote.server.example.com
```

Note If you're going to do this regularly, see recipe 6-5 for advice on how to set your `ssh` options in `~/.ssh/config` so the -A option is automatically set for this machine.

From this shell on the remote server, type this:

```
~/bin/ssh-xfer testfile.txt
```

`testfile.txt` will be put in `~/Desktop` on your local machine. You can change this default location by editing the `XFER_DEST_DIR` value in the `ssh-xfer` patch, before you do the patching.

Note Enabling agent forwarding is a slight security risk, but the convenience may well be worth it! You can also choose to use the patched binary only when you know you're likely to be transferring files and similarly only to use agent forwarding in those circumstances.

6-7. Kerberizing Your SSH Setup

If you Kerberize your SSH setup, you can log on to other machines in your network using your existing Kerberos ticket (that is, without entering your password), which saves time and keystrokes (always important for sysadmins!).

The current version of SSH in Debian/Ubuntu has Kerberos authentication support built in, but you have to edit `/etc/ssh/sshd_config` on the server to allow it to be used. Make sure you have these lines in that file:

```
# Kerberos options
KerberosAuthentication yes
KerberosOrLocalPasswd yes
# GSSAPI options
GSSAPIAuthentication yes
```

Note In some versions of Debian/Ubuntu, the `/etc/hosts` file contains the following line:

```
127.0.0.1       localhost       localhost.localdomain
```

This breaks SSH Kerberos. Instead, edit it to read as follows:

```
127.0.0.1       localhost
```

Now (still on the server side), start up kadmin with **/usr/bin/kadmin -p krbadm** (replace krbadm with your Kerberos admin user if it's different), and enter these commands:

```
ank -randkey host/servername.example.com@EXAMPLE.COM
ktadd -k /etc/krb5.keytab host/servername.example.com@EXAMPLE.COM
```

replacing servername.example.com and EXAMPLE.COM with the fully qualified domain name of your server and with your Kerberos domain, respectively.

Restart sshd with /etc/init.d/ssh restart.

You'll also need to edit /etc/ssh/ssh_config on the client to contain this line:

```
GSSAPIAuthentication yes
```

Now check that you have a current Kerberos ticket on the client machine with klist, and then ssh to the server with ssh servername. You should log in without being challenged for your password. Log out again, delete your ticket with kdelete, and try again. This time you'll be asked for your password as you would usually expect.

Note Bear in mind that Kerberos tickets do expire; if your setup obtains a ticket when you log in via GDM and you customarily leave yourself logged in overnight, then the next morning you'll need to log in to Kerberos again using kinit before you can log into other machines without a password as described here. It's possible to extend the default life span of a Kerberos ticket, but this is unwise because it has obvious security implications.

6-8. Setting and Enforcing a Password Policy with Kerberos

There are two main issues with a password policy: creating it and enforcing it. When setting up a password policy, it's important to bear in mind that forcing people to change their passwords too often can be counterproductive. If your users have problems remembering stacks of new passwords, they'll resort to writing them down instead.

If you're using Kerberos, you can set a minimum length and complexity for your passwords using the policy settings. To check what your current default policy is, type kadmin -p krbadm, and then type getpol default. Your output should look something like this:

```
Policy: default
Maximum password life: 180 days
Minimum password life: 0
Minimum password length: 6
Minimum number of password character classes: 2
Number of old keys kept: 5
Reference count: 40
```

■ **Note** To show all available policies, use listpols.

Most of this is pretty self-explanatory. Number of old keys kept limits the reuse of passwords (so here, a user can't reuse a password until they've changed it five times). The available password character classes are lowercase letters, capital letters, punctuation, numbers, and other characters. Here, the policy insists that at least two of these are used, which is a good minimum. The minimum password length here should be increased, as well; eight or ten characters would be better.

■ **Note** If you don't have a default policy already, you can set one up using addpol default; then use getpol default to find out what the current settings are, and modify it using modify_policy as next.

To modify the password length for the default policy, use modify_policy (which has the alias modpol). Enter this in the kadmin console:

```
modpol -minlength 8 default
```

■ **Note** Setting the character class value to 3 enforces the nonuse of dictionary words, since you then need to have at least one nonletter character in your password.

```
modpol -minclasses 3 default
```

If you set the default policy, any principal added who has a password will have this policy applied by default. You can also set up named policies. For example, you could have one very tough policy for admins and a laxer one for regular users:

```
addpol -minclasses 3 -maxlife 90 days -minlength 12 -history 5 adminpolicy
addpol -minclasses 2 -maxlife 180 days -minlength 8 -history 5 userpolicy
```

To apply this policy to an existing user, user1, use the following:

```
modify_principal -policy userpolicy user1
```

To use a policy when creating a user, admin1, use the following:

```
add_principal -policy adminpolicy admin1
```

If no policy is specified, the default policy will be used.

You can also do this via various PAM modules if you're using an /etc/passwd-based system (see Recipe 6-9). (However, it's a much better idea to use Kerberos! See Chapter 2.)

■ **Note** You can also try making helpful suggestions to your users. For example, you could suggest that they use phrases instead of words (modern systems should be able to handle arbitrarily long passwords) or the initial letters of a phrase or song lyric, with a few numbers or punctuation marks thrown in.

6-9. Setting and Enforcing Password Policy with pam_cracklib

If you're using the standard /etc/passwd and /etc/shadow login rather than Kerberos or another centralized system (see the preceding recipe for Kerberos password policy), you can use the PAM module pam_cracklib to enforce both length and complexity of passwords. This module works by applying a set of rules, covering length and complexity, when a user changes their password.

For length, it uses a single option, minlen (measured in days).

For complexity, it has the options dcredit, ucredit, lcredit, and ocredit, which refer to the character classes' digit, uppercase character, lowercase character, and other character, respectively. A value of –1 for one of these values means "require one character of this type," and a value of 1 means "give 1 credit for this type." The credit system involves giving "length credits" for using nonlowercase characters (this means that you can have a shorter password than the minimum length if it uses nonlowercase characters as well as lowercase characters). However, this can be confusing for users (and reduces the security of the password), so it's better and more straightforward just to require (by setting the value to –1) certain types of character.

Try adding the following line in /etc/pam.d/common-password in Debian-type distros or /etc/pam.d/system-auth in RedHat-type distros:

```
password requisite pam_cracklib.so retry=3 minlen=10 ↵
difok=3 dcredit=-1 ucredit=-1 lcredit=-1
```

The retry value sets a maximum of three attempts at getting an acceptable password. Users can always rerun passwd to try again; this doesn't lock you out after three attempts. minlen sets a ten-character minimum length. difok=3 requires a minimum of three characters different from the last password. Finally, the last three options (dcredit, ucredit, and lcredit) add the requirements that the new password should contain at least one character from each of the character classes of digit, lowercase character, and uppercase character.

However, this policy won't come into effect until a user changes their password, so if their password never expires, they'll probably never change it. To make all your users change their passwords regularly, edit the /etc/login.defs file to set the PASS_MAX_DAYS variable to the maximum time allowed before changing a password (in days).

Finally, however, the change to /etc/login.defs affects only new accounts. To affect existing users, you need to use the command chage:

```
# chage -M 90 -W 7 jkemp
```

This will set the maximum number of days between password changes to 90 for the user jkemp and will warn the user for the seven days in advance before their password will expire. This needs to be done on an individual user basis, unfortunately, rather than as a system-wide policy. You can use awk to generate a script for this:

```
# cat /etc/passwd | awk -F: '{print "chage -M 90 -W 7 "$1}' > maxdays
```

Check over the maxdays file to edit out system users, and then run the script with bash maxdays.

6-10. Checking the Password Policy

Once you've set the password policy, as in the previous recipes, it's also worth occasionally checking that people really are using reasonable passwords and that the policies aren't letting weak passwords through. john-the-ripper (available via most distros) is a password-cracking tool that identifies vulnerable passwords before someone with nefarious intentions finds the weakness.

If you're using /etc/password-based security, the first step is to extract the username/password information from the relevant files using the provided unshadow tool:

```
unshadow /etc/passwd /etc/shadow > /tmp/password.db
```

unshadow will produce a password database only on systems that use /etc/passwd and /etc/shadow for login. For centralized systems, a Kerberos5 module is available, or the supplied unafs utility extracts Kerberos AFS passwords. There's also an LDAP module.

After you've extracted your password database, john has three cracking modes:

- Dictionary mode, which tests passwords based on dictionary words. You can use the provided dictionary or provide your own, and there's an option to enable "word mangling" rules.

- "Single crack" mode, which uses login names and various /etc/passwd values as password candidates, as well as applying word mangling rules.

- Incremental mode, which tries all possible character combinations and will obviously take a very, very long time to run. You'll almost certainly need to stop it manually eventually, unless you have a very short password limit. You can change the parameters for this via the config file.

You can run one of these options at a time (in which case, try "single crack" mode first) or run all of them consecutively with this:

```
john /tmp/password.db
```

To show the results, use this:

```
john --show /tmp/password.db
```

You can then insist on a password change if any of your users have failed the test!

■ **Note** Also remember that you can limit cracking attempts through measures such as locking out specific IP addresses after multiple failed ssh attempts (see recipe 6-13) or limiting the number of times a user can get a password wrong when logging on.

6-11. Limiting sudo

The /etc/sudoers file sets up who can use sudo (that is, who can masquerade as root) and under what circumstances. The basic usage is just to permit a user to have all the privileges that root does, but you can also do far more than that.

It's best to edit /etc/sudoers (you'll need to be root to do this or use sudo with a username that's already in the file) with the command visudo, because that will check that the file can be parsed correctly before it's saved.

■ **Note** visudo won't necessarily use vi as the editor; it'll use whatever is the default editor for the user you're logged in as.

The most basic sudoers line would be to permit a particular user to do absolutely anything with sudo:

```
jkemp          ALL = (ALL) ALL
```

ALL is an automatically defined alias, which means what it says on the tin. This is the format of this line:

```
user          Host = (Runas)          command
```

user is the username that you're running sudo *from*. Host is the machine that you're running sudo on or trying to access. Runas is the user that you want to use sudo to log in as. command is the command you want to run.

So, in that first example, jkemp can use sudo on any machine to authenticate as any user and run any command. Basically, they can do anything they want! (If you look at the /etc/sudoers file, you'll see that this is the same privilege level as root has.)

To make life a little easier (and more maintainable), you can set up aliases in the /etc/sudoers file. So, instead of specifying your user directly, you can set up an alias for them:

```
User_Alias    SYSADMINS = jkemp, pgillin
SYSADMINS     ALL = (ALL) ALL
```

This gives both jkemp and pgillin the same full privileges as before. (This group could just as well contain only jkemp.)

■ **Note** You can also use groups that exist on the system:

```
%admin    ALL = (ALL) ALL
```

This would give all members of the admin group all privileges.

Similarly, you can limit the commands that people are able to run. Let's say that one of your users wants to be able to stop and start their printer. You can allow them to do this with this setup:

```
User_Alias           LOCAL = ksmith
Command_Alias PRINTER = /etc/init.d/cupsd
LOCAL   client3.example.com      PRINTING
```

■ **Note** The (Runas) section is not required; if it's left blank, root is assumed.

---

ksmith will now be able to run sudo /etc/init.d/cupsd restart on their desktop, client3, when required. The Command_Alias can also be a list of commands, and more can be added in the specification line. You should always give the full path to a command (to make sure that it's the command you think it is or at least that someone would have to hack the box first to change the command rather than just writing their own version in their own directory). Also, you shouldn't allow commands that are shells (/bin/bash, /bin/tcsh, and so on) or that you can shell out from, because this is effectively the same as allowing any command.

6-12. sudo: Figuring Out Which Password to Use

The previous recipe discusses some of the basic ways of setting up sudo access. You can also set a variety of options having to do with the use of passwords.

One option is to use the NOPASSWD tag. This allows a user to run a particular command without giving a password:

```
jkemp    client2 = NOPASSWD: /bin/ls, /usr/bin/tail
```

This would allow jkemp to use /bin/ls and /usr/bin/tail without authenticating herself, on client2.

You can also specify PASSWD later in the list to limit this further:

```
jkemp    client2 = NOPASSWD: /bin/ls, /usr/bin/tail, PASSWD:/bin/kill
```

This would allow all three commands, but for /bin/kill, jkemp would have to reauthenticate.

You can also use the Defaults section to specify that a particular user should be prompted for the root password rather than for their own password when invoking sudo. Thus, the following would give jkemp the ability to run any command on any machine as any user via sudo, but would require that she use the root password to authenticate:

```
Defaults:jkemp       rootpw
jkemp  ALL = (ALL)   ALL
```

This is usually not a great idea because one of the advantages of using sudo is that you *don't* have to give out the root password or indeed set one on your system at all. However, let's consider the case of a single sysadmin who knows the root passwords anyway. What happens if their password gets cracked by some evildoer? If sudo is set so that the sysadmin has to reauthenticate with their *own* password, then our evildoer now has root access. If, on the other hand, the sysadmin has to reauthenticate with root's password, then the evildoer now has another password to break before they can get root access.

This logic may also apply if there's more than one sysadmin, assuming that they all already have access to the root passwords. It doesn't apply to anyone who *wouldn't* otherwise know the root password. In this case, stick with the default of using your own password to authenticate.

■ **Note** You can also use the runas_default option to generalize this. This option sets the user that a sudo command should be run as if it's not specified on the command line with sudo -u altuser. By default, this is root. Set it to something else using this:

```
Defaults:runas_default      notroot
Defaults:jkemp       runaspw
```

Now if jkemp types sudo command, it will default to running command as the notroot user and will challenge for that user's password.

6-13. Stopping Brute-Force Attacks with iptables

Brute-force ssh attacks are where an attacker just repeatedly tries to log into your machine via ssh with a series of usernames and/or passwords. They are an unfortunate fact of life if you run any machine that has its SSH port open to the wider world.

Note It's worth considering whether you really *need* the SSH port of each machine open to the world outside your own network; your Kerberos and LDAP servers, for example, probably shouldn't be, and even a web server needn't be open on the SSH port, only the Apache port(s). If you need to log into these servers from home, you can get in via another machine. You could even insist that anyone wanting to log into the network from outside come in via a single gateway machine, but this may be more hassle (from a user management perspective) than it's worth for desktop machines. Users shouldn't be allowed to log into your servers anyway; see recipe 6-3 for information on the AllowUsers directive.

One option for dealing with this problem is to use a solution that monitors how many connections are coming from a single IP address and blocks that IP address if there are too many in a set time period. The iptables limit module is good for this.

First, let's look at a basic iptables setup for a machine with IP address 192.168.100.25 on the 192.168.100.0/255.255.255.0 subnet (that is, machines with IP addresses 192.168.100.*):

```
01   iptables -A INPUT -d 127.0.0.0/255.0.0.0 -i ! lo -p tcp -j DROP
02   iptables -A INPUT -d 192.168.100.25 -m state --state RELATED,ESTABLISHED -j ACCEPT
03   iptables -A INPUT -i lo -j ACCEPT
04   iptables -A INPUT -s 192.168.100.0/255.255.255.0 -d 192.168.100.25 -j ACCEPT
05   iptables -A INPUT -d 192.168.100.25 -p tcp -m tcp --dport 22 -j LOG --log-prefix "ssh:"
06   iptables -A INPUT -d 192.168.100.25 -p tcp -m tcp --dport 22 -j ACCEPT
07   iptables -P INPUT DROP
08   iptables -P FORWARD DROP
09   iptables -P OUTPUT ACCEPT
```

Line 01 drops anything coming in on 127.0.0.0 that isn't using the loopback address. Line 02 accepts any packets related to an established connection with this machine (-d x.x.x.x means that the packet destination is x.x.x.x). Line 03 accepts anything coming in on the loopback address. Line 04 unconditionally accepts any packet from the local network (192.168.100.*) that has a destination of this machine's IP.

Lines 05 and 06 log any SSH packets coming in and then accept them.

Lines 07–09 set the default policy for the INPUT and FORWARD chains to be to drop packets, so anything that hasn't matched one of the previous rules will be dropped. For OUTPUT, we accept everything.

OK, now let's set up the limit module. The easiest way to do this is to create a new chain:

```
iptables -N SSH
```

If you now type iptables -L, you'll see all the chains and your new chain at the end of them. Now let's set the rules for this chain:

```
01   iptables -A SSH -j LOG --log-prefix "ssh:"
02   iptables -A SSH -m limit --limit 3/min --limit-burst 3 -j ACCEPT
03   iptables -P SSH DROP
```

Line 01 logs all connections (see line 05 in the first setup). Line 02 does the limiting work. The limit is set at three connections per minute, but this is an *average*. limit-burst sets how often the average is checked. So here, the rule will be checked after three connections. If those three connections have happened within a minute, the limiting is triggered; no further packets will be accepted until a full minute has passed (whereupon we're back below the three per minute rate). If you set --limit-burst as 6, you could get six connections through as fast as you like, but after that you would have to wait until two minutes had passed since the first connection to have another packet accepted.

Line 03 sets the chain policy to DROP; so, all other packets are dropped.

Finally, we have the issue of when to trigger this. We want to replace line 06 in the first listing, which is also rule 6 in the INPUT chain (execute iptables -L -linenumbers -n to check this). Use this command to replace (-R) rule 6 with this definition:

```
iptables -R INPUT 6 -d 192.168.100.25 -p tcp -m tcp --dport 22 -j SSH
```

This passes all SSH connections (in other words, TCP connections coming in on the SSH port, port 21) to the SSH chain.

You can also get rid of rule 5, since the logging is now done in the SSH chain:

```
iptables -D INPUT 5
```

■ **Note** Remember that after this rule is deleted, the numbering of the rules in the chain will change! It's always wise to use iptables -L --linenumbers to check rule numbers before you make changes.

Now, an SSH packet for this machine will be passed to the SSH chain and rate limited.

6-14. Monitoring for Break-ins with chkrootkit

chkrootkit enables you to have a set of important files monitored for signs of an attacker breaking in, for rootkits, and for worms and other similar nasties. You can set it up to send you information on a regular basis.

It should be available as a package for most distros. On Debian/Ubuntu, install it like this:

```
sudo apt-get install chkrootkit
```

Alternatively, install from source from http://www.chkrootkit.org/.

You can run it manually with /usr/sbin/chkrootkit. You should see a list of files being checked and (ideally!) all having "not infected" after their names. You'll also see the program searching for various specific worms and rootkits and for suspicious files generally. If anything has been found, you'll see the string INFECTED.

■ **Note** It does have a tendency to generate false positives, such as dot files installed in unusual places or servers running on nonstandard ports. Line 03 in the following setup means that false positives will occur only once, however, rather than repeatedly showing up.

What you want, though, is to have this run automatically on a daily basis. If you've installed the Debian/Ubuntu package, this includes the file /etc/cron.daily/chkrootkit that will do this for you, which looks like this:

```
#!/bin/sh -e

CHKROOTKIT=/usr/sbin/chkrootkit
CF=/etc/chkrootkit.conf
LOG_DIR=/var/cache/chkrootkit

if [ ! -x $CHKROOTKIT ]; then
  exit 0
fi

if [ -f $CF ]; then
  . $CF
fi

if [ "$RUN_DAILY" = "true" ]; then
    if [ "$DIFF_MODE" = "true" ]; then
        $CHKROOTKIT $RUN_DAILY_OPTS > $LOG_DIR/log.new 2>&1
        if [ ! -f $LOG_DIR/log.old ] \
            || ! diff -q $LOG_DIR/log.old $LOG_DIR/log.new > /dev/null 2>&1; then
            cat $LOG_DIR/log.new
        fi
        mv $LOG_DIR/log.new $LOG_DIR/log.old
    else
        $CHKROOTKIT $RUN_DAILY_OPTS
    fi
fi
```

To set chkrootkit options, you can set environment variables in /etc/chkrootkit.conf. This is a good default setup:

```
01   RUN_DAILY="true"
02   RUN_DAILY_OPTS="-q -n"
03   DIFF_MODE="true"
```

Line 01 sets daily running (unsurprisingly!). -q runs quietly, and -n skips NFS-mounted directories. Line 03 means that output will be generated only if it differs from the previous day's output. In other words, you will be warned only once! This means that if you have regular false positives, you won't always receive an e-mail; however, it also means that if you miss the first warning (maybe in a particularly heavy email day), you won't get another one. Another option is to integrate it into Nagios (see Chapter 3 for a discussion of Nagios).

6-15. Using cron-apt to Keep Updated

If you're using Debian or Ubuntu, cron-apt is a really useful tool that checks for package updates and will e-mail you to let you know about them. Install the package with sudo apt-get install cron-apt, and then edit your /etc/crontab to include this line:

```
0 4     * * *   root    test -x /usr/sbin/cron-apt && /usr/sbin/cron-apt
```

This will run cron-apt every night at 4 a.m.

To configure it, edit the file /etc/cron-apt/config. Most of this you should be able to leave as is. These are important lines to check and change:

```
MAILTO="admin@example.com"
MAILON="upgrade"
```

Possible MAILON values are always, upgrade (when a package is upgraded), error (when there's an error in the run), changes (when the output changes as the result of an action), and output (whenever output is generated). If it's left empty, mail will never be sent. upgrade is probably the most useful value and avoids clogging up your inbox.

By default, cron-apt will download only the upgraded packages (you then have to install them when you get the email notifying you about them). The actions are controlled by the files in /etc/cron-apt/action.d. The files in this directory will be used as options to apt-get when cron-apt runs. Two are provided by default. The first is 0-update, which runs the following:

```
apt-get update -o quiet=2
```

-o will set an option string (there isn't one given here). The second is 3-download, which runs the following:

```
apt-get upgrade -d -y -o APT::Get::Show-Upgraded=true
```

-d sets this to just download (not install), and -y assumes "yes" to any questions asked. Note that if something really undesirable, such as removing an essential file, is set to happen, apt-get will abort even if -y is set. -o APT::Get::Show-Upgraded=true sets the APT::Get::Show-Upgraded option, thus giving a printed-out list of all packages to be upgraded, which is what shows up in your e-mail.

■ **Note** To automatically run the upgrades, rather than just downloading them, you could remove the -d option in the 3-download line. This is *not* recommended because it's far better to review the changes before they happen, and in most situations, you probably want to run the upgrade on a test box to make sure nothing breaks before you roll it out. Certainly it is a *very* bad idea to automatically upgrade servers.

If you decide to do this, you should remove -y and insert --trivial-only. This will make apt-get use the default option when asked a question, so old config files will be retained rather than overwritten.

■ ■ ■

## CHAPTER 7

Working with Apache

Apache (these days in almost all cases Apache2, that is, version 2 of Apache) is the most popular web server on the Internet (and has been for well over a decade now). It's available as the apache2 package for Debian/Ubuntu. This chapter covers some useful command-line options, module setup, and then various security issues, including https://, htaccess, and Kerberos integration.

7-1. Using the apache2 Command Line

The basic functions of the apache2 command (which may be called httpd in some distros) are to stop, start, and reload Apache2; it's usually run via apachectl (or apache2ctl in some distros):

```
apachectl stop
apachectl start
apachectl restart
```

■ **Note** Debian and Ubuntu use apache2 for this command; some distros instead use httpd. The options should all be the same, though. If in doubt, check the apachectl script to see what the HTTPD variable is set to:

```
HTTPD='/usr/sbin/apache2'
```

Various command-line options are available that enable you to manipulate your configuration without changing httpd.conf. This can be very useful when testing alternative configurations or testing alternative settings. In effect, it gives you an alternative to backing up your old config file and then editing the original, so it will make it possible to run tests faster and switch back to your normal config if you need to make further changes.

It's particularly useful if you manage config files with Puppet (see Chapter 3), because using this method of testing possible changes ensures that the changes will not be overwritten by a scheduled Puppet run while you're experimenting.

After you've finished testing with any of these, type the following to restart with your normal settings:

```
apache2 -k stop; apachectl start
```

Here's a default /etc/apache2/apache2.conf file to start off with:

```
ServerRoot "/etc/apache2"
LockFile /var/lock/apache2/accept.lock
PidFile ${APACHE_PID_FILE}

Timeout 300
KeepAlive On
MaxKeepAliveRequests 100

KeepAliveTimeout 15

User ${APACHE_RUN_USER}
Group ${APACHE_RUN_GROUP}

AccessFileName .htaccess
<Files ~ "^\.ht">
    Order allow,deny
    Deny from all
</Files>

DefaultType text/plain
HostnameLookups Off

ErrorLog /var/log/apache2/error.log
LogLevel warn

Include /etc/apache2/mods-enabled/*.load
Include /etc/apache2/mods-enabled/*.conf
Include /etc/apache2/ports.conf
Include /etc/apache2/conf.d/
Include /etc/apache2/sites-enabled/

ServerAdmin webmaster@localhost

DocumentRoot /var/www/
      <Directory />
    Options FollowSymLinks
    AllowOverride None
</Directory>
```

The first thing to do is to test this config file:

```
apache2 -t
```

This will check that the config files are syntactically correct. It's a very useful one to use *before* you try restarting your production server!

Once you've run that test, just use apachectl start to start Apache with this config (then use apachectl stop to stop it again). Now let's try some of the possible options you can use for testing alternative configs.

■ **Note** In Debian/Ubuntu, you may find that you need to source the Apache environment variables before using apache2 as shown in this recipe, or you'll get error messages such as this:

apache2: bad user name ${APACHE_RUN_USER}

Do this with the following:

. /etc/apache2/envvars

---

1. Start Apache using an alternative DocumentRoot:

   apache2 -k start -c "DocumentRoot /var/www/html_debug/"

   The DocumentRoot processing directive specifies the directory that will be served as the root of your web space. So, when starting Apache with the previous command, if you then went to http://www.example.com, the page served would be /var/www/html_debug/index.html. This is useful if you're testing alternative versions of your web site, because it avoids having to edit the DocumentRoot option.

   You can also use -c to set any other directive. Note that -c processes the directive after reading the config files (so it will overwrite config file settings), whereas -C will process the directive before the config files. Use this if you want to set something that will affect the rest of the config processing, such as setting a custom log file with the following:

   apache2 -k start -C "CustomLog /var/log/apache2/testlog"

   Bear in mind that later directives in the file may override directives set with -C, such as if the standard apache2.conf has a CustomLog directive set, for example. You may be better off using a separate config altogether, as in the next suggestion.

2. Start Apache with an entirely different config file:

   apache2 -k start -f conf/httpd.conf.debug

   This is useful if you're changing a big stack of options at once (and so using -c would be unwieldy) or testing something like SSL (see recipe 7-4).

3. Set the parameter loadmodule, which will then be used when parsing the config file:

```
apache2 -D loadmodule
```

So, if your config file includes this:

```
01   <IfDefine loadmodule>
02         LoadModule my_other_module
03   </IfDefine>
```

then my_other_module will be loaded only if the parameter is set. You can use this for testing modules before adding them permanently by defining loadmodule in the config, or you can use it for testing anything else that you put within an appropriate IfDefine section. The IfDefine section can be temporary (that is, you can remove it after testing) to allow you to switch quickly backward and forward when testing a module or a section of config. When you're happy, remove lines 01 and 03 to avoid the need for the parameter to be passed in.

4. Get information about Apache:

```
apache2 -l
apache2 -L
apache2 -S
```

The first outputs a list of compiled modules so you can check which modules are available and loaded already. The second gives a list of directives (such as the SSL directives discussed in recipe 7-4) and where they apply. This can be really useful for troubleshooting purposes. The third shows the VirtualHost settings as constructed from the config file. Again, this can be useful when troubleshooting to check which settings are being applied to which VirtualHost and that nothing has been missed. Add this section to your config file, and then run apache2 -S to take a look at the VirtualHost settings:

```
<VirtualHost myothersite.example.org>
      ServerAdmin othersite_web@localhost

      DocumentRoot /var/www/myothersite/
      <Directory />
            Options FollowSymLinks +Includes
            AllowOverride None
      </Directory>
      ErrorLog /var/log/apache2/othersite_error.log
</VirtualHost>
```

7-2. Apache2: Dealing with Modules

Apache2 is *modular*, which means there's a core system and then a set of modules that you can include in the main system if you choose. Some of the modules are statically built, which means that they're built in when the server is compiled and can't be removed without recompiling the server. These modules can't be loaded or unloaded on the fly. If you're using the Apache2 package for your distribution, you won't have any control over which modules are built in like this. If you want a different set of built-ins, you'll need to recompile Apache2 yourself. As a rule, you shouldn't need to do this; anything that's missing from the built-in list can be installed dynamically (which I'll describe in a moment). You'll need to recompile if you want to disable any of the built-in modules, but avoid this if possible, since compiling your own software is far less maintainable than using your distro's packaging system.

To get a list of the built-in modules, use this command:

```
apache2 -i
```

Dynamic shared objects (DSOs) are the other type of module. These exist separately from the main binary and can easily be loaded when the server starts or reloads. So, you can take them in and out as you need. Again, your distro package will probably include a few of these modules, and separate packages will be available for other modules.

In general, a Fedora-type system will by default load most of the modules that are provided with the server, whereas a Debian system will load only a few. You'll need to choose to load the rest using the a2enmod tool, which I'm about to explain.

With Debian, you'll find all the module load information in the directory /etc/apache2/mods-available/; this is also where the config files (when needed for a particular module) live, and you can edit the configuration here. To load a module, a symlink is created from /etc/apache2/mods-enabled/modulename.load to /etc/apache2/mods-available/modulename.load.

```
> ls -l /etc/apache2/mods-enabled/
...
lrwxrwxrwx 1 root root 27 2009-07-14 14:20 php5.conf -> ../mods-available/php5.conf
lrwxrwxrwx 1 root root 27 2009-07-14 14:20 php5.load -> ../mods-available/php5.load
...
```

■ **Note** The lines in /etc/apache2/apache2.conf that handle this are as follows:

```
Include /etc/apache2/mods-enabled/*.load
Include /etc/apache2/mods-enabled/*.conf
```

Each modulename.conf file is usually a single line like this:

```
LoadModule modulename /usr/lib/apache2/modules/modulename.so
```

You could, if you like this method of managing module configuration but are not using Debian, set up something similar yourself by manually creating these directories and the appropriate *.load and *.conf files and adding the include lines for both directories. Then remove the LoadModule lines and the module configuration from the main

Apache2 config file. This would have the advantage of keeping your module setup and config separate, which makes adding and removing modules much easier.

You can of course do this symlink adding or removing by hand, but it's better to use the Debian tools provided. To enable a module, use this command:

```
a2enmod modulename
```

To disable it, use this command:

```
a2dismod modulename
```

To get a list of the modules available to enable or disable, just use a2enmod or a2dismod without any argument.

Remember that after you've made any changes, you'll need to reload Apache2 for them to take effect:

```
/etc/init.d/apache2 reload
```

7-3. Setting Up an SSL Certificate for Apache2

When you set up a secure web server, clients have confirmation both that the server is who it claims to be and that the transaction is well encrypted so their data is safe. To do this with Apache, you need to use Secure Sockets Layer (SSL), which is a secure communication protocol. Transport Layer Security (TLS) is the successor to SSL, but they work in basically the same way, so this recipe refers to SSL.

SSL provides a protocol for cryptographically securing browser/web server transactions. In most cases, only the server end is authenticated. Therefore, when the connection starts up, the client can confirm that the server is who or what it claims to be, but not vice versa. However, once the connection is established, both ends are secure, because only the server and that particular client have access to the key that they're exchanging. This is acceptable because in most cases all the server cares about is that the client stays the same throughout the transaction. For client authentication, see the next recipe for how to set up Kerberos authentication.

From the client side, you want to check both that you're sending your data to the site that you think you are communicating with and that no one is grabbing your data on the way through (a *person-in-the-middle* attack). SSL deals with both of these problems.

Here's a quick rundown of the SSL process:

1. The client sends the web server a list of the ciphers it can use.

2. The server picks the strongest cipher that both it and the client support and sends back a certificate with its name and public encryption key, signed by a trusted certificate authority (such as VeriSign).

3. The client checks the CA signature; clients often store popular CAs locally, so this can be done faster and without having to contact the CA.

4. The client sends back a random number encrypted with the server's public key. Only the client knows the number, and only the server can decrypt it, since decryption requires the server's private key. This means that a malicious third party can't get this number.

5. The server and client use this random number to generate a key to use for encrypting the rest of the transaction. So, since the malicious third-party can't get at the random number, they can't get at the data that's encrypted with the key based on it.

The aim of SSL (and modern web browsers) is to make this as straightforward as possible from the client side. This recipe and the next one use Apache2 with `mod_ssl` to get this set up on the web server side.

See recipe 2-3 for how to create an SSL certificate, either self-signed (which is fine for testing or for a local site) or signed by an external CA (a much better bet if you're a reasonably large or public site). The common name (CN) *must* be the same as the address of your web site; otherwise, the certificate won't match, and users will receive a warning when connecting. Note that you can create your certificate either with or without a passphrase. In theory, a passphrase increases server security. However, in practice, if someone can read or copy the private key (and therefore need the passphrase), then they already have root-level access to the system and could obtain the passphrase, for example by using a program like keylogger. A passphrase will protect against script kiddies but not against a serious hacker.

On the other hand, using a passphrase means that your web server won't start unattended (for example, automatically on boot or reboot), because the passphrase must be typed every time the web server starts.

■ **Note** You should *not* set a challenge password. (This is not the same thing as the passphrase!)

To view your certificate, use the following:

```
openssl -x509 -text -in server.crt
```

■ **Note** Set up a diary reminder of the expiry date so that you can renew it when necessary! It's embarrassing when your SSL suddenly stops working.

When you have your certificate back from the CA, it's best to rename it to `my.domain.org.crt` (to fit Apache conventions and to allow for multiple domains with multiple certificates) and to rename the key file similarly. You should then verify the certificate:

```
openssl verify -CAfile /path/to/trusted_ca.crt -purpose sslserver my.domain.org.crt
```

Then check that the certificate corresponds to the private key. The output of these two commands should match:

```
openssl x509 -noout -modulus -in my.domain.org.pem | openssl sha1
openssl rsa -noout -modulus -in my.domain.org.key | openssl sha1
```

Now install my.domain.org.key and my.domain.org.crt into /etc/apache2/ssl, and set the permissions correctly:

```
cp my.domain.org.key my.domain.org.crt /etc/apache2/ssl
chown root:root my.domain.org.key; chmod og-r my.domain.org.key
chown root:root my.domain.org.crt; chmod a+r my.domain.org.crt
```

It's important to make sure that the server key is readable only by root, while the server certificate should be world-readable but owned and writeable only by root. (If you already did this when you generated the certificate and key, you shouldn't need those last two lines.)

7-4. Compiling and Configuring Apache with SSL

Once you've set up your SSL certificate as in the previous recipe, the next step is to get SSL working in Apache. The best bet for this is to use the package provided for your distro. With Debian/Ubuntu, Apache comes with the SSL module available, but it's not automatically enabled. To enable it, use this:

```
a2enmod ssl
/etc/init.d/apache2 restart
```

The generic way to do this is to add this line to your /etc/apache2/apache2.conf or /etc/apache2/httpd.conf file:

```
Include /etc/apache2/mod_ssl.conf
```

You may need to edit this to give the correct location for mod_ssl.conf in your setup. Then restart Apache2.

For configuration, the following instructions assume that you want to run both a secure server (on port 443) and a regular server (on port 80). First, you need to configure the server to listen on both ports. In Debian/Ubuntu, edit /etc/apache2/ports.conf or directly edit /etc/apache2/apache2.conf to include the lines:

```
Listen 80
Listen 443
```

Next, edit /etc/apache2/sites-enabled/yoursite to use the SSL settings. The most maintainable option is to separate the regular and secure server settings out with VirtualHosts.

■ **Note** Any configuration outside the `VirtualHosts` sections (such as setting the `ServerAdmin`) will apply to both (and any other) `VirtualHosts`.

Add the following section to your config file:

```
# ====================================================
# SSL/TLS settings
# ====================================================
NameVirtualHost *:443

<VirtualHost *.443>

        DocumentRoot "/local/www/ssl_html"

        SSLEngine on
        SSLOptions +StrictRequire

        <Directory />
                SSLRequireSSL
        </Directory>

        SSLProtocol -all +TLSv1 +SSLv3
        SSLCipherSuite HIGH:MEDIUM:!aNULL:+SHA1:+MD5:+HIGH:+MEDIUM

        SSLRandomSeed startup file:/dev/urandom 1024
        SSLRandomSeed connect file:/dev/urandom 1024

        SSLSessionCache shm:/usr/local/apache2/logs/ssl_cache_shm
        SSLSessionCacheTimeout 600
        SSLCertificateFile /etc/apache2/ssl/server.crt
        SSLCertificateKeyFile /etc/apache2/ssl/server.key

        SSLVerifyClient none
        SSLProxyEngine off

        <IfModule mime.c>
                AddType application/x-x509-ca-cert       .crt
                AddType application/x-pkcs7-crl          .crl
        </IfModule>

        SetEnvIf User-Agent ".*MSIE.*" \
          nokeepalive ssl-unclean-shutdown \
          downgrade-1.0 force-response-1.0
</VirtualHost>
```

SSLEngine makes the server actually use SSL. DocumentRoot sets the root directory for this virtual host, so you can entirely separate secure content from regular content. You can then set SSLRequireSSL so that, on this virtual host (and thus in this part of the directory tree), SSL *must* be used. This avoids anyone using an insecure connection to access your secure content.

The SSLProtocol directive disables all protocols other than TLS v1.0 and SSL v3.0. SSLCipherSuite is set to use only HIGH and MEDIUM security cipher suites. SHA1 is preferred to MD5 because it is considered to be more secure.

SSLCertificateFile and SSLCertificateKeyFile should be set to the locations where you put your certificate and key files. We're not using client auth here, so SSLVerifyClient is set to none.

■ **Note** The MSIE section is a workaround for some bugs in some versions of Internet Explorer, which can lead to the user seeing I/O errors. Some other older versions of Internet Explorer have bugs with particular ciphers that are harder to work around; see http://httpd.apache.org/docs/2.0/ssl/ssl_faq.html#msie if this is a concern for you.

To run the regular server on port 80, add the following section to the config file:

```
NameVirtualHost: *.80

<VirtualHost *:80>
        DocumentRoot "/local/www/html"
        # Host-specific directory setup, options, etc
        # Most of these options are likely to be set outside the VirtualHosts
        # sections.
</VirtualHost>
```

After you've saved the edited configuration file, restart the web server. If you did use a passphrase when generating your certificate, you'll need to enter it when challenged.

Testing

Create a basic index.html page wherever the root directory of the SSL part of your web server is located, if you don't already have content there.

Then point your web browser at https://www.example.com. You should see an SSL connection opened and the page delivered. If you're using a self-signed certificate, your browser will pop up an alert warning you that the server's identity cannot be verified, and you can choose to view and/or accept the certificate. If using an external certificate, it should all happen without intervention.

Now try to access that content with http://. You should get an error message.

Troubleshooting

If it's not working as expected, first check that your server is actually running using ps -a | grep apache. If that doesn't return anything, try restarting Apache2 (/etc/init.d/apache2 restart), and check for error messages on the terminal or in /var/log/apache2/error_log.

Also check that the permissions on your key and certificate files are set correctly (discussed earlier), as well as the permissions on your test HTML file and its parent directory.

Next, check both the main server logs (at `/var/log/apache2/error_log`) and the SSL logs that you set up in your config file. If you don't get anything useful, try changing the `LogLevel` value in the Apache2 config file to debug, restart Apache2, and test again to get more log data.

If your certificate is in `.crt` format and you're having trouble, you could try converting it to `.pem` format:

```
openssl x509 -inform der -in MYCERT.cer -out MYCERT.pem
```

Then edit this line in your config file:

```
SSLCertificateFile /etc/apache2/ssl/server.pem
```

If you're also running a regular web server on port 80, try fetching a test page via `http://` rather than `https://` to help identify whether the problem is with the web server or with the SSL connection. Note that in the previous setup, the web server's root directory is different for `http://` and `https://`, so you won't (or shouldn't!) be able to access the same content. If your test page in the `http://` root directory works fine, though, and your test page in the `https://` root directory doesn't, then that can help you pinpoint the problem.

If the problem is the SSL connection, a useful tool is `s_client`, which is a diagnostic tool for troubleshooting TLS/SSL connections. The basic usage is as follows:

```
/usr/bin/openssl s_client -connect hostname:443
```

There are numerous other options to this command as well, for which you can check the documentation. If you get error messages, this should help you in locating the problem.

7-5. Securing Your Web Site with htaccess

It's quite common to have a situation whereby you want to restrict part of your web site to a particular set of users. The next recipe shows a way of doing this via Kerberos if you want users to log in as themselves, but if you just want to restrict access to people on the local network, htaccess is a quick and straightforward way to go about this.

Let's say that you want to allow machines only on the local subnet (192.168.*.*) to access the `$APACHEROOT/local` subdirectory. The first file to set up is `$APACHEROOT/local/.htaccess` (note the dot); it should look a bit like this:

```
01  AuthName Local Pages
02  AuthType Basic
03  <LIMIT GET POST>
04      order deny,allow
05      deny from all
06      allow from 192.168.
07  </LIMIT>
```

This will set things up so that the `GET` and `POST` methods require an IP from within this range. Deny directives are read before allow ones (line 04), everything is denied (line 05), and then a specific set of IP addresses is allowed (line 06). Note that it works rather like a regular expression, in that it'll match only whatever is provided. So, this line allows any IP address of the form 192.168.*.*. Problem solved.

But maybe you'd like your local users to be able to access these pages from home as well. In this case, you can add an alternative way of accessing these pages by setting up a special local user. The .htaccess file should look like this:

```
AuthUserFile /etc/apache2/.htpasswd
AuthName Local Pages
AuthType Basic
Satisfy Any
<LIMIT GET POST>
order deny,allow
deny from all
allow from 192.168.
require user local
</LIMIT>
```

Note the Satisfy Any directive; this means you can *either* be in the correct IP range (you can also specify by domain) *or* have the correct username and password. The default is Satisfy All, which would mean that you'd need both to be in the correct domain and to have the correct credentials.

For setting the username up, the key point is the AuthUserFile directive, which sets up a file that Apache will check for the password of your user local as set up in the LIMIT section.

The next step is to create the htpasswd file, using this command:

```
htpasswd -c /etc/apache2/.htpasswd local
```

Note The -c switch is used only to create the file. If you go to add another user, just use htpasswd /etc/apache2/.htpasswd otheruser.

You'll be challenged for the password for the user, which will be encrypted and put in the file. Make sure that only the Apache2 user can read this file:

```
chown www-data /etc/apache2/.htpasswd; chmod og-r /etc/apache2/.htpasswd
```

Note The .htpasswd file can live wherever you like, but for security reasons it should *not* live anywhere in your web data directories. Keep it instead with your Apache2 config. In this case, it doesn't need to be a dot file (.htpasswd) because it won't be visible to the average user anyway; you can just call it htpasswd.

Now try loading a page in that directory from an IP address outside your local subnet; you should be challenged for the username and password. Enter them, and you're allowed in. Pass this username and password on to the users you want to be able to access your machine.

> **Note** This kind of single username/password access, where everyone uses the same authorization, is not very secure! Be careful how sensitive the information is that you protect in this way. However, it's useful if your intention is simply to keep the information off the public Internet at large.

7-6. Securing Your Web Site: Apache with Kerberos

You may have parts of your web site that you want only your users to be able to access or a section that you want people to log into as themselves. If you're running a ticketing system or anything of that sort, then this is particularly useful. For some of these options, htaccess is useful (see recipe 7-5), but if you want individual users to log in as themselves, then tying authentication in with Kerberos is by far the best bet. This means that you don't have to repeat your username/password setup; you can just use what you already have established.

> **Note** This does assume that you already have Kerberos set up! See Chapter 2. Alternatively, you can use the mod_authnz_ldap module (a2enmod authnz_ldap in Debian), which works with LDAP auth and with Active Directory.

The module you want is mod_auth_kerb, which is available from http://modauthkerb.sourceforge.net/ or in Debian/Ubuntu as the libapache2-mod-auth-kerb package.

To install it, add this line to your Apache config file (or for Debian/Ubuntu, run a2enmod mod_auth_kerb):

```
LoadModule auth_kerb_module /usr/lib/apache2/modules/mod_auth_kerb.so
```

You also need to set up a keytab for Apache to use. Run kadmin -p krbadm from your Apache server, and then execute these commands:

```
> addprinc --randkey HTTP/webserver.example.com@EXAMPLE.COM
> ktadd -k /etc/apache2/apache2.keytab HTTP/webserver.example.com@EXAMPLE.COM
```

After this, set the correct permissions for the keytab; it should be readable only by the Apache2 process:

```
chown www-data /etc/apache2/apache2.keytab
chmod og-r /etc/apache2/apache2.keytab
```

> **Note** The only key that should be in this keytab is the Apache one, since the keyfile is slightly less secure because it is owned and readable by the Apache2 user (www-data in the case of Debian/Ubuntu) rather than by root. (Obviously, this is necessary for it to be usable by the web server, but you don't want to expose other keys to that slight insecurity.)

Next, you need to set up the configuration file to use this as the authentication option. Let's say you're setting up a request-tracking system in the directory $APACHEROOT/rt and that this is the only part of the web site that you want to have Kerberos authentication for. Add this section to your site config file:

```
<Location /rt>
    # Kerberisation
    AuthType KerberosV5
    AuthName "Request Tracker"
    KrbAuthRealm EXAMPLE.COM
    Krb5Keytab /etc/apache2/apache2.keytab
    Require valid-user
</Location>
```

The KrbAuthRealm should be whatever you set up as your authentication realm when you were setting up Kerberos (see recipe 2-1). It'll probably be your domain. Krb5Keytab should be set to wherever you saved your Apache2 keytab.

> **Note** You can change that Require to various other values. To restrict access to specific users, use this:
>
> Require user principal1@EXAMPLE.COM principal2@EXAMPLE.COM

That's it! Reload Apache with /etc/init.d/apache2 reload, and go to http://example.com/rt in your browser. You should be challenged for your username and password. If you have any problems, check the Apache2 logs (/var/log/apache2/error_log) for error messages. In particular, make sure that the Apache user can read the keytab file.

> **Note** You can also use this syntax in an .htaccess file in a particular directory. See recipe 7-5 for a discussion of how to use htaccess.

## CHAPTER 8

Making Better Use of the Command Line

You no doubt spend a lot of time on the command line. This chapter contains some tips and tricks to make your life easier when you're typing, including both built-in bash shortcuts and how to write your own autocompletion functions. Working on the command line often also means that you're using files in various ways, including the quick-reference guides to find and xargs (both incredibly useful but occasionally complex to use). The last two recipes will help you operate on files more quickly.

8-1. Using bash Keyboard Shortcuts

A huge number of keyboard shortcuts are available for bash that can make your command-line life much easier and quicker.

Note In fact, these are GNU readline shortcuts, which means that they're usable not just in bash but also in any other applications compiled with readline. This includes, for example, the mysql command line.

You've almost certainly already picked up one or two, but it's worth putting the effort in to get more of them under your fingers. The easiest way to learn them is to pick up one or two at a time and make a point of using them until you're fully familiar with them; then move on to the next couple.

The default setting in most setups is emacs-like editing mode. You can also set bash/readline to use vi editing mode:

```
set -o vi
```

This will put you into a mode that behaves like vi(m) insert mode. To get into command mode, hit Esc (or press Ctrl-[), and then issue your commands as you would on the vi(m) command line. For example, use 3b to move three words backward. Hit i again to go back into insert mode and start typing.

However, note that vi mode doesn't have quite so many useful key bindings defined. You can define your own, though; take a look at the section in the `readline` init file in the bash manual, or type `bind -p` to get a list of key bindings in a form that you can dump straight into your `~/.initrc`). To return to emacs mode again, use this:

```
set -o emacs
```

You can set vi mode to be on permanently by adding these lines to your `~/.initrc` file:

```
set editing-mode vi
set keymap vi
```

The bash man page has many more of the default key bindings documented. You can also type `bind -P` to get a list of possible functions and their key bindings (if any).

- *Ctrl-A and Ctrl-E*: These move to the beginning and the end of the command line, respectively. You're probably already familiar with these.

- *Ctrl-U*: This deletes from the cursor backward to the beginning of the line. This is useful when you've accidentally exited the incremental search with a command line you don't want or if you just get your fingers in a tangle and need to start again. It also works when you're entering passwords, so it's handy when you get stuck halfway and aren't sure how many times to hit Backspace. If you want to put the line you've just cut back again, use Ctrl-Y, which restores whatever is currently in the buffer.

  ```
  > cd /usr/share/some/nonsense Ctrl-U
  >
  ```

- *Ctrl-K*: This is the reverse of Ctrl-U; this deletes from the cursor forward to the end of the line.

- *Ctrl-R and Ctrl-S*: This performs an incremental search backward or forward, respectively, in your command-line history. So, if you hit Ctrl-R and start typing a word (for instance, `find`), it'll start looking for the last command that used the word `find`, and it'll show the results as you type. Keep hitting Ctrl-R to scroll backward through the list of commands that fit the search pattern. If you hit Ctrl-R and then type apache, this is the sort of output you'll get:

  ```
  > [Ctrl-R]apache
  (reverse-i-search)`apache': /etc/init.d/apache2 force-reload
  ```

- *Ctrl-J and Ctrl-G*: These abandon an incremental search either with the line found or with the original line, respectively. So, these commands will put you back to your regular command line, from where you can edit the command you have (the searched-for command line, with Ctrl-J, or the command line you started with, with Ctrl-G) as required.

  ```
  (reverse-i-search)`apache': /etc/init.d/apache2 force-reload
  Ctrl-J
  > /etc/init.d/apache2 force-reload
  ```

- *Alt-. (period) or Esc-. (period)*: Both of these insert the final argument to the most recent command at the cursor point. This is very useful when moving files around and editing them; you can repeatedly apply different operations to the same file. It's also useful for other sorts of file processing. Alt-. falls more readily under the fingers, but Esc and then . is a handy alternative to know if you're using an odd keyboard (Alt-. won't work properly on some keyboards) and in particular if you're using a Mac.

```
> cp /usr/share/doc/README /usr/share/doc/README.local
> vim Alt-.
vim /usr/share/doc/README.local
```

░ **Note** In general, if you have trouble with Alt, try replacing it with Esc. You don't have to hit the second key at the same time as Esc but can hit it immediately afterward if you prefer. In other words, pressing Esc and then . (period) works exactly the same as Esc-. (period).

- *Alt-Ctrl-Y*: This inserts the first argument to the previous command at the cursor point. If you want the *n*th argument, hit Alt-*n* beforehand. So, pressing Alt-2 Alt-Ctrl-Y will give you the second argument to the previous command. (You may find you need to replace Alt with Esc on some keyboards, so you'd press Esc-2 Esc-Ctrl-Y in this example.) It's a lot of keys to remember, but it's useful once in a while, especially if your arguments are particularly long and you're doing something complicated. Also bear in mind that Alt-0 or Esc-0 will give you the first word of the last command, which will probably be the command name and can be useful if repeating a command.

```
> cp /etc/defaults/ldap /etc/defaults/ldap.bk
> vim Alt-C-Y
vim /etc/defaults/ldap
```

- *Alt-?*: This provides history expansion on the current line. (That is, hit this once instead of Tab twice to get a list of possible expansions. This saves a single keystroke but uses more fingers!)

- *Ctrl-T and Alt-T*: These transpose characters and words, respectively. This will pull the character/word behind the cursor over the character/word at the cursor. (Unfortunately, in at least some terminals—for example, gnome-terminal—Alt-T is overridden, so this may not work for you. However, Esc-T should still work.)

```
> cd /urs Ctrl-T
> cd /usr
```

- *Ctrl-W and Alt-Backspace*: Both of these delete the word behind the cursor, but Ctrl-W uses whitespace as a boundary, whereas Alt-BS uses nonalphanumeric characters. So, if you have file.txt and hit Ctrl-W, you'll delete the lot; Alt-BS will leave you with file., which has very obvious uses. (It also works with underscores.)

```
> mv file.txt file.txt Alt-BS
> mv file.txt file.
> mv file.txt file.tex
```

- *Ctrl-_ and Ctrl-X Ctrl-U:* These undo the last change. You can undo all changes made to the line simultaneously with Alt-R.

- *Ctrl-D:* This exits the shell, if at the start of an empty line. This is handled by stty, not by readline, so it should work in any shell. If used in the middle of a line, it deletes the character to the right of the cursor. Using Alt-D or Esc-D will delete a word to the right.

- *Ctrl-C:* This cancels whatever you're running currently. Like Ctrl-D, this is a stty setting and should work with any shell.

- *Ctrl-L:* This clears the screen. This is useful when you don't want it to be obvious what you've been doing! However, be warned that if you're using a terminal that scrolls, your history will be available via scrolling back. This is also useful if something peculiar has happened to the lines and they're not displaying properly. You can also try typing stty sane in this instance.

■ **Note** See recipe 1-2 for discussion of setting up your .bashrc file to improve the way your history is stored.

8-2. Writing Your Own bash Functions

Most sysadmins will already have some aliases set up in their ~/.bashrc file for easy reference to commands they use frequently (and some distributions, including Debian and Ubuntu, include some default settings in /etc/bashrc). Here's an example from mine:

```
alias e='ssh juliet@myemailserver.example.com'
```

Aliases are limited, though, since in bash and related shells you can't pass arguments in from the command line to an alias. There's a "cheat" option, if the argument you want to pass in is always on the end of the line:

```
alias gps='ps -A | grep'
```

This alias will mean that if you type gps apache, the process list will be searched for the pattern apache, so this saves you a little typing. However, this won't work if the argument you want to pass in is in the middle of the line.

The way to do this is by creating a function: functions will take arguments anywhere inside them. For example, say you want to be able to run LDAP searches more readily:

```
function lds() { ldapsearch "($1=$2)"; }
```

Either type this on the command line (in which case it will work only within that particular terminal window until it's shut down) or, to make it a permanent function, add it to your ~/.bashrc and then open a new terminal window.

■ **Note** If you don't want to open a new terminal window, type source ~/.bashrc. However, this can sometimes create problems with settings such as $PATH, because they are repeatedly redefined and thus grow steadily longer.

Then type the following:

```
lds cn jkemp
```

This will run an LDAP search for any entries with a cn value of jkemp (ldapsearch "(cn=jkemp)"). This both saves typing and avoids having to remember which way the (and " go in an LDAP search command (and having to type it accurately once you've remembered it!).

A function is basically a shell script, so you can use a function to do pretty much anything you can write a shell script to do. This means that you can get pretty complicated and even recursive. The following code will go recursively through the directory or directories you enter on the command line, changing any .html files into .shtml files, which is useful if you're moving wholesale to using server-side includes in your web site.

```
01  #!/bin/bash
02  # JK 24.07.2009
03  if [ -z "$1" ]; then
04    echo "Usage: $0 {directories-to-iterate over}"
05    echo "Iterates over all files in directories changing .html to .shtml"
06    exit 1
07  fi
08
09  cwd="$PWD"
10  arg="$1"
11
12  function rename_recursive()
13  {
14    cd "$arg"
15    for file in `ls`; do
16      if [ -d "$file" ]; then
17        rename_recursive "$file"
18      else
19        if [[ "$file" =~ .*\.html ]]; then
20          oldname="`basename $file`"
21          newname="`basename $file .html`.shtml"
22          mv "$file" "$newname"
23        fi
24      fi
25    done
```

```
26    cd ..
27  }
28
29  for dir in $@; do
30      rename_recursive "$dir"
31  done
32
33  cd "$cwd"
34  exit 0
```

Lines 01–07 do the setup and check for at least one argument (the directory to iterate over), line 09 records your current directory so you can get back there at the end, and line 10 assigns the argument to a named variable. Lines 12–27 are the part that does the work. You cd into the directory given by the argument; then in line 15 you get a listing of that directory and iterate over each item in the listing. In lines 16 and 17, you check whether that item is a directory, and if it is, you run the rename_recursive function on it—this is the recursive bit! Otherwise, in lines 19–23, you check to see whether the filename ends in .html and rename it to .shtml if so. Line 25 loops you back to line 15, and once we've dealt with all the items in the directory, you jump back up a directory, and the function is finished.

Lines 29–31 do the initial calling of the function on each argument in turn (so the function will be run, recursively, on each directory you name on the command line), and line 33 makes sure you've wound up back where you started.

8-3. Implementing Programmable Completion with bash

Another trick you'll already be familiar with is hitting Tab to autocomplete filenames and commands. This is great and a massive time-saver, but there are a few ways to extend it.

The first tip isn't, in fact, exactly extending autocompletion, but it helps you locate directories more easily. $CDPATH does for cd what $PATH does for executables. In other words, it'll allow you to type just the name of a directory, and if the parent of that directory is in your $CDPATH, it'll take you straight there. It saves having to type the full path each time.

So, say you regularly want to go to the research subdirectory of your website at /local/www/html/research. Set your $CDPATH like this to include the parent directory:

```
export CDPATH="/home/jkemp:/local/www/html/:$CDPATH"
```

Now just type cd research to get to /local/www/html/research.

However, with that setting, if you're in ~/book/ and want to cd into the research-notes subdirectory of that directory, you need to be wary. If you type research, hit Tab, and then hit Enter without paying attention, you'll end up in /local/www/html/research by accident. In other words, $CDPATH overrides the default completion settings, which would otherwise just look in your current directory. To fix this, add . (the current directory) to the start of the path:

```
export CDPATH=".:/home/jkemp:/local/www/html/:$CDPATH"
```

Now the current directory will be searched first, and then the other directories in the $CDPATH will be searched.

Note This won't tab-complete. You'll need to type the full directory name in (research, in this example), unless you're cding to a directory in your current directory, in which case tab-complete functions as normal.

However, the major improvement available for the regular autocompletion is programmable completion. This more or less borrows from zsh, which has extensive autocompletion and a few other interesting options (it should be available as a package for your distro if you want to investigate).

You can write completion functions all by yourself, but to avoid extensive wheel reinvention, you're better off downloading /etc/bash_completion from http://www.caliban.org/bash/ (also available as a package for most distros and installed by default in Ubuntu as the bash-completion package and Debian in the bash package) and then sourcing that file in your ~/.bashrc file:

```
source /etc/bash_completion
```

Now open a new terminal window, and then try typing ssh at the command line and then hitting Tab. You'll be shown a list of possible hosts, based primarily on your known_hosts file (along with a couple of other tricks). Various other commands are also set up to do this by the /etc/bash_completion file. Experiment with traceroute or ftp.

You can also extend this particular form of completion to other commands or to your own scripts. Take a look at the /etc/bash_completion file. It's pretty big, but you can see that there are a set of subroutines beginning with an underscore (for example, _known_hosts). These are the subroutines that do the work of figuring out the possible autocompletions. Search for a line that looks like this:

```
complete -F _known_hosts traceroute ping telnet host ssh
```

complete -F identifies the function to use for completion. Anything returned by the function (here, known_hosts) is provided as a possible completion option for the commands listed after that function (here, traceroute ping telnet host ssh). -C is a similar option that executes a command and takes the output from that as possible completion. So, if you want to add your command to that list, just add it on the end of this line and re-source the file:

```
> vim /etc/bash_completion
complete -F _known_hosts traceroute ping telnet host ssh mycommand
> source /etc/bash_completion
```

Test your command. It should now autocomplete with hostnames.

Note In general, the functions in /etc/bash_completion fall back on the compgen bash built-in, which passes options to complete (another built-in) to try to generate a word completion. This is the "normal" tab-completion option, but it's quite limited for words such as hostnames using only the $HOSTFILE file, which will usually be /etc/hosts and which is very limited in modern systems that rely on external DNS.

You can also write your own completion function. Here's a very basic function you can add to /etc/bash_completion that looks up a partial hostname in LDAP:

```
01   _ldapcomplete() {
02       COMPREPLY=()
03       cur=${COMP_WORDS[COMP_CWORD]}
04       output=`ldapsearch -Q "(&(cn=$cur*) (objectClass=ipHost))" cn | grep ^cn:`
05       name=${output#* }
06       COMPREPLY=( ${COMPREPLY[@]} $name )
07     return 0
08   }
09
10   complete -F _ldapcomplete ssh
```

Line 02 sets up the array variable that will be used for the completion return (COMPREPLY). Line 03 sets $cur to the value that's been passed into the function, that is, what's already been input on the command line. The COMP_WORDS variable is set up earlier in /etc/bash_completion for use by all functions.

The ldapsearch at line 04 looks for an entry in the LDAP directory, which is a host-type object with a name that begins with the existing input, and then it returns only the cn value of any suitable LDAP entry it finds. The output is piped into grep to strip out all the extraneous LDAP information (the -Q switch is used on the ldapsearch to make the output as quiet as possible). $output will be as follows:

cn: myhost

So, line 05 splits on whitespace and takes the second half of $output to give just myhost. This value is put into COMPREPLY at line 06, and the function finishes. In this case, you'll get only one value, so the line could be this:

COMPREPLY=$name

But to match the rest of the file and to allow for further improvement, you treat it as an array.

■ **Note** This function does not deal properly with multiple return possibilities (it autocompletes only when LDAP returns a single value). To deal properly with multiple returns, COMPREPLY would have to be treated as an array.

Line 10 allows you to actually use the function. It tells the shell that when using ssh, the _ldapcomplete function should be used for hostname completion.

■ **Note** The documentation on the bash man page is pretty good on completion if you want to investigate further.

8-4. Using find

locate is a useful tool for quickly finding files. You can manually update the database with sudo updatedb, although you should use cron to run updatedb regularly for it to be really useful. find is significantly slower, since it searches the directory tree instead of using a constructed database as with locate, but it is more reliable since it doesn't need that database to be up-to-date, and it's far more flexible.

It can, however, be a little confusing to use at first, especially since its error messages aren't always very helpful. This recipe is a quick reference for some of the most helpful find options.

The basic usage is as follows:

```
find [-H|-L|-P] [path] [options] [expression]
```

where [path] is the root directory to start the search from and [expression] is the criteria by which you want to search. Without any other options besides [path], find will keep iterating further into the directory from which the search began, until it runs out of subdirectories and files.

-H, -L, and -P control how find will deal with symbolic links. -P is the default and sets them to be ignored. -L sets them to be followed. -H sets them to be ignored, *unless* the path given on the command line is a symbolic link. In this case, the link will be followed. So, if you wanted to start from the directory /local/bin, which was a symlink to /usr/bin, and used this command:

```
find -P /local/bin --name=foo
```

you would be unsuccessful. Instead, use this:

```
find -H /local/bin --name foo
```

Options

The most useful of these is likely to be -maxdepth:

```
find / -maxdepth 2 -name foo
```

This limits the search to go only two levels below the path given on the command line. So, this would find /usr/bin/foo but not /usr/local/bin/foo.

-mount is also useful, because it sets find to ignore directories on other filesystems; if you have / and /home on different filesystems, you can search just one or the other. For example, you can use it to check how many .bk files you have lying around in the / filesystem but not to look for those in /home:

```
find / -mount -name '*.bk'
```

■ **Note** If you're searching an MS-DOS file tree or a CD-ROM, use the -noleaf option to avoid an optimization that doesn't work on these filesystems.

Expressions

The real power of find lies in the breadth of available expressions:

- -amin n, -atime n: Finds the file last accessed n minutes ago, or n × 24 hours ago.

- -cmin n, -ctime n: Finds the file status last changed n minutes ago, or n × 24 hours ago.

- -mmin n, -mtime n: Finds the file last modified n minutes ago, or n × 24 hours ago.

■ **Note** With the time options, a value of n means exactly n, +n means more than n, and -n means less than n.

- find / -mmin -10: Returns all files in the / filesystem that were modified in the last ten minutes.

- -fstype type: Returns files that are on a filesystem of this type. Valid values include ufs, tmp, nfs, and mfs.

- -name foo: Searches for files whose name matches this shell pattern; so, wildcards and anything else the shell deals with can be used. The following will find your accounting files if you lose them!

  find /home/juliet -name 'accounts*'

- -iname foo: Like -name, but case insensitive.

- -regexp foo: Searches for files whose whole path (not just the filename) matches the regexp foo. The regexp type is by default emacs regexps.

■ **Note** Always quote patterns (so, find / -name 'foo*') to avoid the shell expanding the wild characters.

You can also search for files by type (-type filetype) and size (-size m), as well as by the user (-user username) or group (-group groupname) that owns them.

■ **Note** You can use the exec option with find to run a particular command on the files returned, but it's much more flexible to use xargs, as described in the next recipe.

8-5. Using xargs

xargs is an incredibly useful and powerful command. Basically, it takes a list of strings as input and then executes your chosen command on every string in that list:

```
xargs command
```

Often the input will be filenames, but they don't have to be. It's most commonly used to execute one command on the output from another command:

```
command1 | xargs command2
```

However, you can pipe any kind of input into it, and xargs will do its best to operate on that. The most commonly used command from which xargs takes input is find.

■ **Note** find has a built-in -exec option, but xargs is more efficient (because it operates on groups of filenames rather than on each filename in turn as is the default case with find), and in general the syntax is also clearer to read on the command line.

A couple of options that are useful for testing are -t, which echoes the command before executing it (so you can keep an eye on what's happening and hit Ctrl-C if something is going wrong!), and -p, which echoes it and asks for confirmation.

find with xargs

Use find to locate what you're looking for (see the previous recipe), and use xargs to run the same command on each of the things found.

Traditionally, an advantage to xargs was its ability to handle long command lines before failing, unlike some other commands. For example, the following command is intended to remove all tmp/*.mp3 files (and ignore any subdirectories) but can fail with an "Argument list too long" message:

```
rm `find tmp -maxdepth 1 -name '*.mp3'`
```

The following alternative using xargs does the same thing but avoids the problem by batching arguments:

```
find tmp -maxdepth 1 -name '*.mp3' | xargs rm
```

More modern kernels (since 2.6.23) shouldn't have this issue, but it's wise to make your scripts as portable as possible, and the xargs version is also easier on the eye.

The -n option allows you to manually batch arguments. This line will pass one argument at a time to rm:

```
find tmp -maxdepth 1 -name '*.mp3' -maxdepth 1 | xargs -n1 rm
```

This is particularly useful if you're using the -p option because you can confirm one file at a time rather than all at once.

Filenames containing whitespace can cause problems, because the whitespace is usually taken to denote the end of a filename. xargs and find can deal with this, using GNU extensions to both in order to break on the null character rather than on whitespace:

```
find tmp -maxdepth 1 -name *.mp3 -print0 | xargs -0 rm
```

You must use these options (-print0 for find, -0 for xargs) on both find and xargs or on neither (don't mix the two!), or you'll get odd results.

Another common use of xargs with find is to combine it with grep. For example, the following will search all the *.pl files in the current directory and subdirectories and print the names of any that don't have a line starting with use strict.

```
find . -name '*.pl' | xargs grep -L '^use strict'
```

Enforce good practice in your scripting! (See recipe 1-6.)

xargs and File Contents

It can also be useful to pipe the contents of a file into xargs as input, rather than piping in the output of a command. The following would take the arguments listed in the file diff-files in groups of two and run diff on them:

```
xargs -t -n2 diff < diff-files
```

So, if the diff-files file consisted of this:

```
sample1 alternate1
sample2 alternate2
```

then xargs would run the following:

```
diff sample1 alternate1
diff sample2 alternate2
```

This can be a quick way of comparing large numbers of files. (Use -p instead of -t to get a pause after each diff as well as an echo of the command.)

You can also use a listings file and xargs to concatenate the contents of those files:

```
xargs cat < list-of-files > files-contents
```

This will take input from list-of-files and cat each file in turn into files-contents.

■ **Note** You can generate list-of-files using xargs as well! The following would get all of your LaTeX source files in the current directory into one list, ready to be stuck together:

```
find . -maxdepth 1 -name '*.tex' | xargs echo > list-of-files
```

Moving Files

You can use xargs if you need to rename lots of files (such as with datestamping). This command line will rename each file in the current directory from filename.txt to 20080815-filename.txt:

```
ls | xargs -I {} mv {} 20080815-{}
```

This works because {} is a placeholder meaning "the current argument." (You can use xxx or yyy or any other string instead of {} if you want, as well, and it'll do exactly the same thing.) -I implies -n1, because you want to act on each file individually.

Or you might want to move all the files in directory 1 into directory 2:

```
ls dir1 | xargs -I {} -t mv dir1/{} dir2/{}
```

It's an incredibly powerful tool.

Note You can also use these tricks for other commands. For example, if you have a file containing a list of IP addresses, then this command would run nmap on each IP address at a time:

```
cat iplist | xargs -n1 nmap -sV
```

■ ■ ■

## CHAPTER 9

Working with Text in Files

Sysadmins spend a lot of time paging through text files. In this chapter, the first recipe shows how to use more and less seamlessly on files with different sorts of compression. sed and awk are also useful tools when dealing with text files, and Perl can do even more, especially if you get to grips with some of its command-line options. ASCII isn't the only game in town anymore, though. The later recipes in this chapter look at ways of dealing with UTF-8 to get all the other characters you might conceivably want. Finally, some files aren't text at all but might contain useful information. The final recipe discusses some ways of extracting text from binaries, which can be very useful when bug hunting.

9-1. Using more, less, and Compressed Files

less is a significantly better-featured version of the text pager more. Perhaps most obviously, less allows you to move backward through its output by hitting b (whereas more goes forward only). You can also use the following vi-like commands to navigate through output when using less:

- d, u: Moves forward, backward half a screen.

- j, k: Moves forward, backward one line.

- F: Keeps rereading file and going forward in it. This acts very much like tail -f.

- R: Repaints the screen, discarding buffered input. If the file has changed since you started looking at it, you'll get the new information.

- /, ?: Searches forward, backward. Use Ctrl-K between / or ? and the search term to highlight matches but not move the cursor.

- {, (, [: Finds matching close bracket for the first open {, (, or [in the top line of the screen. (Use k and j to get to the correct line to use this.) This is useful when paging through code.

- m A: Sets mark A at the current cursor point. This is useful when paging through code or other complicated files if you need to compare parts of the file that are more than a screen apart.

- ' A: Goes to mark A (set with m).

- h: Shows help.

■ **Note** Many modern Linux systems substitute less for more automatically. In other words, more is either symlinked to the less binary, or the less binary is used directly.

So, less is great for paging through text files and very flexible, but it won't automatically deal with compressed (zipped or gzipped) text files unless your system has already made the changes I suggest here or something similar, which is the case in recent versions of Ubuntu. This can be a nuisance, particularly when many of the files in /usr/share/doc are gzipped. It's a nuisance to have to run gunzip first, especially because this then leads to half the files being uncompressed and half still compressed.

A straightforward alternative is zless, which will deal seamlessly with gzip, compress, or pack files, allowing you to page through them without having to unzip them:

```
zless file.gz
```

It also handles uncompressed files, and contrary to what's said on the man page, it appears to deal OK with input piped from stdin:

```
ls | zless
```

zless can't, however, handle files that have been tarred as well as zipped (file.tar.gz). This command will allow you to page through file.tar.gz without unpacking it beforehand and thus without leaving unzipped files lying around:

```
tar --to-stdout -zxf file.tar.gz | less
```

However, that's a bit of a mouthful (or keyboard full) to remember. Try this instead:

```
export LESSOPEN="|tar --to-stdout -zxf %s"
```

Now try this:

```
less file.tar.gz
```

You should be able to page through your file without any problems. In fact, this will deal with both uncompressed files and piped input, so you can set this variable in your .bashrc file. However, it won't work on plain .gz files. For those, you should still use zless. (Since this doesn't pick up the LESSOPEN environment variable, it will work as normal.)

If you regularly want to look at tar archives that aren't also zipped (for example, file.tar), you can set this to work the same trick for these files:

```
export LESSOPEN="|tar --to-stdout -xf %s"
```

Unfortunately, you can't have both variables set at the same time! To manage all the various sorts of files, you can, however, define a set of functions in your ~/.bashrc:

```
function tgless() { tar --to-stdout -zxf $1 | less; }
function tless() { tar --to-stdout -xf $1 | less; }
```

You can now use these commands, and all should work seamlessly:

```
less file.txt
tgless file.tar.gz
tless file.tar
zless file.gz
```

■ **Note** There's also a helper application, `lesspipe`, that you can use and that will handle both `.tar` and `.gz`. Since Ubuntu 8.04 `LESSOPEN` is set to use this by default.

9-2. Using the power of sed

sed is a powerful stream editor. It can edit on the fly, reading from a file or from standard input. It's incredibly complicated, and the man page is not helpful, but remember that you can learn to use it a little at a time. Anything you learn when using sed will come in handy when using regular expressions elsewhere, including in languages such as Perl and Ruby. If this quick run-through interests you, entire books have been written about sed from which you can get more information!

Importantly, sed is *not* interactive. You create your changes on the command line as a command and then pipe the file/input stream through. sed will output to stdout by default, or you can redirect it to a file:

```
sed command filename.txt > output.txt
```

It doesn't edit the existing file in place. You can tell it to do so with this:

```
sed command -ibak filename.txt
```

This will edit `filename.txt` in place and save a backup copy of the old file at `filename.txt.bak`.

One of its main uses from a sysadmin point of view is as part of a bash file or as part of a complicated command line.

■ **Note** Remember that sed operates line by line and command by command. So, it will perform all the commands it can on every line before moving on to the next line. It's important to think about the order you want commands to be performed in. If you want to change `foo bar` to `foo baz` and then each `foo` to `goo`, it's important to do it in that order, or there won't be any `foo bar` to find and alter.

9-2a. Deleting Lines

To delete lines, you use d as the command. For example, if you do an LDAP search, you will usually get a handful of comment lines at the start of the output. Here's an example:

```
# extended LDIF
#
# LDAPv3
# base <> with scope subtree
# filter: (uid=jkemp)
# requesting: ALL
#

# jkemp, People, example.com
dn: uid=jkemp,ou=People,dc=example,dc=com
```

If you want to do something with the information, it would be beneficial to lose at least those first eight lines. This command will do that:

```
ldapsearch "(uid=testuser)" | sed 1,8d
```

The syntax for a range is [first-line-#],[last-line-#].
sed's main power is in its regular expressions. To delete all lines that start with #, use this:

```
ldapsearch "(uid=testuser)" | sed '/^#/d'
```

The /pattern/ syntax is used to match regular expressions. ^ represents the start of the line. To also remove all the blank lines, use this:

```
ldapsearch "(uid=testuser)" | sed '/^#/d' | sed '/^$/d'
```

$ represents the end of the line, so here the pattern looked for is a line whose start and end have nothing between them.

9-2b. Substitutions

sed becomes more useful when you start using its editing capacity to edit within lines. The basic syntax for doing this is as follows:

```
sed -e 's/foo/bar/g' filename.txt
```

This will replace all occurrences of foo in filename.txt with bar. The g means that the change is made globally. Without it, only the first occurrence in each line will be edited.

This syntax can be incredibly powerful, because you can use regular expressions and back references with it. For example, say that you use server-side includes in your web pages, so you have lots of lines that look like this in your web site files for various values of filename (header, footer, and so on):

```
<!--#include virtual="/includes/filename.shtml" -->
```

However, for the local/ directory of the web tree, you now want to use a different set of includes, so you want to change filename.shtml to filename-local.shtml in all the files in this directory. This sed line will do the trick:

```
sed -i.bak 's/includes\/\(\w*\).shtml/includes\/\1-local.shtml/' local/*.html
```

The -i.bak edits the file in place, as shown previously. This will also keep a filename.bak backup copy of the original file; to omit this, just use -i. The matched brackets \(and \) mark off the back references. So, the first section looks for the following and then saves filename as the first back reference:

```
includes/filename.shtml
```

The forward slash has to be escaped with a backslash (thus \/) to avoid it being interpreted as the terminator of the search pattern. \w is any word character (alphanumerics plus underscore), and \w* means any number of word characters, terminated with .shtml. See Table 9-1 for a quick description of regexp syntax in sed.

In the second half of the substitution, \1 refers to the first back reference (the file name). So, as required, you get filename.shtml being replaced with filename-local.shtml. Note that you don't have the g option at the end, because there should be only one file name per include line.

___

■ **Note** To make the forward and backward slashes a little less confusing here, you can use another character for the search/replace delimiter, such as s###g instead of s///g. So, the previous command line would become the following:

```
sed -i.bak 's#includes/\(\w*\).shtml#includes/\1-local.shtml#' local/*.html
```

___

Table 9-1. sed Regexp Syntax

Character	Description
.	Any character on the input line.
^	Doesn't match a character but represents the start of the line.
$	Doesn't match a character but represents the end of the line.
\	Use to escape special meaning. \. means a literal ., and \/ means a literal /.
\(\)	Use to mark off a back reference in the first part of the expression.
\n (where n is a number 1–9)	The nth back reference in the previous part of the expression (see the previous table entry and main recipe), as in \1.
exp*	Zero or more strings matching the expression exp (so A* matches zero or more *A* characters).

Character	Description
exp+	One or more strings matching the expression exp (so A+ matches one or more *A* characters).
exp?	Zero or one strings matching the expression exp (so A? matches zero or one *A* characters).
[A-Za-z0-9]	Any alphanumeric character (A–Z, a–z, 0–9).
\w	Any word character (A–Z, a–z, 0–9, plus the underscore).
\W	Any nonword character (punctuation except underscore and space characters).
\d	Any digit character.
\t	Tab.
\n	Newline.
\b	A word boundary: matches if the character to the left is a word character and the character to the right is not, or vice versa.
\B	Not a word boundary: matches if the characters to right and left are both word characters or nonword characters.

You can also make the replacement only on particular lines:

```
sed -e '1,20s/foo/bar/g' test.txt
```

▓ **Note** Remember that sed works only on a line at a time. If you're searching for a long phrase that might break across lines, then you may end up missing some of them. It's possible to use the hold buffer to read multiple lines into memory and check them. See http://www.grymoire.com/Unix/Sed.html for more on this.

9-2c. Appending, Inserting, and Changing Lines

If you have an LDAP setup, you may want to add a line to an entry or to multiple entries. See Chapter 2 for discussion of how to query LDAP, but once you have a file containing the DN of the entries that you want to change in this format:

```
dn: cn=machine1,ou=Hosts,dc=example,dc=com
dn: cn=machine2,ou=Hosts,dc=example,dc=com
```

you can use sed to add further lines. So, if you want to add the following (the -- is a record delimiter):

```
changetype: add
objectclass: localDesktop
--
```

you can use this sed line:

```
sed 'a\changetype: add\nobjectclass: localDesktop\n--' ldapmodify.ldif
```

As it stands, this will also insert the line after any blank lines you may have at the end of your file. To avoid this, use a match first:

```
sed '/dn/ a\changetype: add\nobjectclass: localDesktop\n--' ldapmodify.ldif
```

This will match for the characters dn anywhere in the line and then add the relevant lines after only the lines that match.

To add the specified line before rather than after the searched-for lines, use \i instead of \a.

▓ **Note** http://www.grymoire.com/Unix/Sed.html gives a very useful full sed tutorial.

9-3. Using awk: Snippets and Quick Reference

awk is a command-line text-processing language that, like sed (see recipe 9-1), can be plugged into command lines to process text input and send the output either to files or to another program. It's a great little tool, and it is in fact a complete programming language, but if you're doing more than one or two lines in it, you should probably be using Perl instead. As always with Linux, use the right tool for the job. Technically on most Linux systems you'll be using gawk (the GNU version of awk), but invoking it as awk is fine and normal.

This is the simplest general form of an awk program:

```
awk [search pattern] { [program actions] } file
```

The default action is to print, so if you omit the action, awk will just print the lines that match the search pattern:

```
awk /juliet/ mylist.txt
```

This will print all lines of the file mylist.txt that contain the word juliet. As with sed (recipe 9-2), use forward slashes to delimit the pattern.

One of the advantages of awk is that you can use it on files that contain table-type data, for example, the /etc/passwd file. If you're moving to LDAP, you might want a list of the home directories that users on each system have. To get a list of home directories with their users, you can use this:

```
# cat /etc/passwd | awk -F: '{print $1 "\n" $6}'
```

-F: sets the field delimiter as : (by default it's whitespace between nonwhitespace characters).

You can also use NF, which is a built-in variable that means the number of fields in the line. $NF gives the value of the last field in the record.

To find out what shells are in use in your system and how many users use each, use this:

```
cat /etc/passwd | awk -F: '{print $NF}' | sort | uniq -c | sort -rn
```

Again, you set the field delimiter to : and then print the last field in each record. These are sorted into order, and then uniq -c counts each unique value. Finally, the output from uniq (which will be a shell name and a count for that shell) is sorted into reverse numerical order. That is, the most popular shell is shown first.

If you want to kill all of a particular user's processes at once, you can pipe ps output into awk and use that output to tell kill what to do:

```
# ps axu | grep jkemp | kill -9 `awk {print $2}`
```

This will kill -9 any process belonging to jkemp. This is pretty extreme, so you'd want to be certain that jkemp isn't going to lose any data or that they shouldn't be doing whatever they're doing!

■ **Note** pkill -9 -u jkemp would also do this, but awk is obviously more flexible than pkill, which is a single-use tool.

You can use awk to determine the total size of the JPG files in a particular directory, perhaps to see whether it's worth splitting the JPG files off into a separate directory housed on another disk.

```
ls -l *.jpg | awk '{s+=$5} END {print "Total size: " s}'
```

This takes the fifth field (which is the size of the file) from each line, sums it, and prints the total.

■ **Note** If you have ls aliased to ls -h (to use human-readable sizes rather than block sizes), you'll need to unalias it with unalias ls before using this command line.

To get a rough idea of the popularity of various pages of your website, you can use this one-liner:

```
$ cat /var/log/apache2/access.log | awk '{print $7}' | sort | uniq -c | sort -rn | head -20
```

The access log is space-delimited, and field 7 (in a GET or POST request) will be the page demanded. This data is then piped through sort, the number of occurrences of each unique value (each page) is provided with uniq -c, and this is reverse-order (that is, highest first) sorted. -head 20 means that you display only the first 20 lines to avoid the very long tail of the files accessed a couple of times. Your output will look a bit like this:

```
975 /
533 /~jsmith/mis/nadsat.html
486 /favicon.ico
291 /rt
239 /robots.txt
215 /cgi-bin/jkemp/bugreport.cgi
```

9-3a. awk, if, and Strings

You can search for a string in a particular field and print only that. For example, to print a list of all users who have tcsh as their shell (perhaps so that you can e-mail them to suggest they switch to bash...), use this:

```
$ cat /etc/passwd | awk -F: '{if ($7 ~ /tcsh/) print $1;}'
```

This sets the field divider to : and then prints the first field (username) if the seventh field (shell) matches tcsh. Alternatively, you could generalize this by searching for users whose shell is *not* bash:

```
$ cat /etc/passwd | awk -F: '{if ($7 !~ /bash/) print $1}'
```

The if syntax is as follows:

```
'{if (condition) action; }'
```

You can also use the if/else syntax:

```
'{ if (condition) action; else action; }'
```

See recipe 9-2b for regexp syntax, which is the same as for sed.

9-4. Manipulating File Contents with Perl

The syntax for reading from a file in Perl is shown in this script, which reads from the auth.log file (which logs authorization attempts) and prints to the output file only those lines that do not match the local domain, thus reducing the amount of file you need to check for dubious login attempts.

```
01  #!/usr/bin/perl -w
02  use strict;
03  my $inputfile = "/var/log/auth.log";
04  my $outputfile = "~/authlogout.txt";
05  my $searchstring = "192.168";
06  open (INPUT, "<$inputfile");
07  open (OUTPUT, ">$outputfile");
08  while (<INPUT>) {
09      print OUTPUT if ! /$searchstring/;
10  }
11  close INPUT;
12  close OUTPUT;
```

This snippet will print only the lines that match your search string (set in line 05) to the output file. (Alternatively, use awk to do this; see recipe 9-3.) To append to OUTPUT rather than overwriting, replace line 07 with the following:

```
open (OUTPUT, ">>outputfile");
```

You can put a + in front of the > or < to indicate that you want both read and write access to the file. +< is almost always preferred for read-write updates, because the +> mode would clobber the file first, so there won't be anything there to read from.

9-4a. Perl, Files, and Command-Line Options

A couple of command-line options make Perl particularly useful for editing files, enabling you to do some quite powerful things without having to leave the command line.

Specifically, the -p option sets Perl up as a stream editor, rather like sed (see recipe 9-2) and awk (see recipe 9-3). It prints out each line that it processes as it processes it. -n does the same thing except it suppresses the printing (so if you want output, you have to put in a print statement). This one-liner does exactly the same thing as the previous script:

```
perl -ne 'print if ! /192.168/' < /var/log/auth.log > testout.txt
```

It checks each line of /var/log/auth.log, and if it doesn't find part of the line that matches 192.168, it prints it to standard out, which is then redirected to testout.txt.

Unlike a traditional editor, because Perl is reading the file in only a single line at a time, it can deal with enormous files quite happily and without any memory impact. So, if you have a couple of months of Apache log files to deal with, you can search through them and edit them with a Perl one-liner like this, where you might have to wait for a noticeable time to get vim to open up the file.

To some extent, this does much the same as sed and awk. Perl syntax may be more familiar to you, and Perl is a little more powerful. However, its power also means that if you're doing something straightforwardly text-based, sed or awk may require less coding. To some extent, it depends on which you get along with best!

You can edit a file with Perl as well. For example, say someone wants a long document on a web page to have all the references to *widgets* changed to *wodgets*. Use this one-liner:

```
perl -pe 's/widget/wodget/g' < biglist.html > newbiglist.html
```

The g at the end of the search command means that the search and replace is to be done globally. Otherwise, it'll just be done on the first instance of every line. We use -p here because there's no explicit print statement in the code. We want each line to be printed with the change made (any lines that are not changed will also be printed, which again is what we want here).

■ **Note** You can edit a file in place with the -i option, overwriting the previous version. However, if something goes wrong, you've lost your file, and you'll have to restore from backup or from your version control system repository. If you use -i.bak, it'll save a backup copy as filename.bak before making any changes.

But if you've had to change something in one file on the web server, you'll probably have to do it in more than one file. Happily, this also works with shell wildcards. So, to make the previous change to every file in a particular directory, use this:

```
perl -i.bak -pe 's/widget/wodget/g' *.html
```

Or to do this recursively through all the directories (this might be useful if you change the name of your main CSS file, for example), use this:

```
find . -type f | xargs perl -p -i.old -e 's/old.css/new.css/g'
```

The -type f argument to find limits this to files, so you won't get errors from Perl trying to do this substitution in directories. You can also use Perl to split columned data, in much the same way as you can use awk. This is the -a option, which adds an implicit split (by default on whitespace) inside the while(<>) loop that -p provides. As with awk, you can change the character to split on with -F. So, to get the user and home directory information out of /etc/passwd, use this:

```
# perl -an -F: -e 'print $F[0], "\n", $F[5], "\n";' /etc/passwd
```

9-5. When It's Not ASCII: Dealing with UTF-8

Before talking about how Linux handles various sorts of text, let's establish what text encodings are available:

- *ASCII*: This is the most basic encoding available. It uses 7 bits to encode the 128 characters that it uses, which means that the eighth bit of every byte is left empty. It's limited, but you can rely on ASCII characters being viewable and available very nearly everywhere. (The exception is certain sorts of mainframe, but if you're using these you'll know about it!)

- *ISO-8859-1*: Given that ASCII has only 128 characters (including 33 mostly obsolete nonprinting characters), all the accented characters and some other nonletter standard characters (such as the U.K. pound sign) are missing from it. Thus, people started creating extensions to it. The first extension, aka Latin 1, was ISO-8859-1, which broadly speaking deals with Western Europe. There are lots more similarly numbered encodings, such as ISO-8859-15, and so on.

- *UTF-8*: The extensions system is cumbersome and requires multiple encodings (which may be incompatible) to be stored on your system. UTF-8 aims to fix this by encoding *all* available characters, using between one and four bytes. Western-style characters all fit within the first two bytes. Everything else in the Basic Multilingual Plane, which covers almost all characters in common use in any language, fits within three bytes. The fourth byte is used for characters in the other character planes (various less-common characters from Asian scripts, historical languages, and noncharacter notations such as musical notation). UTF-8 is very space-efficient for Western-style languages and less so for other languages.

- *UTF-16*: This is another way of encoding Unicode characters, using two-byte "words" (almost all characters in common usage fit within one such word). Unlike UTF-8, UTF-16 is incompatible with ASCII files. A legacy ASCII-only program can probably handle UTF-8, but it can't do anything with UTF-16, so programs must be Unicode-aware. Windows and Java are both UTF-16 based, but both use UTF-8 to represent program code for this reason. You're unlikely to encounter UTF-16 in a context where you actually need to do anything with it, whereas UTF-8 is more likely to show up.

- *UTF-32*: Fixed-width version of the Unicode encoding. It's space-inefficient (because it always uses four bytes) and very little used, so you're unlikely to encounter it.

Historically speaking, Linux basically operated on ASCII or, at a push, one of the language-specific extensions such as ISO-8859-1. Increasingly these days, though, UTF-8 is supported instead, so it's a good idea to switch to it wherever possible. Using UTF-8 means that you don't have to use different and incompatible language-specific extensions of ASCII. You can just use the same character set everywhere. It's a particular boon if you have multiple languages on your system or you have users who need to deal natively with multiple languages.

■ **Note** Terminal emulators, and so on, don't offer full Unicode functionality (for example, high-quality typesetting), but the support that is provided means that the Chinese and Japanese ideograms (well as some other alphabets and nonalphabetic languages) can be represented.

To enable UTF-8 support, select a suitable encoding:

```
> export LANG=en_GB.UTF-8
```

9-5a. Entering UTF-8 Characters in X11

First, you'll need to check that you're using a locale that supports UTF-8. Type locale to get a list of supported locales. Mine looks like this on one machine:

```
LANG="en_GB.UTF-8"
LC_COLLATE="en_GB.UTF-8"
LC_CTYPE="en_GB.UTF-8"
LC_MESSAGES="en_GB.UTF-8"
LC_MONETARY="en_GB.UTF-8"
LC_NUMERIC="en_GB.UTF-8"
LC_TIME="en_GB.UTF-8"
LC_ALL=
```

If you don't see the appropriate UTF-8 line on there, you can use dpkg-reconfigure locales and select the correct UTF-8 locale from the list. You may need to log out and back in again for this to take effect.

In GTK+ 2 (so this should work in Gnome Terminal, Mozilla, Firefox, and possibly other applications), you can enter a UTF-8 character using its hex code. Hold down Ctrl and Shift, and enter the four-digit code. So, holding Ctrl-Shift while entering 0123 will give you a Latin g with a cedilla over it (ġ).

This is a bit of a nuisance for any characters you enter regularly, however. For these, you're better off extending your keyboard mapping with xmodmap. (Warning: this can be complicated!)

The first step is to find out what your current mapping is. The command xmodmap -pm will give you output that looks a bit like this:

```
xmodmap:  up to 2 keys per modifier, (keycodes in parentheses):

shift       Shift_L (0x40),  Shift_R (0x44)
lock        Caps_Lock (0x41)
control     Control_L (0x43),  Control_R (0x46)
mod1        Mode_switch (0x42),  Mode_switch (0x45)
mod2        Meta_L (0x3f),  Meta_R (0x47)
mod3
mod4
mod5
```

This tells you what modifiers are currently in use. Shift is defined as either the L or R shift keys, similarly for Ctrl and meta (Alt). Caps Lock is obvious. Mode_switch is usually the Alt-Gr key; if you're using a Windows keyboard, this may be mapped to the two Windows keys (between Ctrl and Alt). You can check by running xev and hitting the relevant key. The keycode will be given.

■ **Note** xmodmap gives the keycode in hex in this section but later in decimal; xev uses decimal. To convert, use bc:

```
ibase=10
obase=16
66
42
ibase=16
obase=10
42
66
```

ibase sets the input base, and obase sets the output base. So, the first three lines set the input in decimal, set the output in hex, and ask for the value of 66 (decimal) in hex (which is 42). The next lines set input in hex, output in decimal, and ask for 42 (hex) in decimal (which of course is 66!).

If you want to change the Mode_switch key (or any other key), put a line in the file `~/.Xmodmap` like this:

```
keycode 119 = Mode_switch Mode_switch
```

119 is the F12 key.

Next, take a look at your existing keyboard map, with xmodmap -pk | less. The output will start off a bit like this:

```
There are 4 KeySyms per KeyCode; KeyCodes range from 8 to 255.

    KeyCode     Keysym (Keysym) ...
    Value        Value   (Name)  ...

       8        0x0061 (a)     0x0041 (A)     0x00e5 (aring)  0x00c5 (Aring)
       9        0x0073 (s)     0x0053 (S)     0x00df (ssharp) 0x00cd (Iacute)
      10        0x0064 (d)     0x0044 (D)     0x08ef (partialderivative)      0x00ce
(Icircumflex)
      11        0x0066 (f)     0x0046 (F)     0x08f6 (function)    0x00cf (Idiaeresis)
      12        0x0068 (h)     0x0048 (H)     0x01ff (abovedot)    0x00d3 (Oacute)
```

The first column is the keycode (in decimal, as discussed earlier). The remaining columns give the four-digit hex code of the symbol that will be entered via this key being pressed in various circumstances (and then the actual name of the symbol in brackets). The first column is just the key, the second is *key*-Shift, the third is *key*-Mode_switch (usually Alt-Gr, as discussed earlier), and the fourth is *key*-Mode_switch-Shift.

So here, my A key has keycode 8, which will produce *a* on its own, *A* with Shift, å with Alt-Gr, and Å with Alt-Gr+Shift.

OK, let's say that we want to change one of these settings: I want my d key (keycode 10) to produce a degree symbol (°) when hit together with Alt-Gr. Create or edit a file called `~/.Xmodmap` that looks like this:

```
keysym d = d NoSymbol 0x00B0        NoSymbol
```

This sets the key to produce d when hit on its own, nothing when hit with Shift (so the existing keymap will apply instead, and you'll get D), ° when hit with Alt-Gr, and whatever the existing keymap says when hit with Alt-Gr+Shift (in this case, ï). Load this keyfile with the following, and give it a go:

```
xmodmap ~/.Xmodmap
```

In this case, you could also replace 0x00B0 with the name of the symbol (degree) for the same result, which might be more readable. Tables of UTF-8 hex codes are available online.

> ■ **Note** gdm/xdm/etc should source ~/.Xmodmap on login. If you find that your keymap isn't available on login and you have to load it manually with xmodmap ~/.Xmodmap, add that command to your ~/.bashrc or ~/.bash_profile so it will run automatically. This has the added advantage that it'll also be run when you log in via ssh. (This will be true only if using ssh -X, that is, if hooking into the X server. Otherwise, you'll need to change the console keymap.)

Another input method for UTF-8 is digraphs, as supported by the program screen. Hit Ctrl-A and then Ctrl-V, and you'll get the prompt Enter digraph. Various digraphs are available for screen (unfortunately you can't add your own). For example, ?? will give you an upside-down question mark (¿). Alternatively, you can use U and the hex code to enter any arbitrary Unicode character. You may find that this doesn't work for you; this is probably because of a lack of support in the terminal program through which you're running screen.

9-5b. Entering UTF-8 Characters in Vim

In Vim, you can enter UTF-8 characters using their hex code, in a similar way to what's available with GTK+. For example, the following will give you a Latin g with a cedilla over it (ġ):

```
Ctrl-V u 0123
```

However, an easier mode (since vim supports UTF-8 natively) is to set up your X system to support entering UTF-8 characters. Then vim will simply handle them correctly as they're passed in. See the previous recipe for this. The hex code method may be useful if you only occasionally want a particular unusual character (that is, one not in your native character set).

You can also use digraphs, which enable you to type a character, backspace, and then another character and have a UTF-8 character generated. To use these, put this line in your ~/.vimrc file:

```
set digraph
```

To do it temporarily, type :set digraph in command mode in vim. To show the digraphs you have set, type this in command mode:

```
:digraphs
```

Typing (for example) U <backspace> " will give you Ü.
You can set your own digraphs using this:

```
:dig[raphs] {char1}{char2} {number} ...
```

where number is the decimal representation of the character you want. Use this on the vim command line, or add it to your ~/.vimrc file.

■ **Note** If you find digraphs annoying (if you regularly have to backspace to correct single characters, you may end up inserting them by accident), type `:unset digraphs` in command mode (or add `unset digraphs` to your `~/.vimrc` file), and use the following:

```
Ctrl-K char1 char2
```

instead of the following to enter digraphs:

```
char1 backspace char2
```

This method is always available, even when digraphs aren't set.

9-6. Getting Readable Text from Binaries

Sometimes it can be necessary to see whether you can extract useful string (text) data from binary files. A good sign that you have a binary file is when you try to cat it and you get a warning that it may be a binary file, although not all systems give you this warning. (Debian lenny doesn't, but current Ubuntu does.) If you go ahead with the cat, you'll get a screenful of gibberish.

■ **Note** If your terminal does get scrambled, type one of these, even if you can't see what you're typing:

```
setterm -reset
echo [Ctrl-V] [Ctrl-O]
```

This sort of terminal scrambling does seem to be less common than it used to be. You can also use `cat -v` to get better output from binary files.

One case may be if you want to get text information out of a proprietary file format. In some cases, your best bet may be to open it in open source software that reads the file format (such as OpenOffice.org for Word documents). However, this can be slow if all you need is text data.

For Word documents, the utility `antiword` (Debian/Ubuntu package antiword, installed with sudo apt-get install antiword) is good:

```
antiword file.doc | less
```

If you want to save it to a file, use this:

```
antiword file.doc > file.txt
```

That's no good if you're looking at something like information from a crash file or a core dump. You may just be able to eyeball it, using cat or a text editor, but this is tough on the eyes.

```
od -c filename
```

This will convert bytes to ASCII characters wherever possible, but this is rarely terribly useful, unfortunately. strings is more likely to be helpful. It grabs any ASCII strings it can out of the file it's pointed at.

```
strings filename | less
```

For example, you may also be in the position of encountering a random binary file and trying to work out where it came from and what it is or does. Getting any readable text information out of the binary can be helpful here. If you're very lucky, you might get help information out of it (try strings /bin/ls | less, and note the help information near the end of the output). To simplify this a bit, you can pipe the output of strings through grep to look for something specific:

```
> strings /bin/ls | grep -A 5 -n Usage
522: Usage: %s [OPTION]... [FILE]...
523: List information about the FILEs (the current directory by default).
524: Sort entries alphabetically if none of -cftuvSUX nor --sort.
525: Mandatory arguments to long options are mandatory for short options too.
526:   -a, --all                  do not ignore entries starting with .
527:   -A, --almost-all           do not list implied . and ..
```

The -A 5 option to grep gives five lines of context after the match is found; -n prints the line number. For example, it's very useful to quickly find out which libraries a particular binary needs:

```
$ strings /usr/bin/latex | grep lib | grep '\.so'
```

The grep '\.so' part is there to restrict the grep lib returns to only those lines that refer to particular binaries (lib*.so.*) rather than also getting lines such as the error lines from libpng that are returned on my system! The \ is needed to treat the . as a literal rather than as meaning "any character."

■ ■ ■

## CHAPTER 10

Things Going In, Things Going Out

This chapter looks at changing your keymapping to match your keyboard, or using special keys; at automating printer setup and useful tricks for printing text files; and at remote graphical login, which can be very useful for certain sorts of debugging. As the title says, it's a collection of things that go into, and things that go out of, your machines.

10-1. Changing Keymaps in X

If you have a fancy brand-name keyboard, you may well have various nonstandard keys on it that aren't as a rule mapped to anything useful under Linux, which is a bit of a waste of a potentially nice feature. It's possible to write additions to your keymap to change that.

Note There is a difference between the console keymap and the xorg/XFree86 keymap. Changing the console keymap will change the xorg keymap as well, so it's often useful to change the console keymap. See recipe 10-2 for a situation where you just change the xorg keymap using xmodmap and xbindkeys, and see recipe 9-5a for more discussion of how xmodmap works and how you can change it.

The first task is to find out what keycode is being sent by the key you want to remap. For example, here I'll show how to remap Shift-2 to send " (like a British keyboard) rather than @ (like a U.S. keyboard), and I'll show how to remap Shift-' to send @ instead of " to match it. Look for your existing keymap file in /usr/share/keymaps/i386. In some systems, you'll find a keymap set in /etc/console/boottime.kmap.gz, and you could take a look at that file to see which keymap it says it is. In Ubuntu, try looking at /etc/default/console-setup or in the /etc/console-setup/ directory. Otherwise, you will probably know which keymap you're using already!

■ **Note** To temporarily change a keymap (for example, to try Dvorak!), you can use the following:

```
loadkeys /path/to/keymap.kmap.gz
```

Or in Debian/Ubuntu, to install a new keymap, use the following:

```
install-keymap /path/to/keymap.kmap.gz
```

Here let's assume we're using us.map.gz. Unzip it (gunzip us.map.gz), and open it in your preferred editor. Look for the (separate) lines:

```
keycode   3 = two       at      at     nul       nul
keycode  40 = apostrophe        quotedbl
```

and change them to the following:

```
keycode   3 = two       quotedbl    quotedbl    nul      nul
keycode  40 = apostrophe        at
```

Save the file, and rezip it (gzip us.map). You may need to restart X and/or your virtual console for this change to take effect.

■ **Note** To find a keycode, you can use the showkey utility. Type showkey, and then hit whichever keys you want to get the keycodes for. showkey will automatically quit after no key has been hit for ten seconds.

10-2. Linking Keys to Programs

Some keyboards have extra keys (often before the function key line) that you may want to use. Or you might want to reprogram the function keys. You can set these up to launch particular programs.

Using either showkeys or xev (the graphical version of showkeys), first find the keycode of the extra keys that you want to reprogram. What you're looking for is the part of the line that gives the keycode value. Let's say it's 130. You'll also note that there's an XLookupString value given (if you're using xev), which for your currently unused keys should be a null string.

The first step is to use xmodmap to give a value to this unused key (this will appear as the XLookupString). We'll use a higher-number function key. Enter this line on the command line:

```
xmodmap -e 'keycode 130=F15'
```

Now rerun xev, and you should see F15 show up when you hit this key.

Next, you need to link F15 to a program-launch event. You can do this graphically (using the create shortcut option on your desktop, which will usually provide a space where you can specify a hotkey) if you want F15 to launch an application, or you can use xbindkeys. (If this isn't already installed on your system, use sudo apt-get install xbindkeys to install the Debian/Ubuntu package.)

Edit ~/.xbindkeysrc to look like this:

```
#Launch Firefox
"/usr/bin/firefox"
 F15
```

Now start xbindkeys. Your new F15 key should now launch Firefox.

To make this happen automatically, you need to create a script in the Autostart folder of your desktop. In KDE, this is ~/.kde/Autostart; in Gnome, you can save the script somewhere and then use the Administration ➤ Sessions menu item, or you can put the script straight into the folder ~/.config/autostart/.

The script will look like this:

```
#!/bin/sh
#file to map special keys.
xmodmap -e 'keycode 130=F15' #launch firefox
#xbindkeys links keys to applications; config in ~/.xbindkeysrc
xbindkeys
```

The xmodmap line has a comment at the end of the line, which is not really necessary here but is useful if you're remapping multiple keys.

Make the script executable with chmod u+x ~/.kde/Autostart/keymapping. Now restart X, and you should find that your new hotkey works as soon as your desktop has finished loading.

Note See recipe 9-5a for how to set keys to enter Unicode characters and for more information about how xmodmap works.

10-3. Automating Printer Setup with lpadmin

You can admin your printers via a CUPS graphical interface by pointing a browser at http://localhost:631. When challenged for a username and password, you can use root and the root password. However, this is impractical (or at least time-consuming) for installing multiple machines. Instead, you can use lpadmin to add your printers.

Whichever method of printer setup you use, you'll need to install the package containing the driver for your printer. Depending on your model of printer, several packages are available for Debian/Ubuntu. cups-driver-gutenprint is a good place to start; there is also a specific package (hpijs; and hpijs-ppds for the model-specific drivers) available for HP printers.

You'll then need to go looking in /usr/share/cups/model/ to locate the path for the driver for your particular printer. For example, for an HP LaserJet 4350, that would be as follows:

```
/usr/share/cups/model/HP/HP-LaserJet_4350-hpijs-pc13.ppd
```

■ **Note** These paths seem to change distressingly often! This was in use at time of writing; it may have changed by the time you read this. Take a look in the /usr/share/cups directory if this path doesn't work.

Now set up the printer like this:

```
# lpadmin -p print1 -L "Room 43" -D "HP LaserJet 4350" ↵
-P /usr/share/cups/model/hpijs/HP/HP-LaserJet_4350-hpijs.ppd.gz  ↵
-v lpd://post4.example.com/post4 -E
```

-p sets the printer name, -L the location, and -D a human-readable description field. -P gives the path to the printer driver, and -v sets the URI location. In this case, we're accessing the printer via LPD, which will almost certainly be what you want. -E enables the printer (meaning it will be open to accept jobs).

After this, you can use lpoptions to set up the default options. To check what options are available for a given printer, use this:

```
lpoptions -p print1 -l
```

Depending on your printer model, this might be a very long list! For options such as memory settings, you'll need to check your printer documentation (or get it to print an information sheet about itself—most printers should have this as an option from the menu buttons on the printer itself) to find out what values your specific printer has. The lpoptions command here just tells you what options can be set via this printer driver. Unfortunately, it's not very helpfully formatted; an example option will look like this:

```
TR-Duplex/Duplex: False *True
```

This first gives the name of the option (TR-Duplex) and how it's displayed in a GUI or web interface (Duplex). Then after the colon is the list of possible values (False or True). The starred one is the current setting. So to set this option, you'd use the following command:

```
lpoptions -p print1 -o TR-Duplex=True
```

You can also try lphelp print1, which produces a much more nicely formatted result; unfortunately, the lphelp script isn't available for Debian/Ubuntu but may be for other systems.

If your printers are duplex-compatible, you should make sure to set duplex as the default, to save paper; and you'll also want to set the default paper size (particularly if you're based in a country that doesn't use Letter as the default size!). Here's the lpoptions setup for my HP LaserJet 4350:

```
lpoptions -p print1 -o Duplex=DuplexNoTumble -o PageSize=A4 ↵
-o InputSlot=Auto InstalledMemory=Mem4
```

Again, -p is the printer name, and you use -o OptionName=OptionValue to set each option. InputSlot=Auto sets the input source to be automatically detected (this will usually mean the manual feed if there's paper in that and then the top tray). The InstalledMemory value is set by getting the option name from lpoptions as earlier and checking it against your printer specs.

Once you've set all of this stuff, you can create a script with two lines per printer (lpadmin to add the printer and then lpoptions to set its default options), and run it on every newly installed machine. The final line should be as follows to make sure that CUPS picks up the new printers:

```
/etc/init.d/cups restart
```

Finally, you can set the default printer. Either do this manually:

```
lpoptions -d printername
```

or give your script a command-line input, which takes the following as the default:

```
01  #!/bin/bash
02  if [ $# != 1 ]; then
03    echo "Script to install all printers and set default printer."
04    echo "Usage: $0 defaultprinter"
05    exit 1;
06  fi
07  defaultprinter=$1
08
09  lpadmin -p print1 -L "Room 43" -D "HP LaserJet 4350" -P ↩
      /usr/share/cups/model/hpijs/HP/HP-LaserJet_4350-hpijs.ppd.gz ↩
       -v  lpd://print1.example.com/print1 -E
10  lpadmin -p print2 -L "Room 243" -D "HP LaserJet 4350" -P ↩
      /usr/share/cups/model/hpijs/HP/HP-LaserJet_4350-hpijs.ppd.gz  ↩
      -v lpd://print2.example.com/print2 -E
11  lpoptions -p print1 -o Duplex=DuplexNoTumble -o PageSize=A4 ↩
      -o InputSlot=Auto InstalledMemory=Mem4
12  lpoptions -p print2 -o Duplex=DuplexNoTumble -o PageSize=A4 ↩
      -o InputSlot=Auto InstalledMemory=Mem4
13  lpoptions -d $defaultprinter
14  /etc/init.d/cupsys restart
```

Note To override the option settings for a single job, you can set options temporarily on the command line. For example, to print in simplex, for the printer we looked at earlier, use this:

```
lpr -P print1 -o TR-Duplex=False myfile.ps
```

10-4. Printing Text Files Readably

Occasionally you need to print a text file: notes to yourself, notes for someone else, or diff output that you want to be able to write on rather than having to use a screen. lp file.txt will straightforwardly dump the text to the printer, but that's often not very readable. Also, it usually wastes a lot of page space, and it may try to print outside the printable area of the page (meaning that parts are cut off).

The utility a2ps creates nice borders and by default prints two A5 pages on A4 landscape (you can change this with the various options). However, it doesn't do double spacing, which makes writing useful notes on the text difficult. The utility pr, however, does do double spacing but doesn't do the page structure stuff that a2ps does.

The solution is of course to stick them together:

```
pr -d -t filename.txt | a2ps --stdin filename
```

This will send output to your default printer. The -d switch does double spacing, and the -t switch suppresses the file name and page header (which come out untidily when piping into a2ps). The --stdin switch to a2ps then sets the page header/title as filename.

Note If using a2ps directly (rather than piping output from pr), it will automatically set the page header/title from the file name.

If you want to create a PostScript file instead so that you can check the layout of the output before printing it, use the -o switch to a2ps:

```
pr -d -t filename.txt | a2ps --stdin filename -o filename.ps
```

You can also double space text using sed:

```
sed G filename.txt | a2ps --stdin filename
```

For more information on sed, take a look at recipe 9-2.

Another option is enscript, which handles both double spacing and margins, as well as font size and other layout options. To double space plain text with a reasonable margin, use this:

```
enscript --word-wrap -s 16 --margins=72:72:30:30 -p out.ps foo.txt
```

--word-wrap wraps long lines at word boundaries (rather than in the middle of a word). -s 16 sets the baseline skip, which is the space between lines, to 16 points. The margins are set in the order left, right, top, and bottom. -p specifies the file to output to (use -P print1 to output to printer print1).

enscript has the advantage as well of handling Unicode, whereas a2ps does not support it at all.

10-5. Using ssh -X to Log in Remotely

The simplest way to get graphical access to a remote Linux machine is to log in via ssh using this:

```
ssh -X user@machine.example.com
```

However, the `sshd` daemon on the machine you're logging into has to be set up to allow this. Add this line to `/etc/ssh/sshd_config` on the remote machine, and restart `sshd` (`/etc/init.d/sshd restart`):

```
X11Forwarding  Yes
```

This allows you to start graphical programs from your logged-in terminal window, but it won't give you a desktop per se. You need to start everything from the command line. It's a good idea to start another `xterm` from the logged-in terminal window immediately, with `xterm&`, and then work from that so that your original window always has a command line available in case something goes wrong in the working window.

10-6. Using GDM to Log in Remotely

If you want to be able to fire up a full login screen remotely (and then kick off a full desktop by logging in from there), you can use `gdm`, the standard Gnome display manager, to handle this for you. The KDE version, `kdm`, will also do the same thing.

For `gdm`, edit `/etc/gdm/gdm.conf` on the remote machine (on some systems this may be located at `/etc/X11/gdm/gdm.conf`). For `kdm`, edit `/etc/kde3/kdm/kdmrc`. In both cases, you must add a line in the [Xdmcp] section so it reads as follows:

```
Enable=true
```

Or edit the `Enable` line appropriately if there's already one there. Save the file, and restart the display manager so the change will take effect.

■ **Note** You can also use the `gdmsetup` utility to configure `gdm` graphically, if you prefer.

On the client side, you can use Xnest, a nested X server, to connect. This is available as the `xnest-xorg` package for Debian/Ubuntu. Another option is Xephyr (the package `xserver-xephyr`). To use Xnest, type the following:

```
Xnest -query remotemachine.example.com -geometry 1280x1024 :1
```

You should get a login screen for your remote machine. You can give the IP address instead of the name if you prefer.

Troubleshooting

If you get a security error, try this on your local machine (this adds the machine to the allowed list) and then the `Xnest` line again:

```
xhost remotemachine.com
```

If you get a "Server is already active for display" error, check that you remembered to put :1 on the end. Otherwise, the server will default to :0, which conflicts with your existing desktop. You can also try :2 if there's a conflict with :1.

10-7. Using VNC or Similar to Log in Remotely

Virtual Network Computing (VNC) is the fuller-featured way of setting up the capability discussed in the previous recipe. But it's a little more hassle. For Debian/Ubuntu, you need to install the vnc4server package on the remote machine and the xvnc4viewer package on the client machine.

Setting up the server as shown here will again allow you to use GDM and VNC together so that you can both log in and log out of your remote machine. First edit the GDM config file at /etc/X11/gdm/gdm.conf. Then add or edit the RemoteGreeter line:

RemoteGreeter = /usr/bin/gdmgreeter

and add a line after the [xdmcp] line:

[xdmcp]
Enable=true

Next, edit /etc/services to add a VNC service. Add this line at the end of the file:

vnc   5900/tcp

Now create a file /etc/xinetd.d/vnc like this:

```
service vnc
{
      disable = no
      socket-type   = stream
      protocol      = tcp
      group         = tty
      wait          = no
      user          = nobody
      server = /usr/bin/Xvnc
      server_args   = -inetd -query localhost -geometry 1024x768 ↵
                      -depth 16 -once -fp unix/:7100 ↵
               -securitytypes=none
}
```

■ **Note** You can run multiple resolutions by adding extra lines to /etc/services. Here's an example:

vnc800 5901/tcp

This copies the `/etc/xinetd.d/vnc` file to `/etc/xinetd.d/vnc800` and then changes the `-geometry` section of the `server_args` line in this new file to `-geometry 800x600`.

Now use `chkconfig` to remove the `vncserver` startup links from the `init.d` directories (because you're now using `xinetd` to run it instead), stop it in case it's already running, and restart `xinetd`:

```
# chkconfig --level 2345 vncserver off
# /etc/init.d/vncserver stop
# /etc/init.d/xinetd restart
```

To connect, use this line on the client machine:

```
vncviewer remote.example.com:5900
```

That should be all you need to get a GDM login screen for your remote machine, running at 1024×768.

If you don't have access to `init` and `inetd`, you can also `ssh` to the machine and then run `xvncserver` from that session. This is a bit less maintainable than doing it as described. You can also use the client `vinaigre` for a slightly better-featured experience, but this isn't available for all systems: `vinaigre remote.example.com:5900`.

■ ■ ■

## CHAPTER 11

Tracking Down Bugs

Chances are you spend a fair amount of your working time in search of bugs. This chapter has some general notes about best practices for finding and fixing bugs quickly, information about useful tools (`diff`, `strace`, and `ltrace`) when bug hunting, and a couple of recipes on how to improve your system logging (so you can locate problems faster) and use logging data.

11-1. Saving Time

A sysadmin's basic aim when faced with a bug report is to track the problem down and fix it as soon as possible. Or, if fixing it will take a long time and the problem is urgent, you want to implement a temporary workaround.

If you're lucky, the person reporting the bug will have given you a good, clear description of exactly what they did, what is actually happening, and what they expected or wanted to happen instead. If you don't have this, then the first thing to do is to clarify these three things. You should do this with the user if at all possible or, if not, by experimenting yourself. Without a clear understanding of what the problem really is, you're at risk of wasting time—possibly a lot of time—finding and fixing something that may not be the real problem. Unfortunately, users aren't always good at explaining the issue immediately. We've all gotten those infuriating bug reports of the "X doesn't work" variety.

The following are good questions to ask when checking that you have a clear bug report:

- What commands/situations trigger the bug?

- What is the expected result?

- What is the actual result?

- Does it happen if you use a different machine? (This is particularly useful information in situations where some directories are on NFS and users are centralized.)

- Does it happen if you log in as a different user? (You'll probably have to find this out yourself, because most users have only a single login.)

- What have you and/or the user tried so far to fix it?

Note You may have heard of the idea of "teddy bear programming." There's a story told in *The Practice of Programming* (among other places) of a university computing support department that had a teddy bear sitting by the door. Students were allowed to take their problem to a human only if they'd already explained it to the bear. It was fairly common that the act of explaining the problem was sufficient to give the person doing the explaining another idea to try or a realization of what might be going wrong. A similar thing sometimes occurs, in my experience, when writing an e-mail to a mailing list and trying to describe the problem clearly and succinctly and anticipating possible queries. Explaining your problem to a co-worker can also work in the same way. The important point is that the act of talking it through can help you come to a better understanding of what's going on, or even to a solution.

Once you have a clear understanding of the problem, the next thing to do is to try to narrow down the problem space. Generate a test case from your initial bug report, and then shrink the test case down as far as you can while still demonstrating the problem. When your increasingly small test eventually stops showing the problem, that's more valuable information in tracking down the bug.

You can also run your test case as another user, as **root**, as the same user on another machine, and as **root** or another user on another machine. All these tests will help establish a space where the problem might be. It's well worth running as many tests as you can *before* you start actually doing any work in changing anything; otherwise, you won't necessarily be able to tell what it is you did that fixed the problem (see Chapter 1).

If the machine you're working on is a desktop machine, if the problem is a config or software-related one, and if it's showing up only on this machine, consider how much time you're prepared to spend on trying to fix it. It's good practice to have your desktops basically interchangeable and to have an install setup that's as straightforward and hands-off as you can possibly make it. My own rule of thumb is that if such a problem is still unsolved after an hour, it's time to kick off a reinstall. (All data partitions are independent from all root and boot partitions in my work setup, so this doesn't cause any data problems.) The exact amount of time may vary for you, but chances are, there's a point at which it doesn't make much sense to keep throwing your time and energy at a problem that will often be fixed by a quick, clean reinstall. This may seem like a bit of a cheat (surely on Linux you should always be able to find and fix a bug "properly"!), but sometimes cheating is the most pragmatic thing to do if your aim is to keep your systems running and your users happy. An alternative, if you just can't bear to cheat, is to have spare desktops around that you can switch in (so the user is happy) and keep the problem box in your office while you beat your head against the issue.

Note Obviously, not all problems will be solved by this! Anything that's showing up on multiple machines or for only one user is probably not going to be fixed by a reinstall, at least not permanently.

The rest of this chapter discusses some useful tools and strategies for bug fixing. My final note on the matter of saving time is that sometimes the quickest way to solve a problem is to step back from it for a while. Make a cup of tea, go for a walk around the block, or go play NetHack for a few minutes (preferably not for the whole day…); just do anything that gives you a little mental space from the problem. Several times I've been hit by the solution for a particularly nasty bug while cycling home from work and concentrating on the traffic rather than on the problem. It's possible to focus so hard on an issue that you can't see a valuable but slightly sideways solution to it. Giving your subconscious some time to chew on things can be incredibly helpful and save you hours of banging your head against the desk.

11-2. Knowing What to Check First

Here's a quick list of things to check for any bug before you start doing any serious problem solving:

- Run df -h: Are any of the disks full? / or /var in particular can cause peculiar problems, but the /home partition filling up can also give rise to errors (as can /tmp).

Note Sometimes a process may create a large log file that is then deleted but not closed by the process, so it remains there until the process drops it (in other words, the disk space won't actually be released). If you think this might have happened, you can use lsof to take a look:

```
lsof | grep /var
```

This will show you any files that are open in the /var/ directories. Here's an example:

```
innd       3360        news  mem     REG  254,6    155656     2129922  ⬅
/var/spool/news/overview/group.index
mutt       26671       juliet  3r      REG  254,1  2694918    1425422 /var/mail/juliet
```

The seventh column shows the file size, and the second column shows the PID of the process. If you find a dubious entry, you can try restarting the relevant process to clear the file properly.

- Run ifconfig: Check that the network interface still has a correct-looking address and hasn't taken itself down.

- Run ping gateway; ping nfs.example.com; ping ldap.example.com; ping kerberos.example.com; ping machine.external.com: Check that all your local servers are still contactable and then that the outside world is contactable.

- Run **top**: Is there a process that's chewing up all or a lot of the CPU? If so, depending on what it is, you may be able just to kill it.

- Run **ps -A**: Are there lots of defunct processes? This can mean various things, but resolving whatever is happening may help you find what your bug is.

- Run **date**: Check that the time is correct. Especially if you're using Kerberos, it's important that the time on the local machine matches the time on the server to within a few minutes.

- Restart X: This is another in the "crude but often effective" box. Use **/etc/init.d/gdm restart** (if you use the GDM display manager; otherwise, replace as appropriate), or hit Ctrl-Alt-Backspace from the display.

- Switch to a console (Ctrl-Alt-F1), and log in as **root**: Are there general login issues? This should show up if there are serious login problems.

- Switch to a console (Ctrl-Alt-F1), and log in as yourself, a test user, or another user (or use **su**): Again, this may show up general login issues, in which case you may want to take another look at whether your servers are up and responding.

- Run **iostat -dxk 5**: This will give you a quick view of what the disk I/O is doing. **-x** gives an extended report, **-d** shows device utilization, **-k** shows KB per second rather than bytes per second, and **5** refreshes every five seconds.

11-3. Looking at diff Output

diff is handy if you're comparing config files from two separate machines. Copy the second file to the first machine (this example uses the **/etc/hosts** file):

```
scp client1:/etc/hosts hosts-client1
```

Note If you have SSH keys set up (see recipe 6-1), you can use this:

```
diff /etc/hosts <(ssh -n client1 cat /etc/hosts)
```

Don't put any spaces between < and (, or it will break!

Then use **diff** to compare the two files:

```
diff /etc/hosts hosts-client1
```

Its output will look a bit like this:

```
01  7c7
02  < 127.0.0.1 localhost
03  ---
04  > 127.0.0.1 localhost localhost.localdomain
05  10a11,12
06  >
07  > 192.168.0.23        ldapserver
```

Lines 01–04 show the first change, and lines 05–07 show the second change. 7c7 means that in this first change line 7 is being compared with line 7. In the first file (/etc/hosts) named on the command line, line 7 is as shown in line 02 of the diff output (marked with <). In the second file (hosts-client1), line 7 is as shown in line 04 of the diff output (marked with >). Line 03 marks the division between the two files. (If multiple lines in a block were altered, you'd get more than one line at line 02 and line 04, and the dividing mark would be more useful.) So, in hosts-client1, 127.0.0.1 is also defined as localhost.localdomain, rather than just localhost.

The second set of changes means that at line 10 the second file also adds lines 11 and 12. Lines 06 and 07 of the diff output show those two added lines: an entry for the LDAP server.

Another form of output is to use the -C option, which gives you a certain number of lines of context for each change. (Unfortunately, this isn't compatible with the -y; option, which is described in a couple of paragraphs.)

```
> diff -C 1 /etc/hosts hosts-client1
*** /etc/hosts     2009-02-02 21:45:58.000000000 +1300
--- hosts-client1     2009-06-03 09:58:50.000000000 +1200
***************
*** 6,8 ****
  ##
! 127.0.0.1     localhost
  255.255.255.255     broadcasthost
--- 6,8 ----
  ##
! 127.0.0.1     localhost localhost.localdomain
  255.255.255.255     broadcasthost
***************
*** 10 ****
--- 10,12 ----
  fe80::1%lo0     localhost
+
+ 192.168.0.23     ldapserver
```

As you can see, this form of output gives you a bit more information about the file and can be a little more readable than the default output. -C 1 gives you one line of context on each side of the change, with the change marked with ! for changed lines and + for added lines (- for removed lines, although this is not shown here). You can specify as much context as you like; or -c gives a default three lines of context.

You can also use diff -y to show the files in two columns: the changes in the second file will be marked with | for changes and > for added lines. If you do this, it'll be easier to read if you also use the --suppress-common-lines option:

```
diff -y --suppress-common-lines /etc/hosts hosts-client1
```

This will show only the lines that differ, so there's less clutter on the screen, and it's easier to read. Here's some example output showing a single line (plus one blank line) added in `hosts-client1`:

```
> 10.0.0.10        extrahost
>
```

However, this way you don't get any context for the changed lines (the `-C` switch is not compatible with `-y` output), which may or may not be problematic, depending on what file you're looking at and what you're looking for.

■ **Note** Another alternative is to use `vimdiff` or `gvimdiff`; both use syntax highlighting to show you the differences in the files. This is rather easier to read, as a rule, than the standard `diff` output, and because it opens up a `vim` editor window showing both files side by side, it also allows you to navigate through the files and edit them as required while highlighting the differences. In particular, if you're using a graphical interface, `gvimdiff` allows you to change the sizes of the windows on the fly, which can be handy for looking more closely at what's going on in the file. `ediff` mode in GNU emacs works similarly.

11-4. Running strace to Look at System Calls

`strace` is a useful little program and is installed by default on most Linux systems. It allows you to take a look at the system calls being made by a program.

■ **Note** It doesn't provide a stack trace, name notwithstanding. It just traces system calls.

It's very useful as a basic debugging tool, helping you work out where a program is crashing or what problems it's having. In fact, it's also interesting to use even if you're not tracing a problem, because it can help you find out more about what your system is doing.

It's important to remember that user programs on a modern system run in a little circumscribed area within the system. They're not permitted to interact directly with the computer (so you can't just shove numbers into registers and have Things Happen, unless you're **root**). Instead, everything goes through the kernel, and it's these messages to the kernel that **strace** is tracking. So, if there's no **strace** output for a while, don't assume that your program is stuck and that that's where the bug is. It might just be working within its own sandbox and not need to talk to the kernel for a while. Having said that, if the **strace** output does pause and you can't obviously see why from eyeballing the program, it's probably worth taking a look at the last few system calls to see whether anything looks problematic.

The basic **strace** command is **strace program**, but **strace -o output.txt program** is a better bet. This will send the (copious quantities of) output to **output.txt** rather than straight to the screen, making it easier to deal with.

■ **Note** Some editors (for example, vim) are able to do syntax highlighting of strace output. This is very useful in making sense of the output because it helps your eye jump to the correct parts.

Here are a couple of lines of output from running strace on a "Hello World" Perl program:

```
execve("./helloworld.pl", ["./helloworld.pl"], [/* 20 vars */]) = 0
uname({sys="Linux", node="client1.example.com", ...}) = 0
```

The basic structure of each line is the same. Each line is a single system call, with the call name at the start of the line, its arguments in brackets, and the return value after the = at the end of the line.

The uname line here demonstrates another feature of strace. Some system calls involve a pointer to a particular data structure. Here, uname returns a pointer to the system information data. strace dereferences the pointer for you and fills in the data. By default, it will print only a little of that data structure; to get the whole thing, use the -v option to strace.

Here's some more sample output:

```
access("/etc/ld.so.preload", R_OK)      = -1 ENOENT (No such file or directory)
open("/etc/ld.so.cache", O_RDONLY)    = 3
fstat(3, {st_mode=S_IFREG|0644, st_size=43270, ...}) = 0
mmap(NULL, 43270, PROT_READ, MAP_PRIVATE, 3, 0) = 0x2b8740901000
close(3)                              = 0
```

The access call shows what file the program is trying to access (for example, /etc/ld.so.preload) and whether it was successful. A value of –1 means unsuccessful, and then there's an error code (E*****: in this case, ENOENT), which is translated for you. ENOENT means "no such file or directory," but strace helpfully looks up the plain-English meaning of the error code, so you shouldn't need to do so. access, if the file does exist, checks whether the program is allowed to access it (for example, if the permissions are correctly set).

■ **Note** The ld files are related to static and dynamic linking. *Static linking* means that a program creates its own libraries and uses those. *Dynamic linking* means that a program uses the system libraries, so you need only one copy of all the standard libraries, not a copy per program. Nearly all Linux programs now use dynamic linking, so any program you run strace on will look for various ld files before doing anything else. Failure to find one of the ld files isn't necessarily a problem. See recipe 11-5 for comments on ltrace and ldd.

open does exactly what you'd expect. It tries to open the specified file. If that file exists, the return value is a positive number. This is the file descriptor, which is the "handle" that the system will use to refer to this file for subsequent system calls. Problems with accessing or opening a particular file are one of the most likely causes of a bug, so pay particular attention to these calls. However, be aware that config files may be looked for in multiple locations, which will generate a cluster of failure-to-open calls that are absolutely normal. Use the -e option (see recipe 11-4a) to trace only particular types of call.

■ **Note** When files are opened to a numerical file descriptor, the numbers start at 3. This is because the 0–2 file descriptors are already allocated: 0 to stdin, 1 to stdout, and 2 to stderr.

---

fstat returns information about a file, with the first argument being the file descriptor, which, as here, will have been set up by an earlier **open** call. The next section, in the brackets, is a **stat** structure, which contains various pieces of information about the file. To get the full information, use the **-v** option to **strace**. What we see here from the **stat** structure is the file protection and the size (in bytes) of the file. The protection uses the same coding as **chmod**, so here it's 0644, meaning owner+group read, owner write, and owner execute. (The other part of the mode field is a flag identifying whether it's a regular file, directory, or something else. S_IFREG means it's a regular file.) **fstat** returns 0 for success. File protection can be another source of problems.

Later in your **strace** output, if you're running an interpreted script in a language like Perl, you'll see some **getuid** and **getgid** calls, which fetch the user and group ID that the process is running as and also the effective user and group ID. If you're running an executable like a C program directly, you won't see these checks, because they'll already have been done before the program started running. A Perl script will also have a **readlink** line like this, which loads up the path to the executable:

```
readlink("/proc/self/exe", "/usr/bin/perl", 4095) = 13
```

/proc/self/exe is a symbolic link to the executable path; the second buffer is the actual path.

If running a compiled program, you won't see a **readlink** call, because the code is executed directly rather than locating an executable to feed it through. You're less likely to see problems at this stage of the code; user/group ID issues should generate a usable error message to **stdout** without having to fire up **strace**.

■ **Note** Linux system calls are very well documented. You can get information on any of the system calls you'll see in strace output via their man pages (man functionname or man 2 functionname).

11-4a. Setting strace Options

Here are your strace options:

- -f: Traces child processes (forks) as they're created.

- -t, -tt, -ttt: Puts the time of day at the start of each line given to the second, microsecond, or second+microsecond and written as seconds-since-epoch.

- -T: Shows the time spent in system calls (that is, the time difference between the beginning and end of each system call).

- -r: Prints a relative timestamp at the start of each system call.

- **-c**: Counts the time, calls, and errors for each system call, and summarizes this information when the program exits. This is helpful if you're debugging and you're not sure where to start, because it'll help you work out where the problem might lie.

- **-e trace=CALLS**: Traces only the system calls you specify, such as **-e trace=open,read,write** (note the lack of spaces) to trace only the open, read, and write system calls. Use this to minimize the amount of output; it may be best used after you've used **-c** to identify the problem area.

- **-p PID**: Attaches **strace** to the process with the specified process ID. So, if you suddenly see a process hanging or eating up lots of CPU, you can find out what it's doing in real time.

- **-s 128**: Increases the maximum string size to 128 (from the default 32) so you are shown more detail of string data.

11-4b. Running strace in a Shell Script Wrapper

Running your command via the command line as shown earlier may not generate "real" conditions and so may not be entirely helpful when trying to track down a bug. Instead, you can write a shell script wrapper for the command and thus run it via **strace**.

Move your existing program **command** out of the way (but don't delete it!):

```
mv command command.old
```

Then create a shell script **command**:

```
#!/bin/sh
#
strace -o/tmp/command_out.$$ /usr/bin/command.old $*
```

The **$$** is the PID of the current process. **$*** picks up any arguments that were used and passes them to the real command but also kicks off **strace** on the command and outputs to a new file each time the script is called. Now run the command with **command**, and then check the output at **/tmp/command_out.****.

■ **Note** Remember to move the real program back where it belongs once you've finished!

11-5. Running ltrace and Library Calls

ltrace works very similarly to **strace** (see the previous recipe). Instead of tracking system calls, it tracks dynamically linked library calls, so it won't do anything useful if your application is statically linked. Most modern software is dynamically linked, though.

For example, here's a section of the output of **ltrace ls** (in other words, **ltrace** run on the binary **ls**) on one of my directories:

```
memcpy(0x61a6d0, "subversion_repos.html", 22)   = 0x61a6d0
readdir(0x61ddf0)                                = 0x61e510
memset(0x629e20, '\000', 184)                    = 0x629e20
strlen("mono-samples.png")                       = 16
malloc(17)                                       = 0x61a6f0
memcpy(0x61a6f0, "mono-samples.png", 17)         = 0x61a6f0
readdir(0x61ddf0)                                = 0x61e538
memset(0x629ed8, '\000', 184)                    = 0x629ed8
```

■ **Note** As with system calls, library calls are also well documented in Linux systems. man memcpy will, for example, give you information on the memcpy library call.

Looking at the output here, the first line is a call to memcpy. This is copying 22 bytes from the memory address containing the string **subversion_repos.html** to the memory address 0x61a6d0. As with **strace**, **ltrace** will dereference certain pointers for you. In this case, instead of giving the pointer to the memory address for the source of the data, it dereferences it to give you the string that's stored at that address (here it's **subversion_repos.html**, which is the name of one of the files that ls is listing). The return value is just the destination memory address.

readdir, on the next line, is a function that returns a pointer to the next directory entry. The argument (here **0x61ddf0**) is a pointer to the directory itself, and the return value is where to look for the next entry. memset writes a given number (here 184) of bytes of a particular value (here **\000**) to the string referenced by the memory pointer (**0x629e20**).

strlen gives the length of its argument string. Here, it's the next directory entry (as returned by **readdir**), and again, **ltrace** dereferences the pointer for you to give you the string value instead rather than just a memory address. The next line uses a **malloc** call to deal with memory allocation, setting up sufficient memory (the string length plus one byte) to hold the next directory entry. Then the whole series starts over again with memcpy and the next directory entry.

Most of the time you probably won't need to use **ltrace** to this level of detail, but this should provide you with enough of a guide to be able to use the man pages as a reference to decipher the **ltrace** output for a program that's causing you problems.

■ **Note** You can also use 1dd to check which shared libraries a particular program requires. If a particular library can't be found, 1dd will report this.

11-5a. Setting ltrace Options

Here are the **ltrace** options:

- -f: Traces child processes (forks) as they're created.

- -t, -tt, -ttt: Puts the time of day at the start of each line, given to the second, microsecond, or second+microsecond and written as seconds-since-epoch.

- **-T**: Shows the time spent in library calls (that is, the time difference between the beginning and end of each library call).

- **-r**: Prints a relative timestamp at the start of each library call.

- **-c**: Counts the time, calls, and errors for each library call, and summarizes this information when the program exits. This is helpful if you're debugging and you're not sure where to start, because it'll help you work out where the problem might lie.

- **-e CALLNAME**: Traces only the specified library calls. Alternatively, **-e !CALLNAME** would trace all calls *except* for the specified one. You can use this to minimize the amount of output; it may be best used after you've used **-c** to identify the problem area.

- **-p PID**: Attaches **ltrace** to the process with the specified process ID. So if you suddenly see a process hanging or eating up lots of CPU, you can find out what it's doing in real time.

- **-S**: Traces system calls as well.

11-6. Logging with syslogd

Many of the programs on your system will send their logging messages to **syslog**, which manages the logging on most Linux systems. **syslog** can be configured to send particular types of log messages to particular locations.

  syslog messages have two pieces of information attached to them: a facility, identifying the source of the message, and a priority. Both of these are system-defined rather than user-defined; see Tables 11-1 and 11-2 for the available values.

Table 11-1. syslog Facilities

Priority Label	Description
auth	Authorization messages and information (aka security, but this is deprecated)
authpriv	Used for user access messages
cron	cron
daemon	Any daemon that doesn't have its own facility
ftp	FTP
kern	Kernel messages
lpr	Printer system messages

Priority Label	Description
mail	For any mail application
mark	Produces timestamps in log files
news	For any news application
syslog	General log messages
user	Any user process; also the default facility
uucp	UUCP messages
local0–local7	Reserved for local use

Table 11-2. syslog Priority Levels

Security Level	Priority	Keyword
0	Emergencies	emerg
1	Alerts	alert
2	Critical	crit
3	Errors	err
4	Warning	warning
5	Notifications	notice
6	Informational	info
7	Debugging	debug

To set up where logging messages are recorded and which ones are recorded, edit /etc/syslog.conf. To log all messages with a severity higher than notifications to a single file, use this line:

```
*.notice        /var/log/messages
```

This is really a bit general, though. Let's break out the mail messages into a separate file:

```
*.notice;mail.none      /var/log/messages
mail.notice        /var/log/mail
```

The first line logs all messages with priority **notice** and above, except for mail messages, which it doesn't log at all (the **none** priority). The second line logs all messages with facility **mail** and priority **notice** and above to a separate file. To extend this to **news** messages, use this:

```
*.notice;mail,news.none          /var/log/messages
mail.notice         /var/log/mail
news.notice         /var/log/news
```

This now excludes the **news** messages from the general file as well and adds them instead to their own log file at **/var/log/news**. You can treat any facility and priority similarly. Remember that you probably want to keep a catchall file (***.priority**) at **/var/log/messages**, even if you think you've broken out all expected facilities into their own log files.

Use = to log only that priority without including the ones above it:

```
=mail.notice        /var/log/mail.notice
=mail.warn          /var/log/mail.warn
```

You can also use – to avoid syncing the log file after each log entry. This is useful if you have a network logging host that gets logins from lots of machines.

Note You can also send messages to a particular user. Here's an example:

```
auth.crit       admin
```

This will send all authorization messages of **critical** or above severity to the admin user.

It's useful to break out messages of particular known types to limit the amount of messages you have to wade through in **/var/log/messages** when debugging, but be aware that this does also increase the likelihood of your missing a relevant message if you're tracking down a more complicated bug or one that you don't understand yet. However, equally it will make it much easier to track down a bug in, say, the mail system, if you need to look at only a single file that has all the mail messages in and nothing else.

Note To watch /var/log/messages in real time, use `tail -f /var/log/messages`. This is incredibly useful when debugging.

11-7. Performing Centralized Logging with syslog

It's also possible to centralize your system logging, setting up a single log host to receive messages from all machines. This has the advantage that if the remote machine is attacked, the attacker won't be able to delete the logs from the central loghost; it can also have security implications, depending on how you set it up. As ever, be aware of the possibilities for attack.

It's wise to carry on logging locally, as well, so that if there's a problem with a particular machine, you don't have to wade through all the remote logs to identify it.

First, set up syslogd on your log host to receive remote messages. On Debian/Ubuntu, edit the /etc/init.d/sysklogd file so that the SYSLOGD line near the top reads as follows:

```
SYSLOGD="-r"
```

■ **Note** To also remove the MARK lines from the files, use SYSLOGD="-r -m0".

Now restart the syslog daemon (/etc/init.d/sysklogd restart).

On the remote (client) machine, edit /etc/syslog.conf to specify which messages you want to send to the logging host. You probably want just to add this line, rather than replacing the existing lines, as discussed earlier:

```
*.err    @loghost.example.com
```

Restart syslogd on the client machine (/etc/init.d/sysklogd restart).

Log messages from your client machine should now be recorded on the log host. Note that the messages will be filtered twice: once on the client machine (with the setup given here, messages from any source with a priority of err or above will make it through) and then again on the log host, where they'll be treated as any other incoming syslog message and filtered to a particular log file depending on the settings in /etc/syslog.conf. So, mail messages would (assuming this was set up as in recipe 11-6) be filtered to the mail log file on the remote host, and so on. Unfortunately, there's no way of filtering messages from a particular host at this point; you'll have to use grep on the log files.

■ **Note** Another option is syslog-ng if you have very complicated logging requirements.

11-8. Plotting Log Data to Locate Problems: perl and gnuplot

If you want ongoing visualization of log data, you probably want to look at a tool like Cacti or one of the other tools built on RRDTool, rather than building your own data plot. However, sometimes you're monitoring something specific and need to get a quick visualization of the output, perhaps to identify whether there is a real problem.

An example is if you're concerned about the response rate of one of your servers, such as your main NFS server, which anecdotally appears to be slow to respond from time to time. To check this out, you can set up a short script to ping it at intervals and get the response rate.

■ **Note** This is only the start of an investigation. You'd also want to check the response to a real NFS request, among other things.

```
01  #!/usr/bin/perl -w
02  # JK 10.01.2008
03
04  use strict;
05  use Net::Ping;
06  use Net::SMTP;
07  use Time::HiRes;
08  use POSIX qw(stfrtime);
09
10  my $server = "nfsserver";
11  my $file   = "/home/jkemp/sysadmin/nfs_response.log";
12
13  # Ping server and record time and response time
14  my $ping = Net::Ping->new();
15  $ping->hires();
16  my ($ret, $duration, $ip) = $ping->ping($server, 5.5);
17  open FILE, ">>$file";
18  print FILE ((strftime "%b-%d-%H:%M:%S", localtime), " ");
19  printf FILE ("%.3f\n", 1000 * $duration);
20  close FILE;
```

This should be fairly self-explanatory. It's being run on a local network, so there's no need to specify a domain in line 10. The use of Time::HiRes (and then setting the ping response as hires in line 15—this is a feature of the Net::Ping module) enables the data to be recorded with millisecond values rather than just in seconds. In line 16, $ret is the success flag (1 for reachable, 0 for not), which we don't use. We also discard $ip, which is the IP address that the pinged host (here nfsserver) resolved to, and keep only $duration, which is the elapsed time of the ping. The 5.5 value in the ping call is the length of time (in seconds) to wait before giving up, if the host doesn't respond.

Lines 17–20 deal with writing the output to file, with the time of the ping and then the ping response duration printed to three decimal places with printf. Note that this is the time *after* the ping, not before it. In this context, this is unlikely to matter, but it could if you wanted to set a $currenttime value before the ping and then use that here. Note that the $duration value is returned in milliseconds, so you multiply it by 1,000 to get seconds.

Run this every minute (or however often you want) with a line in a cron file. This can be your own cron file rather than that of root.

```
* * * * *        /home/jkemp/bin/nfsserver_ping.pl
```

This outputs data (to the file specified in line 10 of the script) in the following form:

```
Mar-19-00:30:02 0.40
Mar-19-00:31:01 3.54
Mar-19-00:32:01 2.68
```

The best way to get an idea of what's going on here is to plot it, which is where **gnuplot** comes in.

gnuplot expects two space-delimited columns of input, which is why line 18 uses the format it does. Check **man strftime** for more details or for other format options to use (the script imports this POSIX module in Line 08). Here the usage is %b (short form of month), %d (date of month in digits), and %H:%M:%S (time in hours/minutes/seconds), separated by hyphens.

Check whether you have **gnuplot** installed on your system, and install the **gnuplot** package if not. Now, here's the gnuplot config file for this data, **nfs-ping.conf**:

```
01 set terminal png size 1200,800
02 set xdata time
03 set timefmt "%b-%d-%H:%M:%S"
04 set output "nfs-ping.png"
05  set xrange ["Mar-25-00:00:00":"Mar-26-00:00:00"]
06 set yrange [0:50]
07 set grid
08 set xlabel "Date\\nTime"
09 set ylabel "Ping Response"
10 set title "NFS server ping times"
11 set key left box
12 plot "nfs-ping-1.dat" using 1:2 index 0 title "ahost" with points
```

■ **Note** In line 05, change the range to match whatever the dates of your own data are. This gives the start and end points of the x range.

Line 01 sets the output as a PNG file and the size of the plot in pixels, and line 04 sets the name of the output file. Line 02 identifies this as a time plot, and line 03 gives the time format as it has been recorded in your data file; you can use **man date** to get more information about how to specify time data. In line 05, the specified time range must be in this format as well. Lines 08–10 set the labels for the axes and the main graph.

Line 12 is the one that does most of the work. The input data file is specified first. **using 1:2** means that columns 1 and 2 of the input data are used to create the plot. **index 0** means that you use the first data set in the file. You can have multiple data sets in a single file, delimited by two blank lines between each. Here's an example:

```
# data for NFS host 1
col1 col2
col1 col2
```

```
# data for NFS host 2
col1 col2
col1 col2
```

You could replace line 12 with the following and thereby plot data for both your NFS hosts on the same plot:

```
plot "nfs-ping-1.dat" using 1:2 index 0 title "nfs1" with points, \
plot "nfs-ping-1.dat" using 1:2 index 1 title "nfs2" with points
```

This would be useful if you were having reports of problems with one host but not the other; you could directly compare the data to help work out where unusual changes were occurring. `points` is the best plotting option for this data; you can also try `lines` as an alternative or one of the many other options (`linespoints`, `dots`, `steps`…).

Now run the following:

```
cat nfs-ping.conf | gnuplot
```

and then take a look at the generated file, `nfs-ping.png`. You can use Firefox or an image viewer such as `ghostview` or `imagemagick`.

■ **Note** gnuplot is a very versatile program and capable of far more complex tasks than this! Check out `info gnuplot` to access the full user manual, or check out `http://www.gnuplot.info/`.

■ ■ ■

## CHAPTER 12

Managing Time and People

Another thing that sysadmins spend a lot of time doing—stereotypes notwithstanding—is dealing with people. Usually, the people are bringing you problems to solve. This chapter looks at how to manage these interruptions of your time and how to keep track of the enormous number of things that get dumped on your desk on a daily basis. Several recipes cover setting up RT, a ticketing system, to help you keep track of what's going on. Finally, there's some tips on keeping your colleagues on your side. Working life is a lot easier if you limit your battles to being against software rather than people!

12-1. Managing the Interrupt-Driven Nature of Sysadmin Work

There's a tendency for sysadmin work to be very interrupt-driven. Bugs and problems crop up all the time, and sometimes those are important enough that you really do need to drop whatever you're currently working on. Sometimes they're not, but your concentration may nevertheless be broken whenever something new is brought to your attention, especially if someone comes to your desk in person. So, it can be difficult to get time to work on major projects, and even smaller projects may suffer because of the time it takes to pick up your train of thought again after you're interrupted.

There are various options and techniques for dealing with this. One possibility, if you can manage it, is to block out specific times of the day or week where you aren't available to be disturbed. If you're working with colleagues, you can arrange for one person to be on call and the others to be left alone. If you're working on your own, you have to manage it a little differently. You could consider turning your e-mail off for a couple of hours at a stretch, moving to a different location in the building for a couple of hours, or working from home. You may want to put some system in place that is triggered if a really important alert occurs; see Chapter 3 for discussion of Nagios. Also, make sure someone knows how to contact you if there's a genuine emergency!

You may be inclined to think, as a solo sysadmin, that making yourself unavailable for blocks of time will lead to everything falling apart. First, your systems really should be able to look after themselves for a while without your input. Second, if you can't spend half a day somewhere else concentrating on other things, what happens when you're ill or on leave? It's useful to have appropriate reporting and escalation procedures in place anyway, and you can see your "not available" time as a way of checking that these systems are working properly.

A lot of this relies on you managing, or reacting according to, the expectations and behavior of your colleagues. It's no good turning your e-mail off and ignoring the phone if the norm in your place of work is to come to your office in person with problems. See recipe 12-4 for some discussion of this.

There are some problems that simply have to be dealt with on the spot, in which case you'll just have to put down whatever you're doing. With others, the best option is to record the issue somewhere, in whatever way you normally use (see recipe 12-2), and then get back to what you were doing as quickly as possible. This also goes for things that suddenly occur to you in the middle of your work on whatever the current big project is. Write it down somewhere, and keep going with what you're doing. Don't allow *yourself* to sabotage your time.

This is also why it's a good idea to keep thorough notes when you're working (see Chapter 1). If you're in the habit of keeping good notes as you're working, then it'll be far easier to pick your work up again when you go back to the first problem. It won't get rid of the time it'll take to get back up to speed (there's inevitably an overhead as you load all the information back into your working memory, as it were), but it'll reduce it, and it'll save you doing things twice.

Another important technique to develop is the ability to identify what's important, what's urgent, and what's both. Some problems are minor (or have straightforward workarounds) and can be left at the bottom of the priority list. Some problems have to be fixed right now, such as a major network outage. Some problems can be planned for in advance to give yourself a bit more flexibility in fixing them. For example, if the main LDAP server has gone down, then it's wise to sort the problem out ASAP, but if you have a backup server in place, then it's not absolutely urgent. The more backups and fail-safes you have in place, the more flexible your ability to respond becomes. However, you must be sure not to rely on the backups for too long. Any incapacitating server problems should definitely be fixed as quickly as is practicable.

■ **Note** Don't allow even the minor problems to be delayed for too long, though, if you can possibly avoid it, particularly if they're user-facing problems. You'll get a lot more help and respect from your colleagues if they know that you'll fix even small issues as soon as you can. See recipe 12-2 for tips on keeping track and avoiding problems falling through the cracks, and see recipe 12-7 for tips on keeping your colleagues on your side. If you find that you simply don't have the time to fix anything that isn't important, urgent, or both, then it may be time to talk to your boss about getting another sysadmin in.

Another way of making sure that you get through the task list is to spend five minutes at the start of each day checking your to-do list and identifying three things that it's important to get done and that you are committed to doing that day. Don't overdo it. It's best to have three things that you definitely can manage to get done, rather than a longer list that you expect not to get through. (And be aware that some tasks are larger than others! See recipe 12-3 for some discussion of dealing with larger projects.) Then make your first priority of the day getting those three things out of the way. If you have enough interruptions that you don't manage to get anything else done, that's OK. Clearing three things at a time will keep the list under control.

You can also batch smaller tasks and dedicate an hour every day or two to managing those. Even on a busy day it's usually possible to carve out an hour, and getting through several smaller tasks in a row can be a very cheering experience.

Note For lots more useful information on time management, try *Time Management for Sysadmins* by Thomas A Limoncelli (O'Reilly, 2005). *Getting Things Done* by David Allen (Penguin, 2002) is also useful, although aimed at people who work more with paper than with computers; there are lots of web sites aimed at reworking it a bit to work better for IT professionals.

12-2. Keeping Track of Work and of Problems

As I said in recipe 12-1, sysadmin work tends to be interrupt-driven. As well as the problems with concentration and time management that this gives rise to, it leads to a higher chance of losing track of issues as they arise. For example, you're busy working on an issue with the web server when one of your colleagues stops by your desk to complain about a problem they're having with their desktop. It's not urgent, so you tell them you'll take a look at it later and go back to the web server debugging. An hour later, you've forgotten all about the desktop problem—until your colleague comes back to you a couple of days after, asking why you never did anything about it.

There are various steps you can take to avoid this happening:

- Get people to record their bug reports via e-mail. If someone comes to you with a problem, ask them to e-mail you with it "to help me keep track of things."

Note If you have trouble keeping on top of your e-mail, there are plenty of resources out there to assist you. Take a look at the 43 Folders web site, or any one of the many other productivity web sites and books available.

- Write things down yourself as soon as you're told about them, either in a notebook or in e-mail. If you use a notebook, make it one that you'll actually check back in, not one that'll lie unread on your desk for days.

- Keep a to-do list of some variety. For example, use your wiki (see recipe 1-3).

- Use a bug-tracking system such as Request Tracker (RT), as discussed in the next recipe. This can mix well with the previous suggestions. Set up an e-mail address that interacts with the system, and you can ask users to send e-mail to it (or forward their e-mails) or e-mail it yourself. This will also help act as a reminder and to-do list.

The important point is that anything that comes in as a problem needs to be recorded in the same place, whatever way it originally comes in to you. You can get others to help you with this (see recipe 12-7 for a discussion of managing your interactions with your colleagues), or you can do it yourself. Don't rely on remembering things; it's far too easy to get distracted.

12-3. Ticketing System: Using RT

An excellent way of keeping track of bugs, requests, and problems is to use a ticketing system, where every issue that arises is entered as a *ticket* that can then be tracked. Several are available, but Request Tracker (RT) is a good option. Tickets in RT can be allocated to someone to fix, given a priority, placed in a particular queue (to separate different types of bug or request; you can set up as many queues as you like), commented on, replied to, and finally resolved and closed. RT can also send progress updates and reminders to the initial requestor and to other people involved with the ticket. It's open source and written in Perl, so there's also plenty of scope for extending it should you want to do that. (It even includes some straightforward built-in options for doing your own customization.)

■ **Note** A ticketing system is particularly useful when more than one person is involved in a project, because it provides a centralized record of what has been done and what is still to do. However, even if you work alone, it's still a useful way of keeping track of issues (as discussed in the previous recipe) and also provides a backup way of recording what was done. You can include a link to an appropriate wiki page in the resolution comment, for example.

Installation

The Debian/Ubuntu package to install is **request-tracker3.6**, which comes along with a stack of Perl module packages:

```
apt-get install request-tracker3.6
```

One slight installation niggle in the Debian package is that **apache** is a dependency, which is a nuisance if you already have **apache2** installed. To use your existing **apache2** install instead, use this:

```
apt-get install libapache2-mod-perl2
rm /etc/init.d/apache
```

The last line will avoid having both Apache and Apache2 starting at bootup, which would be a nuisance.

Follow the instructions in **/usr/share/doc/request-tracker3.6/NOTES.Debian.gz** to complete the basic install and set up the database back end. If you're using Apache2, you'll also need to edit the provided **modperl** file to comment out this line:

```
PerlFreshRestart Off
```

You need to either install a database (which I won't cover here) or install the database client package if you already have a database server on another machine. I'll assume from here on that you're using MySQL on another server.

Basic Configuration

The individual site configuration file is in **/etc/request-tracker3.6/RT_SiteConfig.pm**. The RT_Config.pm file in the same directory shows all the configuration options and their defaults. You can use this for reference, because the idea is that any setting given in RT_SiteConfig.pm overrides the setting in RT_Config.pm. This makes your site setup much clearer.

Here's a reasonable basic RT_SiteConfig.pm:

```
Set($rtname, 'www.example.com/rt');
Set($Organization, 'www.example.com');

Set($OwnerEmail , 'rt-owner@example.com');
Set($CorrespondAddress , 'rt-reply@example.com');
Set($CommentAddress , 'rt-comment@example.com');

Set($Timezone , 'Europe/London'); # obviously choose what suits you

Set($LogToSyslog     , 'error');
Set($LogToFile       , 'debug');

Set($DatabaseType, 'mysql'); # e.g. Pg or mysql
# These are the settings used when creating the RT database,
# You MUST set these to what you chose then.
Set($DatabaseUser , 'rtuser');
Set($DatabasePassword , 'rtpwd');
Set($DatabaseName , 'rtdb');
Set($DatabaseServer, 'mysqlserver');
# THE WEBSERVER:
Set($WebPath , "/rt");
Set($WebBaseURL , "http://www.example.com");

Set($UseFriendlyFromLine , 1);
Set($FriendlyFromLineFormat , "\"IT Manager via RT\" <rt-owner\@example.com>");

Set($UseTransactionBatch , 1);

1;
```

Most of this code is self-explanatory. CorrespondAddress and CommentAddress set the default e-mail addresses used in the From and Reply-To headers of (respectively) correspondence and comment e-mails sent by RT. You can override these for each queue; these are just the global defaults.

The FriendlyFromLine settings make RT use a nicer From header when sending out e-mails than the default, "SenderName via RT."

Reload Apache with **/etc/init.d/apache2 force-reload**, and then go to the RT web page that you have set (http://www.example.com/rt in the previous example). You should see the RT login screen.

Setting Up RT

The first time you log on, change the **root** user password from the default (**password**) via the Configuration ➤ Users ➤ root menu (the menus are along the top). You can also change other root account settings (for example, the e-mail address) here. Next, create yourself a user account via Configuration ➤ Users ➤ New User. Be careful also to select the "Give this user rights" check box, or your user will not be able to interact with tickets or queues at all. This check box just allows you to set rights for a user. The actual setting of rights is done elsewhere (this is discussed in a moment). Click Save Changes to complete the account setup.

Note In RT, anyone using the system is a user. This covers both people who only raise tickets and the sysadmins who resolve them. Of course, someone who resolves tickets can also raise their own tickets! A ticket is RT's way of recording a particular problem or issue. Tickets can have various things done to them: you can attach comments, send e-mails, assign them to particular individuals to resolve, and so on.

Rights are RT's version of permissions, which limit the actions permitted to a particular user or group of users. They're discussed further in a few moments.

To add your first test ticket, you can go to the home page and use the "Quick ticket creation" box at the bottom of the Home page.

Note The life cycle of a ticket looks like this:

1. A user creates a ticket, either via e-mail or via the web page.

2. RT sends a notification e-mail to the address for the queue admin.

3. The queue admin assigns the ticket to someone (possibly themself!). They can also give it a priority, move it to another queue, or even delete it immediately if it is invalid.

4. The ticket can have comments added, the user can be contacted via the ticket, or various other things can happen, all of which will be recorded by RT.

5. In due course, the issue is resolved, and the ticket will be marked "resolved."

A ticket created with the "Quick ticket creation" box, however, won't have any information other than the title, so it's of limited use. For a more comprehensive ticket, there is a button at the top right of the screen called "New ticket in" (with a drop-down Queue box next to it). Hit this, and you will open a full ticket creation screen. Once you've added a ticket, return to the home page to see it listed.

Note You can add custom fields to a ticket if there's information that you want to encourage people to provide (for example, the name of the machine they're working on). Create these via Configuration ➤ Custom Fields ➤ New Custom Field. You can set various validation options or make the field mandatory. Add this field to a particular queue via the Applies To option on the custom field configuration page or by selecting a queue from the Configuration ➤ Queues menu and then adding the field via the Ticket Custom Fields option. To set a custom field to apply globally, use the Global menu. You can also add custom fields to users or groups if that's helpful in your environment.

RT uses queues to organize tickets, and each ticket belongs to a queue. By default there's just a single default queue. To add more than one queue (for example, to enable yourself to separate software from hardware problems, or bugs as opposed to requests), go to Configuration ➤ Queues ➤ New Queue. Fill in as many of the boxes as you like, and click Save Changes. Bear in mind that once you have created a queue, you can't delete it without editing the database directly. You can, however, disable it (by deselecting the "Enable queue" box), which means that it won't be visible on the site.

To edit the queue configuration, select the queue in the Configuration ➤ Queues menu. This allows you to do things such as setting a per-queue reply and comment address, which may be useful especially if you're working in a multisysadmin environment (since you might want different admins to be responsible for different queues). You'll definitely want to set up the AdminCc group for each queue, which defines the people who are watching the queue. You do this from the Watchers page for the queue. The AdminCc group is a preexisting group whose membership is user-defined. This group, once defined, will be contacted in certain circumstances. By default, they'll be contacted when a ticket is created and when any activity happens on it. You can also add any other user to watch a queue or a ticket, which means that they will be e-mailed in the event of any relevant activity.

Note The best way to do this is to first set up a group using the Configuration ➤ Groups ➤ New Group menu item. All you need to fill in is the name and description; then click Save Changes to create the group. Then you can add members to the group using the Configuration ➤ Groups ➤ Select Groups menu item and then the Members menu item (in the left menu pane) in each group's configuration page. You'll be given two lists, one with current members and check boxes for deletion and one with all other users, from which you can select the user(s) to add.

This means that you can set up a "queue watching" group with a given membership and set up each queue such that it's watched by this group. Then if someone leaves the organization or gets different responsibilities, you only have to move them from the group rather than editing each queue individually.

Rights

A fundamental aspect of RT that you need to understand is the rights system. This governs who can do what operations to and with tickets. Here are some example rights (operations that can be undertaken on or with tickets):

- *CreateTicket*: Create a ticket in a queue.

- *ModifyTicket*: Change a ticket.

- *SeeQueue*: Be able to see the queue at all.

- *OwnTicket*: Have a ticket allocated to you to fix.

- *ShowTicketComments*: See the comments on a ticket.

- *TakeTicket*: Allocate a ticket to yourself.

- *ShowScrips*: Look at the scrips that apply to a ticket. See the "Scrips" section for more about this.

■ **Note** The full list is available by selecting Queues ➤ Select Queue ➤ Group/User Rights.

Particularly important is that if a user doesn't have ShowTicket rights, then even if they have created a particular ticket, they won't be able to see it. Similarly, without SeeQueue rights, they cannot see the queues (and thus see other tickets).

In a basic setup, the most straightforward option is to start by giving all rights to the AdminCc group. This will mean that anyone watching the queue via this group (as per the previous setup) will have full queue admin rights. Highlight all the rights next to the AdminCc group (under the Group Rights menu item), and click Save Changes.

After this, you can decide which rights to give to all users. CreateTicket, ModifyTicket, ReplyToTicket, SeeQueue, ShowOutgoingEmail, and ShowTicket make up a good basic set, because these are most of the tasks users will want to do. They'll be able to create tickets (this one is pretty essential!) and modify or reply to their own ticket (and as discussed earlier, ShowTicket is required for them to see their own ticket). They'll also be able to see other tickets in the queue. ShowOutgoingEmail means that they'll be able to see an e-mail that has been attached to their ticket. You can experiment and see what suits your setup best. Some environments might prefer not to have other tickets visible to all users, for example.

Note It is probably a good idea to distinguish between ShowTicket and ShowTicketComments. This enables your admin team to make comments that cannot be seen by users. A comment is a way of adding a note to a ticket. In the default setting, a comment will be forwarded only to people watching the ticket, not to the originator. In contrast, you can also reply to a ticket, which will add a note to the ticket and also e-mail both the originator and anyone watching the ticket.

However, it is *not* a good idea to use this distinction between replies and comments as a reason to be rude behind the back of the ticket originator! It does mean that you can keep technical information in the comments to avoid confusing nontechnical users or add references to other tickets that are related to the back end of your system (and uninteresting to nonsysadmin users).

User rights work in a similar way and are administered via Configuration ➤ Groups ➤ Select Group ➤ Group Rights (to change the rights for all group members) or User Rights (to set rights for group members individually). You can also set various global rights via Configuration ➤ Global ➤ User Rights. Rights that can be given to users include SuperUser rights.

Scrips

The final important part of RT is *scrips*. These are scripts (specifically, chunks of Perl) that run under certain conditions. It is the part of the system that enables one of the benefits of RT: that it can update all interested parties by e-mail.

There are a collection of default scrips that apply to all queues; you can find them under Configuration ➤ Global ➤ Scrips or from the Scrips menu item of individual queues). Looking at the default setup, you will see that these distinguish between Correspond and Comment. On Correspond, there are three scrips. These send e-mails to AdminCcs, Requestor, Ccs, and Other Recipients, whenever a Correspond event happens (that is, when someone replies to the ticket). On Comment, there are only two scrips, one to e-mail AdminCcs and one to e-mail Other Recipients. This is because the default setup does not e-mail comments to the ticket requestor. You can modify or delete these scrips by clicking them. For example, you can alter the template used or alter the action. There are a collection of predefined actions, as shown in Figure 12-1.

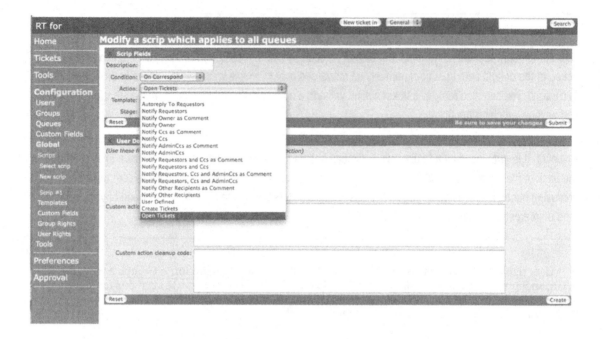

Figure 12-1. The screen to alter a scrip, with list of predefined actions shown

You can also create your own custom conditions and actions, either by creating a new scrip or by editing the existing default scrips. For example, you may want to forward new tickets to your mobile phone but only on weekends (when you're not checking your e-mail). Or you may want to forward them only on weekdays when you're being paid to do work! Basically, anything you can express in Perl, you can add as a scrip.

12-4. Creating RT Tickets via E-mail

As well as RT sending e-mails to users, you can also set it up to accept tickets by e-mail, using the rt-mailgate program. This means both that you can encourage your users to e-mail RT directly (saving yourself time!) and that you can forward user requests and bug reports to be added to the system yourself.

Edit _/etc/aliases_ to include the following line:

```
rt-email: "|/usr/bin/rt-mailgate --queue General ↵
--action correspond --url https://localhost/rt"
```

You next need to make the necessary edits to your mail server configuration to enable the use of pipe commands. For exim4, edit **/etc/exim4/exim4.conf.template** to include the following line (outside the **SYSTEM_ALIASES_PIPE_TRANSPORT** block):

```
pipe_transport = address_pipe
```

Then reload exim4 (`/etc/init.d/exim4 reload`) for the change to take effect.

■ **Note** If you have any authorization set up for RT access (see recipe 12-5), you need to make sure that the "NoAuth" sections of RT are excluded from the authorization. If you don't do this, then the mailgate won't be able to run the required parts of RT (since it doesn't have the correct authorization), and the mailgate setup won't work. This is why there's a separate "NoAuth" section of the RT code! The configuration example in recipe 12-5 does this correctly.

To test this, create a file `testfile` with a couple of lines of text, and execute it from the command line:

```
cat testfile |/usr/bin/rt-mailgate --queue General ↵
--action correspond --url https://localhost/rt
```

A ticket corresponding to the contents of `testfile` should show up on the RT web site. Next, try sending an e-mail to your `rt-email` address from the local command line (`mail -s "testing RT!" rt-email@example.com` and then hit Ctrl-D). Again, the ticket should show up on the web page, and your AdminCc group should receive appropriate e-mails.

If you run your own mail server, this is all you need, because the mail server will handle external mail already. If not, the next step is to grab the mail from the server and deal with it correctly. You can use fetchmail for this, with the following config in a file `rt-fetchmail.conf` (this should be a single line):

```
poll imap.example.com protocol IMAP username rt-email ↵
password passwd smtpaddress example.com mda ↵
'/usr/bin/rt-mailgate --queue General --action correspond ↵
--url https://localhost/rt'
```

`imap.example.com` should be whatever e-mail server you use; `example.com` should be whatever domain your e-mail appears to come from.

The command to do the work of fetching the e-mail is as follows:

```
fetchmail -f /path/to/rt-fetchmail.conf
```

which you should then put in an appropriate crontab (running every one or two minutes should suffice).

E-mail `rt-email` from somewhere nonlocal, wait for the cronjob to run, and a new ticket will appear in RT.

12-5. Creating a Secure Setup for RT

To run RT as a secure or authorized setup (that is, under HTTPS), you need to add some lines to `/etc/apache2/apache2.conf`. Edit the file so it has a section that looks like this (some of this section may already be there):

```
<VirtualHost *:443>
    ServerAdmin admin@example.com
    ServerName www.example.com

    DocumentRoot /local/www/html
    Options +Includes
    AddType text/html .shtml
    AddOutputFilter INCLUDES .shtml

    <Directory />
    Options FollowSymLinks Includes
    AllowOverride None
    </Directory>

    <Directory "/local/www/html">
    Options Indexes +Includes FollowSymLinks
    AllowOverride FileInfo AuthConfig Options

    Order allow,deny
    Allow from all
    </Directory>

    Include /etc/request-tracker3.6/apache2-modperl2.conf

    SSLEngine on
    SSLCertificateFile /etc/apache2/ssl/apache.pem

</VirtualHost>
```

The important line is the one that references the RT include file! Restart Apache2 (with /etc/init.d/apache2 force-reload), and you should be able to access RT via HTTPS.

You can also integrate RT with Kerberos to use Kerberos sign-on to access the RT web pages.

Note This doesn't strictly form part of the single-sign-on process; your users will have to enter their passwords. But it does avoid the need to remember a separate password.

Create an apache2 keytab via krbadm, and add this section in the <VirtualHost *:443> section of your Apache config:

```
<Location /rt>
# Kerberization
AuthType KerberosV5
AuthName "Request Tracker"
KrbAuthRealm EXAMPLE.COM
Krb5Keytab /etc/apache2/apache2.keytab # or appropriate location
```

```
Require valid-user
</Location>

# We don't use kerberos auth for the "noauth" areas of RT - these are the
# areas that run outgoing mail and other similar things.
<Location /rt/NoAuth>
Order allow,deny
Allow from all
Satisfy any
</Location>

<Location /rt/REST/1.0/NoAuth>
Order allow,deny
Allow from all
Satisfy any
</Location>
```

Next, you need to edit RT_SiteConfig.pm to add these lines:

```
Set($WebExternalAuto , 1);
Set($WebExternalAuth , 1);
```

Reload Apache2 (/etc/init.d/apache2 force-reload) to implement the changes, and then try logging on with your Kerberos password.

■ **Note** The $WebExternalAuto line also sets RT up such that if a new user logs in or sends a request by e-mail, a user account is automatically added. This saves you time!

12-6. Getting Big Projects Done

As discussed in recipe 12-1, sysadmin work by its nature tends to be interrupt-driven. As well as sometimes making it hard to keep track of, this can also mean that it's hard (or seems hard) to find time to sit down and work on larger projects, such as replacing servers, introducing new pieces of software, or doing web site revamps if that's part of your job (as it may be in a smaller company), and so on.

There are a couple of solutions to this. Probably the first thing to do is to make sure that only the projects that really need to be large undertakings are in fact time-consuming. Server replacement, for example, such as when acquiring a new desktop machine, should be straightforward and automated as far as possible. (Of course, setting up the automation itself may come under the heading of a large project!).

In general, make sure that you're being as time-efficient as possible. The general rule is that by the second time you do something, you should be looking at automating it. Some issues may come up only once; it's rare for something to come up only twice. It's much more likely that it'll return again, at which point any time taken in automating it becomes valuable.

You should seek to minimize the amount of effort it takes just to keep things running smoothly. By centralizing your systems (see Chapters 2 and 3), keeping good notes and records (see Chapter 1), and keeping your systems secure (see Chapter 6), you should aim to have as much as possible of your setup not requiring regular attention. This will help give you more time for the user problems that will inevitably come up and for the larger projects when they do arise.

The larger projects are also where some of the fun of sysadmin work comes in—the opportunity to look at new software and find new ways of running things more effectively. So, even after you've made your operations as smooth as possible, it's important to find ways of protecting a certain amount of your time from unimportant interruptions. Some options for this are discussed in recipe 12-1. An ideal option is to set up and protect a certain amount of time every day or every week during which you avoid interruptions unless something genuinely dramatic has happened.

Another good option is to break things down. Any large project has a series of small steps (starting with some research, moving on through installing the software, configuring it, configuring clients, working out a backup solution, and so on). Keep a list of them, and tackle one at a time when you have an hour or so free. If you cover one of those steps every day or so, you'll get through the whole project in the end.

Finally, remember to keep comprehensive notes! It's just as important when you're researching new things or working on a prospective big change as it is at any time. It still saves you time every time you return to the problem, and it'll help you when you come to make changes at a later stage or when you need to repeat the project (perhaps for a backup of the new type of server system you've just set up).

12-7. Dealing with Your Colleagues

A lot of sysadmin work, in particular in small companies, is about working with other people as well as with computers. The problems that arise are often about users interacting with computers (whether that's in the sense of them discovering a bug in a program or of them actually managing to break something). It's worth your while to consider the best ways to make your life easier when dealing with those other people, as well as how to make your life easier when fixing machines.

Make sure that you don't lose track of people's problems (see recipes 12-2 and 12-3). If your colleagues regularly have to remind you about their issues, then they're likely to lose a certain amount of faith in you, which can have negative repercussions in the long run (especially if your manager is one of the colleagues who is losing faith!). This also makes it easier to minimize the daily interruptions. People will need to tell you about their problems only once and then can trust that you'll resolve them.

Don't let minor issues slide. Make sure that you get on top of them ASAP. This, again, will tend to reassure your colleagues about your preparedness to fix things for you and will generate more goodwill when you do have to delay a fix or when there's something particularly recalcitrant going on, because they know that you will be doing your best to get it sorted!

Make it easy to contact you in various ways. Email, phone, and/or a ticketing system like RT (see recipes 12-3 to 12-5) are the basics, but you may want to include others such as IM.

One of the most important things to remember is to keep people updated with what's happening with their issue. Let them know how long a problem is likely to take to solve, and inform them if that changes (for example, if what looks like a straightforward issue turns out to in fact resemble a many-tentacled monster from the deeps...). Be honest. If you don't know what's going on, say so, and if you're not sure whether something is fixable (such as whether a particular file from a particular date will still be available on backup), say so. Don't make promises you aren't sure you can keep! In general, it's better to be cautious about what you promise. It's much better to have someone made happy when it turns out that you can after all fix something than have them disappointed when it turns out that you can't!

Own up when you screw up. If (when...) you manage to catastrophically break something, do your best to fix it, but if you can't (or if the screw-up has already been noticed), own up to your responsibility. And then move on immediately to inform your manager what you're doing to ameliorate the problem!

It's a good idea to have policies agreed with your colleagues and your line manager (and further up the management chain). These policies should cover your security arrangements, what you do and don't support (for example, is there some user software that you support only on a "best-efforts" basis and other software that is more important?), which servers and services are the most important and therefore should be prioritized if there are problems, what the expected service standards are for various things, and anything else you can think of to agree on ahead of time. The more explicit your support agreements are, the easier it is to prioritize your own work, and it also becomes easier to deal with aggravated users because you can point to your policy.

Finally, keep an ongoing note of everything you achieve (either as you do it or by reviewing your notes every week or month). This is useful for a couple of reasons. First, you may want to send out a general weekly or monthly e-mail letting your colleagues know what has changed. This also enables you to remind them to get in contact with you if there's anything they are having problems with. Second, when it comes to the end of the year and you want to discuss your performance and compensation with your manager, it's useful to have this list so you can dazzle them with just how good you are. This is especially handy for sysadmins because a fair chunk of the work is inevitably small bug fixes, which means it's easier to lose track of larger achievements.

Perl Tips

See recipes 1-5 to 1-7 for some discussions of good scripting habits. Here are a few more Perl notes that you may find helpful.

Perl Modules and CPAN

One of the most useful things to know about for Perl is CPAN (http://cpan.org), the repository of Perl modules. To install a module directly from CPAN, use this command line (ideally as root):

```
# perl -MCPAN -e "install Module::Name"
```

However, if possible, it's better to install the module as a Debian/Ubuntu package because you'll get any updates automatically (when the package is updated) and because it also becomes easier to manage the install or removal of the module. Numerous Perl modules are already available as packages, and a reasonably large number of modules are included in the standard Perl install. To check whether a module is installed already, use this one-liner from the command line:

```
> perl -e "use Module::Name"
```

No output indicates that the module is present; if it's not present, you'll get a "Can't locate Module::Name" message.

If the module isn't installed already, the next step is to see whether it's available as a package. The standard Debian/Ubuntu naming convention is for the package containing the module Module::Name to be called libmodule-name-perl (so Authen::SASL is libauthen-sasl-perl), so try sudo apt-get install libperl-module-name.

If the module doesn't already exist as a Debian package, a more maintainable alternative to installing directly from CPAN is to package it yourself using the dh-make-perl package (later you'll also need the devscripts package, so the following installs that as well):

```
> sudo apt-get install dh-make-perl devscripts
```

Next, download and unpack the module source. My example module here is Finance::Bank::Smile, which is an interface to online banking for my U.K. bank, Smile. The CPAN page is http://search.cpan.org/~rpanman/Finance-Bank-Smile-0.05/, so I download and unpack the source and then generate the files needed to create the package:

```
> wget http://search.cpan.org/CPAN/authors/id/R/RP/RPANMAN/Finance-Bank-Smile-0.05.tar.gz
> tar zxf Finance-Bank-Smile-0.05.tar.gz
> dh-make-perl Finance-Bank-Smile-0.05/
```

If you look in `Finance-Bank-Smile-0.05/debian`, you'll see various package-related files n there. You can edit these by hand, but the defaults should be fine for a personal, local package.

■ **Note** Get more information about all of this at the Debian New Maintainer's Guide:
`http://www.debian.org/doc/maint-guide/`.

Now build the module:

```
> cd Finance-Bank-Smile-0.05; debuild
```

In your original top directory, there will now be a correctly named DEB file, `libfinance-bank-smile-perl_0.05-1_all.deb`. Install with the following:

```
> sudo dpkg -i libfinance-bank-smile-perl_0.05-1_all.deb
```

■ **Note** It's useful to bear in mind that CPAN doesn't have any checks applied to uploads. Anyone can upload anything they want. So, be careful when installing modules that you don't know or that aren't widely used. To get information on Perl modules, try `http://cpanratings.perl.org/`.

Useful Modules

Here's a quick list of some modules that you may find useful:

- `Authen::SASL`: Provides SASL authentication modules (including GSSAPI, which enables Kerberos authentication). See recipe 2-10 for details.

- `Data::Dumper::Simple`: Dumps out your Perl data structure as a string or set of strings and will recurse if need be. This is very useful for debugging. Regardless of what you think a variable must contain (even if you're really, really sure...), the best thing you can do if it's all going wrong is to actually *look*. `Data::Dumper::Simple` is a slight improvement over regular `Data::Dumper`, because it includes the name of the variable by default:

  ```
  use Data::Dumper::Simple;
  print STDERR Dumper($file, %datahash);
  ```

- `Date::Parse`: Converts a string time to epoch seconds (which is the format that Perl uses in most situations but which isn't very human-readable).

```perl
use Date::Parse;
my $time = "2009-07-10 10:57:00";
my $secs = str2time($time);
```

It'll also parse regular language dates (e.g., "10th July 2009 10am"), and it tries to get your local time zone right.

- `DBI::*`: Provides a huge quantity of various database independent interface modules. There are many, many options and possibilities, but here's a brief example of the `DBD::MySQL` module (note that you need only to use `DBI()` to get this module):

```perl
#!/usr/bin/perl -w

  use strict;
  use DBI();

  # Connect to the database.
  my $dbh = DBI->connect("DBI:mysql:database=test;host=localhost",
                         "jkemp", "mypassword",{'RaiseError' => 1});

  # Create a new table 'mytable'. (No errorcatching, because this must not fail.)
  $dbh->do("CREATE TABLE mylist (id INTEGER, item VARCHAR(200))");

  # INSERT some data into 'mylist'. $dbh->quote() is used to quote the string.
  $dbh->do("INSERT INTO mylist VALUES (1, " . $dbh->quote("first list item") .
")");
```

- `File::Find`: Traverses a directory tree.

```perl
use File::Find;
my $directory = "/home/jkemp/";
find ( \&wanted, $directory );
sub wanted() {
    # here's where you specify which sorts of
    # files you want to be found
}
```

- `File::Glob` Extends standard file globbing to use BSD-style globbing (the Perl built-in uses `csh`-style globbing). Most notably, this handles whitespace in patterns better.

- `Getopt::Long`: Handles command-line options in your script, if you have complicated options. Here's a simple example:

```perl
use Getopt::Long;
my $verbose = '';
GetOptions ('verbose' => \$verbose);
```

It can also handle options with values, options with multiple names, and a wide variety of other possibilities. (It may also be overkill for a basic script, but it's useful for more complicated ones.)

- `LWP::Simple`: Grabs a web page with a single command.

```
use LWP::Simple;
my $document = get("http://www.itv.com/sport/tourdefrance/default.html")
    or die "Couldn't get TdF page";
if ($document =~ /Armstrong/) { print "Highly unusual lack of Lance!");
```

- There's very little error handling (you get **undef** on failure and the content on success), but it does what it does admirably straightforwardly.

- `Mail::Sendmail`: Provides a simple module for sending mail from a script. It'll use whatever your default mail server is.

```
use Mail::Sendmail;
%mail = ( To      => 'me@gmail.com',
          From    => 'me@example.com',
          Message => "Talking to myself..."
        );
sendmail(%mail) or die $Mail::Sendmail::error;
```

- `Net::LDAP and Net::LDAPS`: Provides various LDAP interface options. See recipe 2-10 for details.

- `Net::Ping`: Provides a simple module that you can use to ping other hosts and get the return time and other information.

```
use Net::Ping;
my $ping = Net::Ping->new();
my ($ret, $duration, $ip) = $ping->ping($server, 5.5);
```

- `Perl::Tidy` (aka **perltidy**): Tidies up badly formatted code (useful if you're taking over someone else's code and that person didn't have your own high readability standards) and will also output nicely formatted HTML with the -html option.

```
> perltidy badscript.pl
```

Be warned! The more horrendous the input was, the higher the possibility that **perltidy** will break it. Make sure that you test properly before and after to ensure that the code is still doing the same thing.

- `Text::Table`: Prints output in a nice table. You create the table and then load the data in, and `Text::Table` handles the alignment and presentation. It's basic but useful.

- `Time::HiRes`: Implements high-resolution (microsecond) timers. This is often used by other modules, such as `Net::Ping`.

```
use Net::Ping;
use Time::HiRes;
my $ping = Net::Ping->new();
$ping->hires();
```

Perl Syntax Notes

Here are a few brief notes about a couple of the corners of Perl syntax that I often find myself having to refer to the documentation for. Remember, however, the Perl maxim: there's more than one way to do it!

open with |

To get command output, you can use open with a pipe, as shown in recipe 4-2:

```
open FILEHANDLE, '-|', 'command';
while (<FILEHANDLE>) {
    # do stuff!
}
```

This will pipe the output from command into FILEHANDLE, which the while() loop then iterates over line by line. If you use '|-' instead, the output from FILEHANDLE is piped to command.

?:

This syntax, which basically provides an if-then-else shorthand for assignments, can be useful. If the value before ? evaluates as true, then the value after ? is used for assignment; otherwise, the value after : is used. So this statement:

```
my $a = $ok ? $b : $c;
```

is a shorthand for this:

```
my $a;
if ($ok) {
    $a = $b;
} else {
    $a = $c;
}
```

Use this with caution; it can be a neat way of doing things, but if you find yourself scattering parentheses everywhere and/or having to look at it more than once to understand it, go back to the longer version.

SWITCH Statements

There's no official `switch` statement in Perl because there are several ways of doing the same thing already. One neat way is to use the fact that a labeled **BLOCK** is basically a loop that runs exactly once. So, you can use a snippet that looks like this:

```
SWITCH: {
        if (/^A/) { $value = "A"; last SWITCH; }
        if (/^B/) { $value = "B"; last SWITCH; }
        if (/^C/) { $value = "C"; last SWITCH; }
        $value = "";
    }
```

Note There's now a `Switch` extension to Perl that you can access with `use Switch;` at the start of your script, but it can be a little slow.

Index

XYZ

You Need the Companion eBook

Your purchase of this book entitles you to buy the companion PDF-version eBook for only $10. Take the weightless companion with you anywhere.

We believe this Apress title will prove so indispensable that you'll want to carry it with you everywhere, which is why we are offering the companion eBook (in PDF format) for $10 to customers who purchase this book now. Convenient and fully searchable, the PDF version of any content-rich, page-heavy Apress book makes a valuable addition to your programming library. You can easily find and copy code—or perform examples by quickly toggling between instructions and the application. Even simultaneously tackling a donut, diet soda, and complex code becomes simplified with hands-free eBooks!

Once you purchase your book, getting the $10 companion eBook is simple:

❶ Visit **www.apress.com/promo/tendollars/**.

❷ Complete a basic registration form to receive a randomly generated question about this title.

❸ Answer the question correctly in 60 seconds, and you will receive a promotional code to redeem for the $10.00 eBook.

233 Spring Street, New York, NY 10013

Offer valid through 4/10.